TRIBES, TREATIES, AND

CONSTITUTIONAL TRIBULATIONS

VINE DELORIA JR. & DAVID E. WILKINS

TRIBES

TREATIES

AND

CONSTITUTIONAL

TRIBULATIONS

UNIVERSITY OF TEXAS PRESS, AUSTIN

A portion of this work was previously published as "The Application of the Constitution to American Indians" in *Exiled in the Land of the Free*. Clear Light Publishers: Santa Fe, New Mexico, 1992.

Requests for permission to reproduce material from this work should be sent to Permissions, University of Texas Press, P.O. Box 7819, Austin, TX 78713-7819.
www.utexas.edu/utpress/about/bpermission.html

♾ The paper used in this book meets the minimum requirements of ANSI/NISO Z39.48-1992 (R1997) (Permanence of Paper).

Library of Congress Cataloging-in-Publication Data

Deloria, Vine.
Tribes, treaties, and constitutional tribulations /
by Vine Deloria, Jr. and David E. Wilkins. — 1st ed.
p.   cm.
Includes bibliographical references and index.

ISBN 0-292-71608-7 (pbk. : alk. paper)
1. Indians of North America — Civil rights — United States —
History.   2. Indians of North America — Legal status, laws, etc. — United
States — History.   3. Constitutional history — United States.
I. Wilkins, David E. (David Eugene), 1954–   .   II. Title.
KF8210.C5D45   1999
342.73'0872 — dc21   99-26402

CONTENTS

Almost every known human society bases its beliefs and institutions upon historical precedents, seeking to remain within the boundaries originally established by its founding ancestral line. Nevertheless, in the course of national existence human memory fades and mythological interpretations of the beginnings of human society take hold in the popular imagination. Eventually the past, in spite of all efforts to the contrary, becomes idealized in our view of national origins, and the hard facts of history, in particular those incidents and activities of which a nation is not proud, become deeply buried in the national psyche. Present views of reality are believed to have always prevailed, and bringing a corrective viewpoint to prominence is seen as disruptive and often heretical, as if the past existed only to reflect current prejudices.

So it is with American Indian nations and the U.S. Constitution. Today, when the idea and ideal of equality and the vision of homogeneity is popular and acceptable, many people assume that the Constitution provides ample direction for the solution of all social problems. Indian tribes in this view are simply another racial/ethnic minority—the original proprietors of the continent, but not qualitatively, legally, or politically any different than other racial/ethnic groups who have suffered various and continuing measures of discrimination in their effort to gain full citizenship status.

When confronted with the constitutional clauses that seem to distinguish tribal nations from other identifiable racial/ethnic groups, many people remark politely, if naively, that while the Constitution does indeed mention Indian tribes [1] and Indians generally, [2] the passage of time and the ratification of assorted treaty provisions, as well as the enactment of specific laws that enfranchised individual Indians or targeted particular classes of Indians or specific tribes as American citizens, [3] have negated or at least significantly diminished whatever distinctive status or rights Indians were thought to have retained. The best thing for tribal members to do, for those who support this logic, is to accept their present status as American citizens and work to make American society a better place in which to live.

These same people would not, under any circumstances, suggest that the progress in human rights and economic benefits that the majority has made over the past two centuries, due primarily to an expansive interpretation of the same constitutional clauses, be reduced, negated, or eliminated. Indeed, their tempers rise whenever someone suggests the unconstitutional basis for social security, federal insurance of home mortgages, or any of the benefits that have been made available through the liberal and contemporary interpretation of obscure constitutional wordings.

American Indians, therefore, face the worst of all possible situations when they attempt to clarify their status and rights. People who would grant great flexibility in determining the meaning of the commerce clause when applied to their own welfare find it incomprehensible when Indians expect the same pattern of interpretation of the same words when applied to their lands, their treaties, and their rights to self-government and the separate national existence this clause suggests. Even the most sympathetic non-Indians cringe at the thought of a coherent and consistent interpretation of Indian rights. They know, of course, that American history is replete with instances in which the Constitution and laws of the United States — and the three branches of the federal government that are charged with upholding the Constitution and drafting, implementing, and interpreting laws — have utterly failed to do justice to American Indian nations.

When we examine the relationship of American Indians as individuals and as tribal nations in their collective capacity to the Constitution, and subsequently to the U.S. government, we discover two basic avenues for discussion. We can pore over the constitutional debates, examine the correspondence of the founding fathers, review the arguments of *The Federalist Papers,* and investigate the activities of the first few congresses to determine what the Constitution originally meant when applied to American Indians. What, we ask ourselves, did the founding fathers intend the relationship with American Indian tribes to be? And how far toward or from that desired result has American history taken us? Such studies are useful in providing a context within which the constitutional relationship with Indian tribes can be examined and understood, but to be able to infer from what we gather, it is unrealistic to assume foresight on the part of the founding fathers that can provide us with answers to today's problems. To reach intelligible conclusions, we would have to vest Washington, Jefferson, and others with prophetic powers that would do Nostradamos proud. We may uncover some principles of congressional intent of constitutional interpretation, but we cannot use these ideas to make sense of what consequently happened or to clarify the status and rights of Indians today.

The other avenue of approach is to study the ways in which the Constitution has been applied — or not applied — to American Indians as individuals and to the lands, treaties, and rights of Indian tribes as separate sovereign nations. This method combines legal and political theories with the events and incidents of our history. Its basic value is that it can be used not only to demonstrate the unfolding of constitutional ideas over a long period of time, identifying the process of erosion of the status of the tribes within the constitutional framework, but also clarify the shorter periods of time within which the necessities of history forced novel applications of constitutional principles as the only immediate solution to pressing intergovernmental problems involving tribes, states, and the federal government.

This book will concentrate on the manner and circumstances under which the Constitution of the United States was applied to American Indians — in both their individual and collective capacities — and to their lands, treaties, and rights; it will concentrate on the ways in which Indian peoples were often excluded from the just application of constitutional principles, particularly when they were excluded from the protections offered by the Constitution. In directing our attention to the specific incidents that mark this avenue of discussion, we will come to see that a massive corrective effort is needed to bring forward the misapplications and omissions of American history so that we can create a coherent and consistent interpretation of the relationship of tribal nations to the U.S. government (and the constituent states) and to the Constitution. Existing federal Indian law — that congeries of treaties, agreements, statutes, court cases, administrative regulations, etcetera — although assumed to be a logical unity, will more accurately be seen as a terribly fragile edifice, held together more by the historical and geographical circumstances of American Indians in their relation and proximity to western peoples, institutions, and rules than by any consistent or logical principles of jurisprudence that all Anglo-Saxon law is presumed to possess.

In order to give adequate expression to the many facets of this avenue of approach, we will first examine the status of the Indian tribes when they initially encountered Europeans, the ideas and legal/political doctrines that were used to explain their relationship to the "civilized world," and the intellectual, emotional, and normative inheritance from this era of world history that provided the context within which the founders of the American republic derived their confederate and constitutional references to Indians. We will then examine the original basis for dealing with Indian tribes as articulated in the Articles of Confederation so that we can understand the shift in emphasis that occurred with the adoption of the Constitution as the organic document of the United States.

An examination of the various constitutional phrases that mention Indians or Indian tribes will give us some basis for seeing how Indians came to mind when the constitutional fathers dealt with the question of the smaller, culturally and politically distinct indigenous nations on their western frontier. We will see the dangers the tribes posed when they had sufficient independence and military capability and could choose to ally themselves with any of the European nations who had imperial designs on parts of the North American continent. These explicit constitutional clauses, however, only give us one-third of the context within which the relationship of American Indians and the United States began. In order to carry out its constitutional responsibilities, the government of the United States had to exercise a wide variety of political powers in comprehensive but changing geographical and historical settings. It was inevitable that in unexpected ways the expansion of the United States and its solutions to its own domestic problems would involve its relationship with Indian tribes. Consequently, there are numerous constitutional clauses and phrases that, over the course of American history, have come into importance and affected the status and rights of American Indians. Finally, and perhaps historically most important, is the relationship of the three branches of the federal government to Indian tribes. To what degree and in what measure has each branch dealt with Indian tribes, and to what degree has the Constitution provided each with authority to do so?

After examining these constitutional issues so that we have a proper bearing on the Constitution as a document authorizing the exercise of political power, we will trace the manner in which both explicit and implicit constitutional clauses have been interpreted when confronting the reality

of American Indian existence and rights. This investigation will be sufficient to provide a context within which an examination of the application of the constitutional amendments can be scrutinized. Did the amendments, which provide all American citizens with certain inalienable rights
and privileges, include or exclude American Indians? What effect, if any,
did the various Indian naturalization measures — especially the 1924 Indian Citizenship Act,[4] which unilaterally bestowed U.S. citizenship to Indians — have on the status of tribes and their members? To what degree
and with what effects did Indian inclusion or exclusion in the American
social contract contribute to the development of a clear and reliable definition of the place of American Indians within the American political
system? Or, on the contrary, has Indian inclusion or exclusion simply fostered a continual confusion and uncertainty about the status of indigenous peoples in the American political and constitutional matrix?

Finally, although many states are playing a far more active (though constitutionally debatable) role in tribal affairs, Indian tribes are the clear focus of federal concern and action, whether malevolent or benign. How
has the status of Indian tribes changed as both explicit and implicit constitutional principles have been applied to them? Which changes can be
justified within the scope of constitutional powers and which reflect only
the political expediency of the day and have no legitimate authority apart
from the application of irresistible force that has been available to and often wielded by the federal government? Determining the contemporary
status of Indian tribes is one major test that can be invoked when examining the application of the Constitution to those tribes. Absent an informed
consent by a tribe to be included within the constitutional framework, any
action of the United States, no matter what the intentions, violates the basic premise of the social contract — that government depends upon the
consent of the governed. The degree to which American Indian nations
and Indian persons have or have not received recognition and protection
from the U.S. Constitution is, in large measure, an accurate gauge of the
capability of the Constitution to meet the needs of American society.

TRIBES, TREATIES, AND

CONSTITUTIONAL TRIBULATIONS

CHAPTER 1

EUROPEANS AND THE

NEW WORLD

ISCOVERY of the New World shook the foundation of Old World jurisprudence and initiated a movement to establish a body of international law. For centuries Europeans had lived with a makeshift edifice of political theory that fluctuated between a recognition of the divine right of kings and an admission that dynastic struggles presented the continent with a political fait accompli that could only be endorsed and sanctified by the Catholic Church. In the limited conceptual universe of fifteenth-century Europe, this arrangement was accepted because there was no reason to believe that the world was any larger than Europe and the remote places of which Europeans had knowledge. Columbus's voyages considerably expanded these limited horizons and made it necessary that Europeans find a way of understanding the world in its totality. Who were the people living on the other side of the ocean, and what relationship did they have with Europeans who at the time of discovery shared, if nothing else, a universal belief in the Christian interpretation of the world and of human history?

The Catholic Church was quick to respond to this intellectual dilemma; in the spring of 1493 the Pope issued the famous bull *Inter Caetera*,[1] in which the Church granted to the kings of Castile and Leon all the lands and countries the Spanish had discovered or might discover in the future.

The lands, of course, were not the Pope's to grant, but in the European mind of the time the Holy Father was understood as Christ's vicar on earth, and hence if any authority existed to bolster European political claims against the peoples of the New World, it would have to be found in a religious context. The Church's purpose for granting an undetermined portion of the earth to a minor European country was to ensure that the gospel be preached to all nations — and the Spanish were expected to do precisely that. Very quickly the Spanish composed a legalistic document, the *Requerimiento*,[2] which was to be read to the indigenous groups of the New World as they were contacted by Spanish explorers. The *Requerimiento* recited the history of the world as Europeans then understood it and called upon the natives to submit themselves to the authority of the Spanish monarchs and the Pope or face the "justifiable" wrath of the Spanish military. No people go to war or seek to divest others of life and property unless they have devised a moral justification for their actions; the *Requerimiento* became the Spaniards' legal and moral excuse for dispossession of the indigenous peoples of the New World. It also provided the intellectual context within which international law began to develop.

The subsequent debates among Spanish theologians regarding the nature of the natives (whether or not they were by nature free persons or slaves), the seemingly endless series of papal bulls that sought to refine and clarify the rights of Europeans in newly discovered lands, and the correspondent responsibilities Europeans assumed in making claims against the indigenous peoples need not concern us here.[3] What is important to note is that the doctrine of discovery, as the papal franchise came to be called, was cited by European monarchs as justification for claiming a clear legal title to lands in the New World on the basis of the fact that the monarch had authorized certain adventurers to search out new lands on his or her behalf. With the exception of the Spanish, who made conversion an integral part of their colonial activities, most of the European sovereigns laid claims to lands in the New World without accepting the corresponding responsibility to spread the gospel to the natives. Discovery thus became a secular, legal theory that was of benefit only to the European countries. Since the natives were not Christians, they were precluded from legally defending themselves or forcing the Europeans to recognize their rights to their lands.

Spain, England, France, Holland, Sweden, Russia, and Portugal all established colonies in the western hemisphere, and, insofar as there was any international law, their claims to territory were generally respected by each other. Colonies became important pieces of real estate in the wars that ravaged Europe during the succeeding three centuries. Some colonies changed hands many times as victors in the European wars, using the doctrine of conquest, imposed harsh terms on their defeated enemies and confiscated their colonies. When colonial areas changed hands, it was believed that the successful nation acquiring the colony inherited the original claim under the doctrine of discovery of the nation they had defeated. So there was never a time, even when the natives had done a good deal of the fighting, that original legal title could vest in the hands of the true owners of the soil.

In the struggle for North America, England was generally the victor, although both France and Spain maintained the fictional posture that they owned portions of what is now the United States — even after the American Revolution. After the Seven Years' War (1756–1763), Great Britain stood alone on the eastern seaboard, and France was able to argue a presence in North America only by the secret device of ceding most of Louisiana to Spain just prior to making peace with England. Spain had settled portions of the Florida, Georgia, and Carolina coasts but lacked the will and resources to defeat the troublesome Creek and Choctaw nations, so it contented itself with establishing favorable trading relationships with the southeastern Indian tribes. Spain faced no competition in the American Southwest or on the California coast in its claims to those territories.

Since the English had been substantially dependent upon the Indians, particularly the Iroquois Confederacy, in defeating the French, they wisely recognized the national status of the major Indian tribes of the interior and generally forbade their colonies from dealing with the Indian tribes on any consistent or substantial basis. In 1763 the King established via a royal proclamation a boundary line running along the Allegheny Mountains beyond which English colonists were forbidden to go. The king also organized departments of Indian affairs that were responsible primarily to the Crown and its advisors — not to the colonial governments. The English treatment of the natives had something of the flavor of the original papal intent, in that private contributions toward the conversion and civilization of the natives were encouraged. But commerce rather than Christianity dominated English colonial concerns.

The fathers of the American Revolution and Constitution had a definite English heritage insofar as they understood the nature of their Indian relationships. First, there was no question that they believed they owned the clear legal title to the lands of the continent they had wrestled away from Great Britain. Second, they recognized the wisdom of the English propensity to treat the larger Indian confederations as having recognizable and respected national status. Indians who were not accorded the respect to which they believed they were entitled did not fight as allies and were likely to appear in battle on the other side of the line.

In the negotiations of peace concluding the Revolutionary War, the British insisted that the territory between the old proclamation line (roughly the Ohio river) and the Great Lakes be designated as the Indian country with the thought that it would provide a buffer state between the United States and Canada. Apart from the Kentucky bluegrass country, which Daniel Boone and James Henderson had already invaded, Americans coveted nothing as much as the annexation of Canada, and with that area predominantly French, Great Britain was walking something of a tightrope in securing its remaining North American possessions. As one of the last points to be discussed during the treaty negotiations, England finally acceded to American demands and left the status of this area — and of its inhabitants — unresolved and nebulously described in the document ending the war.

A curious situation then developed. Many northern tribes in the area west of the Mississippi and north of the Illinois River drew closer to the English, even though the fur traders they encountered were French, half-breed French, and eastern Indians. These loyalties persisted until the War of 1812, and many American explorers and traders arriving at Indian villages in Minnesota, Wisconsin, and on the upper Missouri River were surprised to find the British flag flying over their heads. Thus American flags and peace medals from the president became part of the American fur trade and diplomatic encounters.

Finally, there was no question that the Americans believed the Indians were heathen savages who had little to recommend them and who, if they were to live near or among white settlements, needed to be transformed into "civilized" human beings. Indeed, while still in its early colonial phase, Massachusetts divided its Indian population into wild tribes and converted Indians who lived in "Praying Towns," which received a measure of political status and self-government according to Puritan views of these matters.[4] Since Indians truly did not understand Anglo-Saxon property law and were otherwise benign and trusting according to their own habits, Americans began to think of them as children needing firm guidance in their business transactions — hence the idea of the colonial or state government acting as a trustee to ensure fair treatment. It was not long before the idea developed that the non-Indian governments — at all levels — should sell Indian lands to settlers at reduced prices as an exercise of the trusteeship. In "civilizing" the Indians, tribal lands of vast acreage were declared "surplus," and land holdings were reduced to small plots where Indian families were expected to live like their white neighbors.

The heritage of the European/Euro-American claim of legal title to Indian lands has remained constant from 1492 until the present day. The nomenclature used to discuss Indian land rights has changed a bit, and we now describe Indian lands as being held "in trust" by the United States, a euphemism that simply avoids the necessity of remembering that Indians, with some rare anomalies, are not thought to own the legal title to their lands and can be dispossessed by the U.S. government at any time.[5]

The moral responsibility of the European nations and later Euro-Americans to bring the gospel and European civilization to the natives has not radically changed since the 1500s either. It has been a sporadic interest of the federal government during the course of American history, never forgotten but rarely a major concern. More often this idea has served as a justification for policies (e.g., Indian removal, allotment and assimilation, termination) that are actually in the best interests of the political and economic forces of the United States, so that the responsibility of the nation to educate, convert, and elevate the Indians socially, economically, and spiritually has been the cloak that hides a multitude of sins.

The recognition of the status of the Indian tribes as nations has changed little between 1763 and the present. In large part their status as defined by the federal courts, Congress, and the chief executive has created a confusing body of law illustrating the continuing effort of the United States to escape this part of its English inheritance. It is important to note, however, that the revolutionary and constitutional fathers accepted without question the English view of the national status of an Indian tribe.

The first evidence of this recognition can be found in a July 1775 congressional speech composed to address the powerful Indian nations on the frontier. It pleads with them to remain neutral and asks them to regard the Revolution as merely a "family quarrel" among the English. A treaty council was held at Fort Pitt in July 1775 in an effort to get the Delaware and Shawnee to remain neutral. In late August and September the Six Nations met with American representatives at German Flats and Albany because the Americans, realizing the strong relationship between the Iroquois and the Crown, hoped to postpone any attacks on the New York and Pennsylvania frontiers. The Americans would meet each year with the Delawares and Shawnees until 1778.

Previous treaties had been conferences in which both parties prepared talks or speeches that they gave to the other party, and after an exchange of views often taking two weeks or more, each party made final speeches that summed up the points under discussion. The treaty would then be considered valid for the points on which agreement had been reached. The United States escalated the diplomatic process in 1778 by drawing up a paper that would be the first Indian treaty written in formal diplomatic style: the Delaware Treaty of September 17, 1778.[6] Article 6 of the treaty declared, "And it is further agreed on between the contracting parties should it for the future be conducive for the mutual interest of both parties to invite any other tribes who have been friends to the interest of the United States, to join the present confederation, and to form a state whereof the Delaware nation shall be the head, and have a representation in Congress."[7]

It might be argued that the promises made by the United States were only words of expediency made in a time of great stress, and as such, the promises were not worthy of belief, nor did they actually invite a permanent relationship between the Delawares and the revolutionary government. Yet this situation in 1778 was not one of desperation for the Americans. They had signed two treaties with France earlier in the year, and there was every indication that Spain might be enticed to enter the war on the colonists' side. Sir John Butler had led his loyalists and Indian allies on a sweep of the Wyoming valley in Pennsylvania in July, devastating the interior of that colony and sending a wave of terror through the outlying settlements of the frontier. The Delawares had been favorably inclined to side with the Americans since the early treaty at Pittsburgh, when the Ohio tribes voted to remain neutral.[8]

The purpose of the 1778 treaty was to secure permission of the Delawares to pass through their country so that an American force, including pro-American Delaware and Shawnee, could capture Detroit. Had the Delawares had only a minor political status at that time, it would not have taken any diplomacy, let alone a formal treaty arrangement, to move through their country and attack Detroit and other British posts in Canada. But now with the terrible winter of Valley Forge behind them, with their courageous fight at Monmouth in June, the Americans were ready to go on the offensive. So we have no reason whatsoever to believe that the offer tendered to the Delawares was insincere.

The offer of statehood was subject to congressional approval, but we must not think of Congress in the light of present-day conditions. The Continental Congress was little more than a selection of representatives sworn to prosecute the war to its desired ending: victory for the Americans and independence. It was within the political understanding of the day that the Delawares might want some formal connection with the United States so as to be relieved of their relationship with the English king and to be free from the bullying tactics of the Iroquois, most of whom were the staunch allies of Great Britain. Had the Delawares immediately petitioned for statehood, it would have been a very interesting turn of events. The United States at that time was governed by the Articles of Confederation, and this document gave "states" considerably more flexibility in dealing with Indians than did the later Constitution. The Delawares might well have become the brokers of all federal relationships with the western tribes, and settlement of the interior of the continent might have been radically different.

The Revolution resolved the question of political independence only for the Americans. It did not affect the posture of other European nations toward Indian tribes. After the war the British conducted several treaty councils with the tribes of the Ohio and Great Lakes country. British trading companies dominated the fur trade of the interior and Great Lakes area for several decades. The Spanish quickly made treaties with the strong southeastern tribes, most notably the Creek and Choctaw,[9] and in 1785 made an important treaty with the Comanche, which had to be conducted at several locations in the Southwest because the tribe controlled nearly one thousand miles of territory considered by the Spanish to be their borderlands.[10] Russian trading companies made treaties with California tribes to secure their title to land. And following the Mexican Revolution in 1820, the new Mexican government immediately began making treaties with tribes who resided primarily in the area later settled by the United States, and continued to do so until the 1870s.[11]

It has been argued by some people that Indians, by aligning with Great Britain and being much smaller than the United States, became conquered nations at the end of the Revolution. This view can only be maintained through an ignorance of the historical situation. In 1783, at the urging of the Secretary of War, Congress passed the following resolution:

> Resolved, That the Secretary of War take the most effectual measures immediately to inform the several Indian nations on the frontiers of the United States that a peace has been concluded with Great Britain and to communicate to them what cessions of forts and territory have been thereby made to the United States, assuring them at the same time that the different posts will soon be occupied by the American troops, intimating also that the United States are disposed to enter into friendly treaty with the different tribes.

The resolution was supported by an order that stated:

> That the Secretary of War transmit the proceedings of Congress herein, with copies of President Dickinson's and General Irvine's letters to the Commander in Chief, who is directed to request Sir Guy Carleton to take such measures as may second the views of Congress, and prevent the commission of further hostilities by the Indian nations in with Great Britain against the citizens of the United States.[12]

Contrary to American expectations, the British did not rush to turn over the trading posts to the Americans, nor did any large force of Americans seek to control these posts. The Americans did, however, make in good faith peace treaties with Indian nations who had sided with England. Thus did the Six Nations at Fort Stanwix in October, 1784; the Wyandot, Delaware, Chippewa, and Ottawa in January 1785; the Cherokee in November 1785; the Choctaw in January 1786; and the Chickasaw and Shawnee in January 1786 all make peace treaties with the United States.[13]

Large numbers of Americans were moving into the Kentucky bluegrass lands, and trade with Indians in that region was difficult to regulate even with the peace. The struggle between the large states with massive although poorly defined western boundaries and the "landless" states—Maryland,

Pennsylvania, Delaware, Rhode Island, and New Jersey—over how the lands between the Ohio and Great Lakes were to be governed and settled aggravated the peace on the frontier. Lawless acts by settlers drove the tribes toward conflict, and Congress was impelled to act. In March of 1788 Congress reported the following:

> That the confederation of a large number of tribes of Indians, to op-
> pose the settlement of the lands, North of the river Ohio, is a subject
> of great importance, and seriously claims the attention of the United
> States. That said tribes of Indians have expressed the highest disgust, at
> the principle of conquest, which has been specified to them, as the
> basis of their treaties with the United States, and in consequence of
> which, the limits of their hunting grounds and territory, have been cir-
> cumscribed and defined. That the practice of the British government,
> and most of the Northern colonies previously to the late war, of pur-
> chasing the right of the soil of the Indians, and receiving a deed of sale
> and conveyance of the same, is the only mode of alienating their lands,
> to which they will peaceably accede. That to attempt to establish a
> right to the lands claimed by the Indians, by virtue of an implied con-
> quest, will require the constant employment of a large body of troops,
> or the utter extirpation of the indians [sic]. That circumstanced as they
> are at present, being in alliance with, and favorably treated by, the
> British government, the doctrine of conquest is so repugnant to their
> feelings, that rather than submit thereto, they would prefer continual
> war. That the principle of waging war for an object which may be ob-
> tained by a treaty, is justly to be questioned. That at the ensuing treaty,
> it is highly probable, the indians will, in the first instance, object to
> the right of the United States to the country North of the Ohio. If the
> Commissioners, who are to hold the treaty, are bound by instructions
> to adhere rigidly to the principle of conquest, and the limits of territory
> stated at the former treaties, an abrupt departure of the Indians, and
> hostilities in consequence thereof, may be expected. Your secretary
> humbly apprehends that the United States may conform to the modes
> and customs of the indians in the disposal of their lands, without the
> least injury to the national dignity. Were an opposition to the custom
> of the indians in this respect to be a material part of the national char-
> acter, it would not be highly estimated in the opinion of the world.[14]

The message is quite clear. If the American treaty commissioners implied that the tribes had been conquered, which of course they had not, such an assertion would have provoked a massive Indian war — Great Britain being the chief beneficiary. The United States could not have withstood world opinion on such activities. Hidden in this message is the possibility that many European nations, seeking to control the fledgling American nation, would have given support to the Indians. "Conquest" was a political slogan, not a practical reality, and even as late as 1868 at Fort Laramie,[15] the American treaty commissioners were careful not to imply that the Indians were being conquered.

There are many other bits of evidence indicating that the Indians have not been a mere matter of domestic policy, but for our purposes we can conclude by restating some of the basic themes that formed the context for dealing with Indians. The applicability of the Constitution to Indians and Indian tribes must be examined in this setting because these themes always formed the basis for attitudes that influenced the manner in which legislation and policy were formulated. Out of the colonial heritage then, three principles emerged:

1) The land was believed to ultimately belong to the United States, although Indian tribes were recognized as holding a lesser title of occupancy that they could cede to the federal government without duress.

2) Indians were culturally and intellectually inferior to Europeans and Euro-Americans.

3) Indian tribes must nevertheless be treated as nations capable of entering into diplomatic negotiations and making war.

These were interrelated tenets and indicated both the cultural arrogance and political pragmatism of American policy makers. Although these attitudes are nowhere found in the Constitution or law books, they were the dark-colored glasses through which Indians were seen.

CHAPTER II

THE ARTICLES OF

CONFEDERATION

O N April 17, 1754, hostilities between England and France broke out when a French force seized the fork of the Ohio and Monongahela Rivers (an area that later became Pittsburgh) and erected Fort Duquesne. George Washington was dispatched with a small force to counter the French move but was ultimately driven out of the Ohio valley. In mid-June British colonial officials advised the colonies to make a treaty with the Iroquois, and so delegates from New England, New York, Pennsylvania, and Maryland met at Albany, New York, to do so. Recognizing that the situation required more than a basic treaty arrangement, the delegates after ample debate finally adopted a "Plan of Union," which gave a comprehensive structure for governing the Atlantic seaboard where the English were settled.

A grand (federal) council with legislative power (though colonial assemblies were to retain their own legislative powers for internal affairs) was proposed, as well as a president-general to act as an executive officer. Together they were to have responsibility for Indian affairs and were to supervise relations with Indians, levy taxes for general purposes, and negotiate new land purchases not within the existing boundaries of any of the colonies. It was at this conference that Benjamin Franklin pointed out the smooth functioning of the Iroquois Confederacy and urged his fellow delegates to adopt similar policies.[1]

Although the Plan of Union created by the Albany Congress was rejected by the British government, it did establish the paradigm that patterned all subsequent discussions of political unity and organization. The Articles of Confederation, drawn up and adopted in November 1777, reflect the Albany proposal as tempered by the demand to speak directly to the state of rebellion in which the colonies were engaged. A good deal of the substance of the Constitution is found in the articles, but it is also evident that the colonists did not understand the sophistication of the Iroquois Confederacy.[2] The stumbling block that emerges in the articles is the document's inability to deal adequately with the question of sovereignty, an issue that later is better, but not completely, resolved in the Constitution.

Colonies, now states under the articles, insisted on maintaining a measure of foreign relations for themselves. Article 6 declares that "No State without the consent of the United States in Congress assembled, shall send any embassy to, or receive any embassy from, or enter into any conference, agreement, alliance or treaty with any king, prince, or state. . . ." Article 9 gave the United States in Congress assembled the sole and exclusive right to make war and peace and enter into treaties — but the states in their own interest could still maintain ambassadors, thus effectively negating and hampering the exercise of sovereignty by the United States.

States could not wage war under Article 6 without the consent of Congress "unless such State be actually invaded by enemies, or shall have received certain advice of a resolution being formed by some nation of Indians to invade such State. . . ." This provision is not altogether clear since it was the white settlers who were invading the lands of the Indians rather than Indians seeking to take the colonists' property. By allowing the individual states to wage war against the Indians on their own initiative, the articles created a situation in which the danger of conflict on the frontier was maximized — with few expected beneficial results available to the Indians or to the individual states.

The central government under the articles was given the responsibility of "regulating the trade and managing all affairs with the Indians, not members of any of the States, provided that the legislative right of any State within its own limits be not infringed or violated. . . ." This seeming delegation of authority, when placed in the context of a confederation of colonies with charters granting them lands "to the South Seas," was in fact no delegation at all. Since many of the colonies claimed lands in the interior based upon colonial grants from the Crown made at a time when no Euro-Americans knew the geography of the continent, the reservation of the power to restrict the actions of the federal government with respect to Indians meant that Georgia and some of the other colonies could establish their own political relationships with tribes who lived thousands of miles from the Atlantic coast. And conceivably, several states would be dealing independently with a large Indian tribe that occupied lands to which each of the states laid claim.

The dangers, clearly foreseeable in the manner that the articles allocated responsibility for Indian matters, did not arise for several reasons. The Committee on Indian Affairs monitored the actions of states very closely. In September 1786 Congress admonished Virginia to avoid conflict with the Cherokee and Shawnee for fear of uniting the frontier tribes in the southern part of the country.[3] The states were encouraged to get instructions from Congress before trying to deal with Indians. For example, a request from Pennsylvania was favorably received by the Continental Congress in the proceedings of Saturday, September 20, 1783:

> [T]hat the legislature of Pennsylvania be informed, in answer to the request of the delegates of that State, in consequence of instructions from the said legislature of the 13th instant, that Congress have no objection to a conference being held on behalf of the State of Pennsylvania, with the Indians on their borders, respecting a purchase to be made by and at the expence of the said State, of lands within the limits thereof; *provided no engagements relative to peace or war with the said Indians, be entered into by the said State, the power of holding treaties on this subject being vested by the Confederation solely in the United States in Congress assembled.*[4] [Emphasis added]

In other words, dealing with Indian tribes had two levels of activity — land purchases and war and peace. But even land purchases had to have federal approval and some federal presence to prevent frontier wars that might arise.

Most states were more concerned about resolving the question of the western reserved lands than gaining more land on their borders. Some colonial grants had extended to the South Seas — a rather extravagant gesture by the Crown to entice people to settle the colonies. Landless states — Maryland, Delaware, Pennsylvania, New Jersey, and Rhode Island — insisted that the federal government should have title to the lands north of the Ohio, so not much was done in the way of land purchases during the period of the Articles of Confederation.

Nevertheless, some states did insist on conducting their own Indian relationships. New York, for example, considered itself supreme in dealing with the Indian tribes residing in its boundaries and intended to eventually rid the state of so-called hostile tribes. In an effort to carry out Indian removal and to show its alleged superiority over Indian matters, the state went as far as arresting agents of the Confederated Government who were seeking to negotiate a peace treaty with the tribes.[5] North Carolina adopted a similar posture of superiority regarding its relationship with the Cherokee, and Georgia negotiated treaties directly with the Creek during this period. But with the passage of the Trade and Intercourse Act, federal authority became supreme.[6]

The major actions of Congress during the years under the Articles of Confederation testify to the national status the tribes enjoyed. The Ordinance of 1786, for the "Regulation and Management of Indian Affairs," sought the "safety and tranquility" of the frontiers. It created two districts — north and south of the Ohio River — to be placed under the charge of two superintendents. Part of the superintendents' job was "whenever they shall have reasons to suspect any tribe or tribes of Indians of hostile intentions, they shall communicate the same to the executive of the state or states whose territories are subject to the effect of such hostilities." The ordinance further prohibited citizens of other nations from living with any Indian tribe, though there was virtually no possibility of enforcing the ban because the frontier was so expansive. Passports to travel in Indian country were to be issued by the superintendents, and trading licenses, good for no more than one year, were required of all traders. The whole thrust of the ordinance was to establish rules for American citizens, not for Indians or Indian tribes.[7]

Georgia did not pay much attention to the ordinance, but encroached on Indian lands and made treaties for its own convenience with the Cherokee and Creek. Pennsylvania and New York preferred to set up desks at federal treaty proceedings and, as the unwary Indians passed by, to have them sign papers ceding lands to these states. The land cessions demanded in the South affected a considerable amount of territory; they usually involved securing bottomlands along an extensive portion of a river because big plantations required easy transportation of cotton and other agricultural crops to seacoast cities. Thus a year after the ordinance, when the question of providing a government for the territories north of the Ohio became necessary, Congress passed another ordinance, this one containing a clear statement of policy.

The Northwest Ordinance of July 13, 1787,[8] created a governor for the territory and a general assembly to pass laws modeled after the domestic laws of existing states. No fewer than three nor more than five states could be created in the designated area, and while new states were to be admitted to the union on an "equal footing" with the original states, they were restricted, as a territory and as new states, from interfering "with the primary disposal of the soil by the United States . . . nor with any regulations Congress may find necessary for securing the title in such soil to the bona fide purchasers." Article 3 contained statements of morality unusual in an act of Congress and spelled out the policy toward the Indian inhabitants who were, after all, the original owners of the soil that was to be distributed so casually. The article reads:

> Religion, morality, and knowledge, being necessary to good government and the happiness of mankind, schools and the means of education shall forever be encouraged. *The utmost good faith shall always be observed toward the Indians; their lands and property shall never be taken from them without their consent; and, in their property, rights, and liberty, they never shall be invaded or disturbed, unless in just and lawful wars authorized by Congress; but laws founded in justice and humanity shall, from time to time, be made, for preventing wrongs being done to them, and for preserving peace and friendship with them.*[9] [Emphasis added]

This article can be understood as a transitional phase in the conception of Indians: the need for avoiding war is evident, but the tone is one of protecting the Indians from the depredations of American settlers.

Insofar as the article and ordinance clarify the status of Indians, it is clear that in restricting conflict to "just and lawful wars" the congressional thinking was to follow the tenets of international law, adopting the very phrase that was used by the early Spanish explorers reading the *Requirimiento* to the natives of Central America and Mexico prior to attacking them. Congress never did bother to examine whether the wars it waged against the tribes in the West were just or lawful; it merely appropriated funds to wage these wars. Presumably this sentiment concerning the northern Indians also extended to the southeastern Indian tribes; following the adoption of the Constitution, the provisions of this ordinance were generally incorporated in a succeeding act that covered the territories south of the Ohio River.[10]

The Articles of Confederation were superseded by the adoption of the Constitution in 1789. Vigorous debate in the Constitutional Convention was followed by contending parties, the "Federalists" (pro-Constitution) and "anti-Federalists" (anti-Constitution), debating in newspapers and publicly distributed pamphlets the differences between the articles and the proposed new document. The anti-Federalists, content with the arrangement under the articles, did not raise the question of the Indian relationship, assuming perhaps that the states could deal with the question. The Federalists saw Indians as having both international and domestic relevance. In *Federalist* No. 42 James Madison attacked the unwieldy procedure required by the articles:

> The regulation of commerce with the Indian tribes is very properly unfettered from two limitations in the Articles of Confederation, which render the provision obscure and contradictory. The power is there restrained to Indians, not members of any of the States, and is not to violate or infringe the legislative right of any State within its own limits. What description of Indians are to be deemed members of a State is not yet settled, and has been a question of frequent perplexity and contention in the federal councils.[11]

Madison objected to the vague wording that failed to define the status of Indians within state borders. Although the Six Nations lived within the state of New York, the real problem was the vast tracts of land still occupied by the Creek and Cherokee in Georgia, the most aggressive of the former colonies claiming all the land described in its charter. This question was slightly touched upon when discussions on representation and direct taxation were the subject of debate. While some people could argue that there was never a clear idea of which Indians would be under the jurisdiction of state governments and which ones were to remain independent of state political control, the content of the discussion assumes that taxable Indians would be those individuals who had left their tribes.

Of considerably more importance was the fact that the Indian tribes living on the frontier could align themselves with those European nations who still coveted lands in North America and had the capability of conducting war against the American settlements. Madison, writing to Thomas Jefferson on October 24, 1787, reported a rumor about a possible conflict as part of his pro-Constitution argument. "We hear from Georgia that that State is threatened with a dangerous war with the Creek Indians. The alarm is of so serious a nature, that law-martial has been proclaimed, and they are proceeding to fortify even the Town of Savannah. *The idea there, is that the Indians derive their motives as well as their means from their Spanish neighbors*" [emphasis added].[12] Alexander Hamilton, writing as "Publius" in *Federalist* No. 24, best summarized the perceived status of the Indian tribes on the frontier. After warning that British and Spanish settlements were ringing the frontier, thus possibly preventing American growth across the Appalachians, Hamilton projected a scenario for the future, possibly the first instance of American paranoia over the threat of foreign countries:

> The savage tribes on our Western frontier ought to be regarded as our natural enemies, their natural allies, because they have most to fear from us, and most to hope from them. The improvements in the art of navigation have, as to the facility of communication, rendered distant nations in a great measure, neighbors. Britain and Spain are among the principal maritime powers of Europe. A future concert of views between these nations ought not to be regarded as improbable.[13]

In his next offering Hamilton repeated his warning. "The territories of Britain, Spain and of the Indian nations in our neighborhood do not border on particular States, but encircle the Union from Maine to Georgia. The danger, though in different degrees, is therefore common. And the means of guarding against it ought, in like manner to be the objects of common council and of a common treasury."[14] Hamilton saw war with Indians in an international setting: "Indian hostilities, instigated by Spain or Britain, would always be at hand. Provocations to produce the desired appearances might even be given to some foreign power, and appeased again by timely concessions."[15]

This fear of foreign intervention did not decrease with the adoption of the Constitution. The Act of June 30, 1834,[16] provided that "if any citizen or other person residing within the United States, or the territory thereof, shall send any talk, speech, message or letter, to any Indian nation, tribe, chief, or individual, with an intent to produce a contravention or infraction of any treaty or other law of the United States, or to disturb the peace and tranquillity of the United States, he shall forfeit and pay the sum of two thousand dollars." Even during the American Civil War, the settlers in the West lived in fear that the Indians on the frontier would unite with the South and push them from their homes.

Indians could not have been conceived to be within the scope of constitutional provisions and still be conceived to be independent and conspiring with foreign treaties in alliances seeking warfare with the United States. Because the United States linked the Indians with foreign nations as possible enemies, the only recourse for the federal government was to secure land cessions and treaties of peace with them and gradually extend American jurisdiction over lands to the west. The laws mentioned in the Ordinance of 1787 were for the protection of the Indians, not for their exploitation, so we must read the treaty texts in that light even though some very unequal bargains were forced on the tribes.

The federal government under the Articles of Confederation had little real authority. In almost every important area in which a nation would be expected to act as a unified entity, sovereignty was split between the national government and the individual states. Particularly in the South, confederation was more a convenience than reality. The southern states were always vulnerable to the machinations of the Spanish colonies in the Floridas and Louisiana, and Spanish colonial officials went out of their way to cultivate the good feelings of the powerful Creek Confederacy, keeping the level of paranoia in Georgia and the Carolinas at a fever pitch. The contemporary heritage of the days of the Articles of Confederation is the propensity of states to assert their sovereign rights in defiance of the national government. And although the Constitution resolved the issue of splitting both sovereignty and subject matter in the allocation of powers between the federal government and the states, the tradition had been established that under certain ill-defined conditions, states could occasionally take matters into their own hands when it came to dealing with the Indians.

CHAPTER III

THE CONSTITUTION AND

AMERICAN INDIAN TRIBES

The Federalist Papers

Establishing a form of government that would work efficiently was a far greater concern of the constitutional fathers than dealing with the Indian tribes within the states and on the frontier. As a result, we have few comprehensible insights into how the framers of the Constitution viewed tribes or individual Indians, and we know little of what they had in mind regarding the future activities of the United States in relation to tribal nations. *The Federalist Papers* address some of the topics of debate waged by the successful advocates of the Constitution. By examining how these essays represent the public arguments presented on the part of constitutional advocates, we can determine how the popular mind understood the role and status of Indian peoples in the new constitutional framework.

A surprising amount of theoretical discussion is presented in the Federalist/anti-Federalist debates. The constitutional fathers were cognizant of the intellectual debates concerning the nature of government that had substantially altered the European political landscape in the preceding centuries. The French philosopher Baron de Montesquieu,[1] in particular, seems to have been influential; his idea that a republic must of necessity embrace a small territory in order to be effective was cited many times by the anti-Federalists.[2] Their chief worry was the question of whether the Constitution was improving a confederation or in fact creating a national government. The speech of George Mason at the ratifying convention of Virginia may be cited as a fair representation of the concerns of the anti-Constitution delegates:

> Is it to be supposed that one national government will suit so extensive a country, embracing so many climates, and containing inhabitants so very different in manners, habits, and customs? It is ascertained, by history, that there never was a government over a very extensive country without destroying the liberties of the people: history also, supported by the opinions of the best writers, shows us that monarchy may suit a large territory, and despotic governments over so extensive a country, but that popular governments can only exist in small territories. Is there a single example, on the face of the earth, to support a contrary opinion? Where is there one exception to this general rule? Was there ever an instance of a general national government extending over so extensive a country, abounding in such a variety of climates, where the people retained their liberty?[3]

The concern was not that the United States would not eventually expand and include more states and territory but that the effort to create a national government was doomed to failure because of the already extensive lands and peoples that constituted the new nation.

Considerable debate raged over how to organize the territory lying north and west of the Ohio River. Virginia had long-standing claims to the area and was willing to surrender its lands on the condition that other states having expansive territorial descriptions in their charters do likewise. The Northwest was a puzzle to the Americans, as it had been to the English before them. Every scenario looked forward to the political organization of the area as a separate state, but how should the state be qualified to join the nation? A three-tiered process was finally approved whereby the territory would at first be governed strictly by federal officials appointed by the president and approved by Congress.[4] As the population increased and it became possible to organize a legislature, self-government of a sort was to be allowed. When the population reached a certain level, the territory could apply for admission to the union. The new state government would then partially satisfy the Montesquieu problem of governing too large an area by a strong central government. This process was approved and in place *before* the Constitution was adopted.

The ordinance for settling the Northwest did not look at the question of the Indians; it contemplated a time when the territory would be settled by whites. People assumed that the lands would be purchased from the Indians — but where would the Indians go? One does not need to be prophetic to see that absent a definite provision — something other than the sentiments contained in Article 3 of the ordinance — the Indians would have to be moved out of the area. If anyone looked to the small remnant reservations in Connecticut, Massachusetts, New Jersey, Virginia, Delaware, and South Carolina as forecasting a policy of reserving lands to create small enclaves for Indians, the subject never arose in the constitutional debates.[5]

Instead, the concern when dealing with the Indian question was one of preventing frontier wars and allowing the federal government to supervise trade with the Indian nations so as to make the Americans competitive with the English and Spanish on the distant frontiers established by the Treaty of Paris. Because of the lack of foresight, the realistic alternatives to dealing with Indians were but three: 1) new state boundaries could be drawn excluding the Indian lands; 2) no more treaties could be made, and the Indians would eventually become citizens of the new states; or 3) "Indians" as a subject matter could be made an exclusively federal matter and treaty making would be continued.

No effort was made to exclude Indian lands from the new state boundaries for a number of reasons. Land cessions were not always in clear, manageable tracts. Creating geographical enclaves in the midst of states, or between them, would only produce lawless areas where mischief would be fostered. It was difficult enough to keep the settlers from invading Indian lands beyond the agreed boundary established by the Treaty of Fort Stanwix in 1784. The United States did not have the military power to abrogate any treaties at the time of the constitutional debates. Indeed, in the 1790s a coalition of Ohio tribes inflicted two devastating defeats on American armies sent into the Ohio country to chastise the tribes. The opinions of foreign nations at the abrogation of Indian treaties would have provided the European nations with the excuse they needed to meddle in American affairs.

So Indians became a federal matter. John Jay, in favor of a strong federal government, produced the argument that probably determined the outcome of the issue. He wrote that "not a single Indian war has yet been occasioned by aggressions of the present federal government, feeble as it is; but there are several instances of Indian hostilities having been provoked by the improper conduct of individual States, who, either unable or unwilling to restrain or punish offenses, have given occasion to the slaughter of many innocent inhabitants."[6] Whether a conflict could be provoked by England or Spain, initiated by the Indians, or caused by lawless settlers, the feeling was that Indian matters should be handled by the national government.

Much comment has been heard about the malicious institution of slavery, which was once formally written into the Constitution and required a war to erase its stain. The failure to look ahead and contemplate the real alternatives to the Indian problem was as great a sin—but one of omission, laziness, and allegiance. It created a situation in which the states and territories would frequently be the opponents of the federal government when Indians were the subject of debate.[7] Because Congress was comprised of senators and representatives of the several states, the opportunities for Indians to consistently receive an impartial hearing in the federal legislature were few. Elected officials were at times torn between their responsibilities as federal representatives and their need to get reelected by their predominantly non-Indian constituents. There was seldom any question where their sympathies lay. The only appeal could be to the sense of national honor, and that was a slim reed upon which tribes could base their hopes.

Learned commentators reviewing the genius of the Constitution frequently argue that the division of sovereignty between three branches of government was sufficient to ensure that the rights of minorities were not abused.[8] The further division of political power between the national government and the states meant that even more protections would be guaranteed because almost all the states modeled their governments after the federal example. This analysis, however, is extremely naive. The constitutional checks-and-balances system protects a temporary political-minority point of view.[9] It allows for the exploitation of any small or dissident group that has any kind of continuing existence in the American social fabric.

Racial minorities, small religious sects, and often the laboring class have had great injustices heaped upon them by the coordinate efforts of these three branches of government because such groups are always in the political minority and are not formally represented anywhere.

Explicit Clauses Dealing with Indians

American Indians are named specifically in two sections of Article 1 of the Constitution. In section 2, paragraph 3, in the formula for determining the apportionment for representatives to Congress and direct taxes, we find the phrase "excluding Indians not taxed." The wording seems to be a variation of similar phrasing found in Article 9 of the Articles of Confederation, which gives to Congress the exclusive right and power to regulate trade and manage affairs with Indians "not member of any of the States." Indeed, the constitutional phrase only makes more specific the distinction between Indians having no relationship to states and individual Indians considered to be regular citizens over whom the states might extend tax liabilities. The phrasing of section 2 appears once again in the Fourteenth Amendment to the Constitution, and the interpretation of the phrase in both instances is reasonably obscure.

Section 8, paragraph 3 contains the major clause by which most actions dealing with Indians have been undertaken. It gives to Congress the power "to regulate Commerce with foreign Nations, and among the several States, and with the Indian Tribes." Most litigation dealing with Indian matters revolves around the interpretation of this clause,[10] and from it springs the massive edifice of legislation, court decisions, and administrative rules and regulations that compose the structure and substance of the federal relationship with Indians and Indian tribes. We will deal more specifically with the meaning and implications of this paragraph later.

One direct reference to Indians contained in the Articles of Confederation was omitted from the provisions of the Constitution. Article 6 prohibited any state from making war unless it was actually being invaded or "shall have received certain advice of a resolution being formed by some nation of Indians to invade such State, and the danger is so imminent as not to admit of a delay, till the United States in Congress assembled can be consulted." This omission cannot be credited wholly to the plenary nature of the commerce clause. The same article gave states the right to send embassies to other states and preserved for states a certain measure of external sovereignty. In the allocation of the diplomatic functions of the federal government, exclusion of the states' right to make war on Indians must be seen as advancing the status of the federal government rather than as an internal reform.

The simple language that mentions Indians in the Constitution does not give any indication of the manner in which the Constitution was to be specifically applied to Indians. Indeed, a careful, plain reading of the clauses indicates that relationships with Indians are an external matter for both the states and the federal government. Congressman Lloyd Meeds (Democrat, Washington), writing his dissent in the final report of the American Indian Policy Review Commission in 1977, said that the Constitution admitted only two sovereigns, the states and the federal government. He could, therefore, find no constitutional basis for supporting Indian tribal sovereignty.[11] In this contention he was absolutely correct, but only insofar as the Constitution identifies the specific sovereigns that created it, the states; establishes and restrains the sovereignty of the federal government; and establishes procedures to admit new states as sovereigns. There is no mention of France or Spain in the Constitution either, but that does not deprive them of the power to make treaties with the United States and have their provisions enforced.

Tribes are preexisting sovereigns whose existence is not beholden to the Constitution or to the federal or state governments. Moreover, the explicitly Indian-related phrases in the Constitution deal with the situation that confronted the United States at the time they were written. When the U.S. Constitution was adopted, Indian tribes, as independent sovereigns, were wholly free to align themselves with any sovereign they wished or to remain nonaligned if they so chose. England and Spain were aggressively courting the larger Indian confederacies, and it was not until the end of the War of 1812 that the United States finally assumed a position of primacy among the sovereigns competing for midcontinent Indian allegiance. On the Pacific coast it was not until the settlement of the Oregon question in the middle of the nineteenth century that the Indian tribes were precluded from dealing with other sovereigns.

Implicit Clauses Dealing with Indians

The Constitution allocates the sovereign powers of our nation between the constituent states and the federal government. In general, according to the explanations offered by advocates of the Constitution in *The Federalist Papers,* most internal affairs of the people are reserved to the states, with the primary exception of the commerce clause, which underscores the need for a uniform commercial system to ensure the free flow of commerce between and among the states. All foreign affairs and the power to deal with the property of the United States are vested in the federal government. The constitutional clauses that imply a power or responsibility to deal with Indians are applicable to the degree that the federal government, finding itself confronted with a new and specific problem involving Indians, looks beyond explicit authorizations and finds that an existing constitutional power originally meant to deal with an entirely different question can be cited as justification for actions it might take in solving the new problem.

There are two aspects to the exercise of such powers that must be noted. On the basis of former acts and the history of former dealings with Indians, Congress, the president, or the federal courts can *assume* that a certain implicit power applies because it has been used before in similar situations. Or — and this difference is critically important — confronted with a new situation for which there does not seem to be an existing constitutional power or congressional act, Congress, the president, or the federal courts can *imply* that an existing power can be used to justify and authorize actions that are contemplated.

The act of assuming or implying that a power or authority exists finds its validity in previous practice, and here precedent plays an important role. Such an act is always subject to the scrutiny of the different branches of the federal government and *should* be subject to some kind of constitutional control or limitation. The course of American history has demonstrated that where Indian tribes have no recourse within the American political system, new laws and new theories of the relationship between the United States and Indians are allowed to go unchallenged and — whether in fact constitutional or not, and whether in fact just or not — become part of the law of the land insofar as it describes the status and rights of American Indians.

Changing either the assumptions about the applicability of a constitutional power or the implications of the applicability of that power has traditionally meant that one of the three branches of the federal government has made a statement of reasonable clarity unchallenged by the other two branches. Clearly this situation has dangers of severe magnitude for Indians. If Indians are not regarded as a subject of pressing national importance — after 1890 they began to play a minor role in domestic affairs — there is no rational basis for one of the branches of the federal government to confront another branch that has done an injustice to Indians. Checks and balances is a valid method of governing only when the subject under discussion has tangible and profound implications and importance for the government as a whole. In the absence of a sense of overwhelming importance, the tendency of the tripartite form of government is to stand back and allow one branch to dominate a certain subject matter, in both a de facto and a de jure manner. This level of domination sometimes reaches the point of actually excluding the other two branches.

Some examples from American history make this situation clear and comprehensible. In the earliest decades of American political existence, it was assumed that the treaty-making power was applicable to Indian tribes and foreign nations.[12] The major difference between dealing with Indian tribes and foreign nations was the necessity of sending formal diplomatic missions to the foreign nations while only sending agents and treaty commissioners to the Indian tribes. With the passage of time and the subsequent expansion of the territory of the United States, Indian lands and tribes became enclosed within the exterior boundaries of the country. It could not be argued with any degree of credibility that Indian tribes remained "foreign," because their geographical location was obviously within the boundaries of the country. Because of their location, then, and solely because of this geographical dimension — even though politically and legally tribal nations remained foreign to the United States — Indians became, in the eyes of many people, a matter of domestic concern. Consequently, in 1871 Congress prohibited the future recognition of any Indian tribe as a political entity with which the United States could make treaties.[13] This unequivocal stand taken by Congress was not challenged by either the judiciary or the executive branches and became law.

From the beginning of the republic until a major Supreme Court decision in 1903, *Lone Wolf v. Hitchcock*,[14] it was assumed that the United States was reasonably restricted in its power to affect the use and status of Indian lands,[15] although the federal government had virtually no restrictions on its power insofar as the imposition of federal criminal jurisdiction onto Indian lands was concerned.[16] Indians, under the doctrine of discovery, had clear equitable title to the lands they occupied, and until they voluntarily chose to sell all or a part of their lands, it was the responsibility and duty of the United States to protect them in the undisturbed enjoyment of their territory.[17] However, in *Lone Wolf v. Hitchcock*, the Supreme Court ruled that the federal government, in the exercise of congressional powers, had, and had always had, plenary powers over Indian lands and property. Plenary power was implied through the application of convoluted judicial logic in defiance of the historical record and specific articles of a treaty written and explained by federal representatives.[18] But the doctrine of plenary power was not challenged or disclaimed by either the Congress or the president and so has come to be regarded as constitutional law.

When implied powers are assumed, the historical record should act as a limitation on their exercise. Precedent plays a critical role in defining the permissible limits within which the implied power can be exercised. When an implied power is the creation of a particular problem-solving situation and there is no good historical precedent or record to which the power can be referred and judged, then the articulation of the power becomes an open-ended proposition. It is, in fact, new law making, a change in the meaning, scope, and intent of the Constitution, and is capable of giving birth to an endless series of additional implied powers or novel applications of the newly articulated power—with virtually no limitations.

In the case of American Indian peoples, the original assumption is that the federal government is authorized and empowered to protect the Indians in the enjoyment of their lands. Once it is implied that this power also involves the ability of the federal government by itself to force a purchase of the lands, there is no way the implied power can be limited. If the government can force the disposal of lands, why can it not determine how the lands are to be used? And if it can determine how the lands are to be used, why can it not tell the Indians how to live? And if it can tell the Indians how to live, why can it not tell them how to behave and what to believe?

And so forth. For small, economically and politically weak groups like Indian tribes, the only slight limitation placed on the federal government is the outcry of the affected tribe, and at times of the general public, at the outrageous conditions the U.S. government has created and perpetuates — conditions that place tribes in precarious positions vis-à-vis states, the federal government, and society at large. Or, as former Commissioner of Indian Affairs Francis A. Walker put it, "the Government is only bound in its treatment of [the Indians] by considerations of present policy and justice and not by the Constitution." [19] The force of implied power simply rolls along of its own internal logic.

Implied powers ebb and flow according to the manner in which the nation sees itself and conducts its business. Almost any clause can be seen, in the right context, as authorizing federal activity consonant with the intent and scope of the Constitution. Depending upon the set of circumstances confronting the federal government and upon its vision of its role in governing the country, the various clauses move in and out of favor according to the political philosophy of those in power. Ultimately, then, implied powers of the Constitution are the trump cards of elected officials, and the government is one of persons, not of laws.

The implied powers of the Constitution that have at one time or another been believed to be applicable to American Indians, their rights, and their properties include the following:

1) the power to lay and collect taxes

2) the power to establish a rule for Naturalization of citizens

3) the power to establish Post Offices and Post Roads

4) the power to constitute Tribunals inferior to the Supreme Court

5) the power to make all Laws which shall be necessary and proper for carrying into Execution other powers

6) the presidential power to grant reprieves and pardons

7) the power of judicial review

8) the power to make new states

9) the power to dispose of and make all needful Rules and Regulations respecting the Territory or other Property belonging to the United States

10) the power to protect states from domestic violence

We shall deal specifically with the application of these powers in the field of Indian affairs below. There is one additional implied power that, because of its importance in Indian matters, must be recognized. Article 6, clause 2, declares that "all Treaties made, or which shall be made, under the Authority of the United States, shall be the supreme law of the land." Assuming, as both the Indians and the United States did, and as history attests, that the treaty-making power extends to the relationship with Indian tribes, then it follows that the treaties made with Indian tribes are the supreme law of the land. The logic of this reasoning attaches to both the treaty document and to the enforcement of its specific provisions. But treaties have been honored in the breach more than in the enforcement. Nevertheless, insofar as we can discuss the application of the Constitution to Indian tribes, their status, rights, and property, it is necessary that we include this subject in our discussion. Consequently, federal legislation dealing with Indians is separate from and has a superior status in comparison to general national legislation and must be treated as a unique subject. As the Supreme Court remarked in *The Kansas Indians*,[20] "the conduct of Indians is not to be measured by the same standard which we apply to the conduct of other people." If we follow the policy originally articulated in the Northwest Ordinance, which is the only clear policy statement made by Congress, all activities dealing with Indians or Indian matters must reflect a high moral standard.

CHAPTER IV

THE RELATIONSHIP OF INDIAN TRIBES

TO THE THREE BRANCHES

OF THE FEDERAL GOVERNMENT

Branches of the Federal Government

The Constitution authorized three coequal branches of the federal government—the legislative, the executive, and the judicial—each with specific functions to perform and restricted powers to exercise. In theory, the smoothly coordinated functioning of these three branches, each vigorously pursuing justice and the welfare of the citizenry, is sufficient guarantee of the rights and liberties of the states, the citizens, and all nations and parties who rely on the promises of the United States. Depending upon the circumstances, anyone approaching the federal government must deal with one or more of these branches—at least, that is what our political scientists and experts in government tell us.

Contact between American Indian tribes and the United States began within two months of the outbreak of hostilities at Concord and Lexington, when the Continental Congress prepared a speech to be made to the western Indian tribes advising them that the quarrel between the colonists and the King of England was a family matter and asking for their neutrality. Under the Articles of Confederation the Congress conducted all Indian affairs using committees and appointed commissioners. With the adoption of the Constitution and the election of a president responsible for treaty making, the executive branch began to play a major role in the Indian relationship. American Indians first formally approached the judicial branch in 1831 and 1832 when two Cherokee cases were filed in the Supreme Court as a court of original jurisdiction.[1]

Over the years the role of each of the branches of government with respect to Indians has changed dramatically. The legislative branch has become the dominant actor in the lives of Indians, and the judicial branch is nearly as important in its role in interpreting the laws of Congress that deal with Indians. The role of the president and the executive branch have changed most fundamentally. With the expansion of the federal government, the bureaucracy itself exercises significant veto power over the president's program and affects congressional lawmaking as well. By stalling the implementation of laws, writing the rules and regulations under which programs operate, and manipulating budget items, the bureaucracy appears to have become a fourth independent branch of government.[2]

In order to understand adequately the application of the Constitution to American Indian tribes, it is necessary to examine the historical relationship of Indian nations to each branch of government. Insofar as each branch understood and fulfilled its responsibilities under the Constitution, we can observe how the Constitution can be said to apply, or not apply, to Indians. To the degree that any branch, or the branches acting in conjunction, redefines its role and responsibilities toward Indians, we can ask whether or not this change is in accord with constitutional principles and powers and whether or not it represents the assumption of unconstitutional powers and the subsequent confiscation of Indian rights and property. We cannot deny that it is necessary that roles and powers of government should change to deal with new conditions. But the process of change should not be whimsical. It should have solid philosophical/jurisprudential logic and contribute to the growth of a logically consistent body of law and policy.

Unfortunately, history shows nothing of the kind. As Indians have become less of a military threat and own considerably less land, the perspective of people serving in the respective branches of government has become harsher and more contemptuous. "Federal Indian law," stripped of the hypocritical veneer given to it by law professors, has become a hodgepodge of personal grudges, ad-hoc policies, inconsistent judicial decisions, and a general exercise of ignorance about Indians, framed in statutory language. Political scientists may wax eloquent about how smoothly our government functions when instructing their colleagues and students, but we all know it is an institution that honors the Constitution more in the breach than in the faithful performance. Therefore, instead of saying what the branches of government are *supposed* to do, we will examine vignettes of what they have *actually* done when dealing with American Indians.

Indians and the Executive Branch

The Constitution gives the president no direct responsibilities for Indians. In his capacity as primary actor in the diplomatic process of treaty making, however, the chief executive very early became involved with American Indians in supervising treaty negotiations at the direction of Congress and in administering the provisions of ratified treaties. The language of treaty making during colonial times involved characterizing the kings of England and France, and ultimately the president of the United States, as "Great Fathers" with both red and white "children" with whom they wanted to live in peace; peace always being made possible, it seemed, by the red children's selling land to the white children.

This imagery also reflects the practice by many Indian nations of designating one elder as the primary chief of the people, a largely advisory position for the most part but one signifying the moral posture of the tribe toward outsiders. No Indian negotiator would think of concluding an agreement without personal reassurance that the moral integrity of the people on the other side was reflected within the agreement. No constitution can describe the aura of moral authority bestowed on the individual occupying its highest office and on the citizens of the country. Most political scientists miss this aspect of government completely.

George Washington played the role of the "Great Father" better than most of his successors and lent dignity to the task of dealing with the Indian nations, but few of the later presidents would devote much time to entertaining delegations in the same manner. On August 8 and 10, 1789, Washington appeared before an ad-hoc Senate committee appointed to confer with the president on the protocol to follow in the ratification of Indian treaties, in making appointments to the various offices dealing with

Indian matters, and in the form of communication to be used between the president and the Senate on these matters.[3] Later that same month, on August 22 and 24, the president met again, this time with the entire Senate, to discuss the treaty problems with the Indian nations inhabiting the southern states.[4] Unfortunately, as the task of government grew more complex, presidents were not able to indulge themselves in open dialogue on Indian matters.

Thomas Jefferson, while developing the view that the Indians should be moved west across the Mississippi where they would be relatively immune to the white man's vices, secretly purchased Louisiana from Napoleon, uncertain whether the purchase was a constitutional act and apparently oblivious to its ultimate impact on Indians. Andrew Jackson had an extreme anti-Indian stance stemming from his military days. He pushed through Congress the Indian Removal Act of May 28, 1830,[5] which enabled the federal government to place the veneer of legality over a policy that encouraged treaty violations by setting in motion a punitive alternative should tribes wish to remain east of the Mississippi. Abraham Lincoln, on the other hand, insisted on reviewing the kangaroo court-martials of the Minnesota Sioux and reduced the number of death sentences significantly, although for political reasons he could not overturn all the proceedings of the Minnesota court.[6]

In 1870, at the very end of the treaty-making period, President Grant initiated a "Peace Policy"[7] in spite of the pressures brought on him from old comrades — military careerists who sought to have Indian affairs placed under the control of the army. This policy of humanitarian concerns, inspired by the Quakers, failed not because of Grant's support but because of the hypocrisy revealed by the churches arguing for "real" Christians to supervise the civilization of the Indians. From 1870 to 1880, it was the custom for presidents to invite Indian delegations to the White House.[8] So we have many pictures of visiting tribal groups who met with the president, received silver peace medals, and went back to their people believing they had received inviolable pledges of justice from the government. Included with these tours, however, were side trips to naval installations, army barracks, and other locations where the military might of the United States was deeply impressed on the chiefs. Intimidation rather than good will was the diplomatic method of dealing with American Indians during this time.

Francis Leupp, commissioner of Indian affairs from 1905 to 1909, wrote a book, *The Indian and His Problem,* shortly after his tenure as head of the Bureau of Indian Affairs (BIA). He was impressed with the generally warm and open attitude of some of the presidents when dealing with Indian matters. Leupp recounted that:

> . . . on the 4th of March, 1897, . . . President Cleveland was warned that a tricky paragraph had got into the pending Indian appropriation bill, favoring a certain private mining scheme on a remote reservation. He refused therefore to sign the bill, and it died with the Congress and the administration.[9]

Leupp did not, as we shall see, find Congress equally as concerned.

Franklin D. Roosevelt ensured that Indians were included in the New Deal programs even though separate services for Indians existed. Thus Civilian Conservation Corps camps brought substantial wage employment to the reservations for the first time, replacing part-time and seasonal work. Roosevelt also appointed sympathetic men to offices responsible for Indian matters, most notably Harold Ickes (secretary of the interior) and John Collier (commissioner of Indian affairs), and even intervened on behalf of the Seminoles when the Bureau of Animal Husbandry threatened to kill deer on the Seminole Reservation in Florida on the excuse that they carried cattle ticks. Roosevelt's letter to Claude Wickard, secretary of agriculture, is a classic example of positive leadership in the executive branch:

> Dear Claude:
>
> Tell your Bureau of Animal Husbandry that I do not want any deer killed on the Seminole Reservation in Florida until this war is over. Tell them to have the proposed amendment put on by the House eliminated in the Senate — $5,000. Tell them that if the thing stays in the bill I will impound the money. The point is that no one knows whether these unfortunate animals are hosts to cattle ticks or not. The investigation ought to teach us more about it. You might also tell the Bureau of Animal Husbandry that they have never proved that human beings are not hosts to cattle ticks. I think some human beings I know are. But I do not shoot them on suspicion — though I would sorely like to do so!
>
> Always sincerely,
> (Signed) FRANKLIN D. ROOSEVELT [10]

In 1966 Lyndon Johnson appointed the first American Indian to a federal post since the Grant administration and demanded that the Bureau of Indian Affairs be cleaned up. He later established by executive order the National Council on Indian Opportunity, chaired by the vice-president, which for a short while shared policy recommendations with Indian leaders.[11] And Richard Nixon took the lead in restoring lands that had been wrongly confiscated by the government or erroneously excluded from the reservations by faulty surveys.[12] He also materially assisted with the repeal of Menominee termination[13] and secured passage of the Alaska Native Claims Settlement Act.[14]

Detrimental errors made by some chief executives in applying constitutional principles to American Indians include the refusal to demonstrate leadership in the formation of Indian policy and the acquiescence to actions of another branch of government that were clearly morally wrong. Andrew Jackson's role in substituting his own personal racial agenda for previous solemn promises was despicable but part of the risk every government takes in having individual leaders. But what do we make of Dwight D. Eisenhower's signing terminal legislation and a statute that allowed states to unilaterally assume civil and criminal jurisdiction over Indian reservations,[15] thereby voiding many treaty guarantees by simply walking away from responsibility? Eisenhower signed the bill while remarking that the act was "a most un-Christian thing to do."

Although there was an outcry against Jackson's agenda, by Eisenhower's era, Americans simply assumed that the president had no moral agenda to which he could be held responsible. Ronald Reagan waited until the last two months of his two-term tenure in the White House to meet with a group of Indians about the posture of his administration. A straggling few Indian leaders attended the sessions, probably because they had never been to the White House before, and listened to Reagan stumble through a prepared speech while movers were packing furniture and personal belongings to prepare the executive mansion for the Bushes.

In general, the beneficial acts of presidents have been remembered far more often than their perfidy. The benign image of the president and the exaggeration of the scope of his powers has remained reasonably strong in the minds of American Indians, so that their expectations of receiving justice from the president through his active intervention on their behalf has not eroded very much in the course of American history.

This belief was evident as recently as May 1994, when President Clinton invited scores of Indian and Alaskan Native political leaders to meet with him on the White House lawn. Mustering both the symbolic and substantive power of his office, Clinton reaffirmed the government-to-government relationship between tribes and the United States and stressed his support for tribal self-determination and the trust obligations of the federal government. Clinton vowed "to honor and respect sovereignty based upon our unique historic relationship," and he pledged to protect the right of tribes to exercise their religious freedoms.[16] This gathering was hailed by the White House and throughout Indian country as a major event, but it did little to derail Congress's plan to cut social, health, educational, and legal support for tribes, an agenda with which Clinton agreed.

For a short period of time a president did exercise a kind of constitutional power when dealing with Indians. Beginning in May 1855, President Franklin Pierce set aside tracts of land by executive order as Indian reservations.[17] No constitutional power existed for the president to act in this manner until the passage of the General Allotment Act in 1887,[18] when language in that legislation seemed to authorize the recognition of reservations established through that device. The president could, in the exercise of this power, also abolish reservations he had created. This power, despite its expansive nature, did not vest legal title in the Indians and thus was not primarily used for the benefit of Indians. It was actually an administrative ploy to handle the rapid settlement of some of the western regions and to provide land for tribes "separated from evil example or annoyance of unprincipled whites who might be disposed to settle in their vicinity."[19] In other cases, executive orders were used on behalf of tribes with whom the United States did not wish to sign treaties.

Congress acquiesced in this practice as long as land was plentiful and settlers few in the western territories. In 1919, however, at the urging of white settlers and state officials, Congress declared that "hereafter no public lands of the United States shall be withdrawn by Executive Order, proclamation, or otherwise, for or as an Indian reservation except by act of Congress."[20] Eight years later, in 1927, Congress further narrowed the president's power to deal with boundaries and Indian reservation land titles when it declared that "hereafter changes in the boundaries of reservations created by Executive Order, proclamation, or otherwise for the use and occupation of Indians shall not be made except by Act of Congress: *Provided*, that this shall not apply to temporary withdrawals by the Secretary of the Interior."[21]

Some real but unrecognized questions arise in this short history. The constitutional argument is subtle here. Presumably there is no public-domain land owned by the United States except that which has been purchased by the federal government from an Indian tribe or tracts that have been abandoned by a number of tribes and are therefore "unclaimed." Since the government was rounding up Indians and placing them on reservations, it can hardly be said that anyone had actually abandoned their lands. The president was therefore confiscating Indian property when he segregated out a small tract of land for a tribe and recognized the remainder as public domain. Nowhere in the Constitution do we find this power, and while Congress eventually limited the practice, it certainly acquiesced long enough for it to become an accepted administrative device.

In the alternative, even assuming that the United States does own both the legal and equitable titles to the land — thus precluding all Indian claims whatsoever, claims generally rejected by courts and commentators — what happens when the president sets aside public lands for Indians? It would appear that the president was giving away property of the United States without any constitutional or congressional authority. When Congress forbade this practice, it gave no reason for doing so. The problem was that for a period of time, two branches of the government refused to confront each other over dubious practices, and the third branch, the Supreme Court, had no authority to call them into question absent legislation in which the problem was raised. The question of aboriginal land title was raised on several occasions in the Indian Claims Commission,[22] and, allowing for some few exceptions, litigant tribes usually had their aboriginal occupancy areas recognized, at least for the purpose of resolving their claims for compensation for the taking of the lands.

The relationship between Indian tribes and subordinate officers and agencies of the federal government is somewhat different than their relationship with the president. In the early days of the republic, Indian matters were allocated throughout the government according to their subject matter. Thus, the preservation of treaty texts and supervision of territorial affairs involving Indians were responsibilities of the State Department; general Indian matters and the distribution of annuity goods were handled by the War Department; treaties were negotiated by presidentially appointed commissioners; land matters and the procurement of annuity goods, as well as the later operation of trading houses and factories, were the responsibilities of the Treasury Department. The Indian relationship with the United States affected several departments of the government, and the exercise of the commerce clause was spread to a number of constitutionally authorized administrative agencies. This condition reflected partially the national status of the Indian tribes and partially the embryonic condition of the federal government in its formative stages.

In 1834 the situation changed radically. Congress passed two acts that reduced the focus of Indian affairs to a single department's bureau and systematized its rules for conducting commerce with the Indians. The first act, "to regulate trade and intercourse with the Indian tribes,"[23] not only provided an overview of existing laws regulating trade but also featured congressional initiatives to resolve the problems of criminal jurisdiction and the status of tribes and agencies. This act can be understood as the primary move away from a negotiated relationship toward an eventual administrative solution to Indian problems. Equally as important in this respect was the companion act, "to provide for the organization of the Department of Indian Affairs,"[24] which created an administrative structure within which programs for Indians would be administered. The combination of the two acts meant that the rights of most Indian tribes became a matter of administrative option rather than nationally enforceable law.

In 1849 the Bureau of Indian Affairs was transferred to the newly created Department of the Interior.[25] From that time until 1950, when Congress passed two major educational statutes, the School Facilities Construction Act (P.L. 815)[26] and the Federally Impacted Areas Act (P.L. 874),[27] the BIA was the primary representative of the United States to Indian tribes. In effect, the creation of the BIA meant that the legislative and executive functions of the government were merged together in an administrative agency, creating a new creature with wholly new powers. In time, the bureau came to dominate every aspect of Indian life. Yet its authorization could not be challenged constitutionally because it was created in part to fulfill federal treaty provisions and in part to administer programs for the benefit of Indians, a mission well within the exercise of congressional plenary power. The problem was that none of the branches of government had conceived of the federal government possessing plenary power over Indians except in the political sense.

One of the most pernicious transfers of authority within the executive branch was the Indian Delegation Act,[28] which authorized the secretary of the interior to delegate some of his power to the commissioner of Indian affairs and for the commissioner to do likewise until power to make decisions was reduced to a much lower level. Every decision made within the bureau continued to be reviewed by everyone higher on the bureaucratic food chain, however, and the net result was to create an unconscionable lag time for decisions affecting Indian lives and property. The moral implications were even worse. Now blame could be distributed over such a wide range of offices that no one could ever be held accountable to any standard of performance whatsoever.

By the 1960s the executive branch and its agencies were well on their way to once again creating a governmentwide service network to serve Indian tribes. In national laws addressing poverty, revenue-sharing, and the environment, Indian tribes became recognized agencies for the reception of federal funding. This expansion was not due to the recognition of Indian tribes as treaty-making entities standing outside the constitutional framework. Rather, Indian tribes, because of their public nature and semi-corporate status established by the adoption of constitutions and bylaws under the Indian Reorganization Act,[29] were made eligible to be sponsoring agencies under federal social reform laws that sought to serve all American citizens. In the administration of many programs, the tribe, although the official sponsor, had to provide services for nontribal members within the geographical area the program served.

On the other hand, special legislation enabling tribes to provide to their members services that would otherwise have been provided by the federal government created a strange twist in the relation of tribes to the executive branch. Under the provisions of the Indian Education and Self-determination Act,[30] popularly known as "638," and the Tribal Self-Governance Act,[31] tribes could perform many BIA functions, in effect making them a part of the executive branch as far as these programs were concerned. But no one was certain whether the Indian Delegation Act of 1946 covered the appointments clause of the Constitution, which restricted the executive branch in delegating its powers and responsibilities to a nonfederal entity. In the 1960s a federal court ruled that tribal courts, established as part of the Indian Reorganization Act programs, were sufficiently federal to enable an Indian to file a writ of habeas corpus seeking relief from a tribal-court judgment.[32]

At the present time, when there is perceived misconduct by the executive branch regarding its refusal to act on behalf of Indians, the remedies available to Indian nations include, among others, the right to file suit in the federal courts to compel an executive officer to act on their behalf or to prohibit the same from acting to their detriment. But these suits have only occasionally been successful[33] and have in no way diminished the federal government's self-described power to eliminate tribal governments if it so chooses.[34] Because Indians are the exclusive concern of the federal government through the allocation of the commerce clause, executive officers are given unusually wide discretion in the exercise of their powers. Any appeal is ultimately an appeal to basic morality and not a constitutional remedy.

Indians and the Legislative Branch

Comprehensively describing the relationship of American Indians to the federal legislative branch is a massive study in itself. We can only sketch out the basic outlines of the relationship here, but simply identifying the areas in which Indians and the legislative branch interact should be sufficient. Historically, there have been three areas of congressional action that affected Indians and their rights and property: 1) congressional acts that seek to establish the laws under which Indians will be related to the federal government, 2) appropriation acts that provide funds and instructions for the expenditure of funds, and 3) acts that deal with the rights and property of states and citizens that have some relationship to the rights and property of Indians.

Congressional actions in the first category usually involve treaty and agreement promises and provisions. At the beginning of the republic, when the presence of Indian tribes on the frontier made Indians an important national topic, Congress gave serious consideration to the provisions of treaties; its major policy direction was to ensure peaceful relations with the tribes. Evidence of this attitude can be seen in the careful treatment of the boundary line that marked the lands remaining to the tribes as Indian country and separated the Indian lands from the territory the United States had acquired in treaty cessions. In a series of trade and intercourse acts beginning in 1790[35] and concluding in 1834,[36] Congress faithfully attempted to define the boundaries of Indian lands and federal public lands to reflect each of the changes brought about by treaty cessions. By 1834 the line was so tortuous and complicated that Congress settled on a general definition of what the term "Indian country" meant: "That all that part of the United States west of the Mississippi, and not within the states of Missouri and Louisiana, or the territory of Arkansas, and, also that part of the United States east of the Mississippi River, and not within any state to which the Indian title has not been extinguished, for the purpose of this act, be taken and deemed to be Indian country."[37] Thereafter Congress made no attempt to define the scope and extent of Indian country, and it became a technical term used by the federal courts and administrative agencies to roughly determine the locations at which federal authority would be presumed to be in effect.

A similar example can be seen in the handling of treaty and agreement annuities and payments. Beginning with the first Indian treaty in 1778[38] and continuing until the Snyder Act of 1921,[39] Congress laboriously listed item by item the funds to which individual tribes were entitled in its annual appropriation acts. The Snyder Act, which appropriated funds for expenditure for Indians under a broad authority given to the Secretary of the Interior, was enacted in order to simplify the appropriation of moneys. This act greatly expanded the moneys available for Indians because it released the government from a strict adherence to the provisions of treaties, most of which had been authorized at a time when minimal funding was adequate to enable the federal government to fulfill its treaty and trust obligations to tribes.

In addition to the treatment of lands and treaty annuities, a major problem confronting Congress was the task of securing an adequate system of civil and criminal law over areas where the tribes and white citizens interacted with each other and over the reservations themselves when it appeared that tribal governments were no longer able to provide a measure of social order. It was not until Congress adopted the policy of forced assimilation in the 1880s and began to deal arbitrarily with the status and disposition of tribal lands that serious constitutional questions concerning the scope of congressional power began to arise. We will discuss these questions below when we examine the specific constitutional clauses that have been cited as authority for certain kinds of congressional acts.

Indian treaties were generally not self-executing. That is, following the signing, ratification, and proclamation of an Indian treaty, few provisions automatically took effect and became law. Since most treaties involved some kind of land cession and required some kind of annuity payment, Congress was required to pass enabling legislation to appropriate the funds or, in the case where lands were opened at a certain price and the proceeds were to be deposited in the Treasury to the credit of the tribe, Congress had to act to establish the procedures under which this task was accomplished. And in many instances where the treaty called for the establishment of schools, trading posts, hospitals, and other social services, Congress had to authorize construction and the creation of specific positions within the Bureau of Indian Affairs. Thus, appropriation acts became the most important aspect of the legislative agenda for Indians.[40]

Some constitutional questions should be raised with respect to the manner in which congress used the appropriation statutes to change the status and rights of Indians. There are two aspects of this area that warrant discussion. First are the occasions when Congress reduced the amount of treaty annuities owed the tribes or changed the term of years during which the annuities would be paid. On these occasions it was customary to send a federal delegation back to the tribes concerned and secure signatures of the chiefs and headmen approving the reduction. A good example is the provision for annuities in the 1851 Fort Laramie Treaty[41] with the Sioux and other tribes. The term of years for the distribution of an annual amount of $50,000 in annuities to the Indians was originally a period of fifty years. But Congress subsequently reduced it to ten years with a stipulation that the president could recommend an additional five years if he so chose. The record, moreover, is confused regarding the legality of securing the signatures of chiefs following this reduction in the term because the changes were not made in an open council.[42]

Second, Congress quite frequently attached radical policy-change riders to appropriation acts, provisions that substantially altered the rights of Indians with little congressional debate and no tribal consent. The best example of this practice is the prohibition against further treaty making inserted in the 1871 appropriation act following a minor item appropriated for the Yankton Sioux.[43] That such a major change in the direction of Indian policy could occur almost as an afterthought raises substantial constitutional questions. We will deal with the major arguments later. It is sufficient here to note that in the relationship between Indians and the United States, the propensity of Congress to attach fundamental policy changes to legislation that it was their responsibility to pass under the treaty relationship raises serious questions about the fairness of the procedure and whether or not some of these congressional initiatives were in fact unconstitutional exercises of power, not simply the product of the exercise of plenary power.

In the continuing conflict between the claims and rights of non-Indian American citizens and the Indian tribes with whom the United States has treaty relationships, there is no question but that Congress has heavily favored non-Indian citizens, often in derogation of explicit treaty responsibilities. Almost from the beginning of the republic until the present time, Congress has frequently protected Indian rights only to the degree that they do not conflict with the wishes and interests of non-Indian citizens and/or the federal agencies that often have a conflicting or competing interest to the Indian tribes. Land preemption laws granted good title to Indian lands to non-Indian interlopers who refused to obey federal land laws and moved into Indian country before the lands were purchased by the United States. Homestead acts, railroad subsidy grants, swamplands grants, irrigation districts, and the establishment of national parks and forests all entailed the confiscation of millions of acres of Indian land without any consideration for the existing rights of Indians. One solitary case, *U.S. ex rel the Hualapai Indians v. Santa Fe Pacific Railroad Company*,[44] raised significant questions about the manner in which Congress granted lands to others before it extinguished the title of the Indians, but neither Congress nor the executive branch, nor even later courts, had any enthusiasm for following the directions of the Supreme Court in this matter.

In the first century of American political existence, when the Indians could have most constructively dealt with congressional committees, there were few opportunities to do so. With the exception of representatives from the Five Civilized Tribes, who were sent to Washington to oppose

specific pieces of legislation, few Indians ever saw a senator or congressman; their dealings when in our nation's capital were almost always with
the president and members of the executive branch. The 1867–1868 Peace
Commission[45] had several senators as members, but their concern was
that congress would accept the treaties they were negotiating. During this
period some congressmen were known to tribal leaders because of the
proximity of their homes to reservations or because of past commercial
dealings. These elected officials were hostile to Indian interests; they had
been elected and reelected many times to seek removal of the tribes or
confiscation of Indian lands. And even in the 1890s, congressional committees were hard-pressed to understand the conditions under which Indians
lived. This situation continued until the 1920s, when numerous tribal delegations became more forthright and began to appear in Washington in an
effort to secure federal legislation opening the court of claims to them.[46]

Former Indian Commissioner Francis Leupp, seeking to applaud the few
members of Congress who did work intelligently on Indian legislation, unwittingly left us an accurate description of the real functioning of the legislative branch. Leupp observed:

> When it is remembered that all laws and appropriations are passed by
> the votes, or the silent consent, of more than five hundred members of
> the two houses of Congress, that *probably not more than one-fifth of
> these know anything at all about Indians, and that, of this small group,
> it is doubtful whether a dozen know anything of tribes outside of the
> borders of their own States respectively,* it argues pretty well for the in-
> dustry and interest of a few men that we obtain any Indian legislation
> of real value.[47] [Emphasis added]

In other words, instead of Indian legislation being the product of intelligent debate, it is, and generally has been, a matter of indifference and ignorance in considering bills. The process has been at the mercy of the for-
tunes of chance.

Leupp was even more specific in his criticism of the manner in which
Congress dealt with Indian legislation, citing an example of the haphazard
manner in which the legislative branch fulfilled its constitutional duties.
Describing the Burke Bill,[48] which had been carefully considered in com-
mittee and discussed ably on the floor of the House of Representatives,
Leupp writes that a member:

who feared lest it might contain something which would conflict with the existing laws affecting the Five Civilized Tribes [Cherokee, Creek, Chocktaw, Chickasaw, and Seminole], proposed an amendment excepting from its operation "the Indians of the Indian Territory." Although the House had been legislating on Indian Territory affairs for so many years, *neither the proposer of the amendment nor any other member present* seems to have been aware that there were any Indians in the Territory besides the Five Civilized Tribes; so the amendment went through without opposition.[49] [Emphasis added]

But even with this ignorance and inattention by Congress, Indian legislation does not simply appear out of nowhere. It has a systematic origin and established procedures, both of which, as we might suspect, are often corrupted by informal practices, so that pretending there is some constitutional duty being performed is sheer hypocrisy.

Leupp noted that most Indian legislation was submitted to the Department of the Interior and formally introduced at the request of the executive branch. But then corruption frequently marched in and took over the process:

If a political henchman was to be rewarded, and none of the other budget bills afforded a means of taking care of him, he was permitted to become an "attorney" for some Indian tribe, and his fees appropriated in the Indian bill; or if there had been a deadlock between the two houses on any question, and only a few votes were needed in one or the other to break it, those votes could occasionally be procured by wedging something into the Indian bill at the last moment for the gratification of wavering members who had Indians in their bailiwicks.[50]

This practice may be practical politics, but it does not derive from any constitutional article, phrase, or clause. The reality is a great deal more grim. "It is the unwritten law that any Senator who is a member of the Indian Affairs Committee may have practically whatever he asks for in his own State, if within the power of the committee to grant it," Leupp observed. "Thus it sometimes happens that a dubious item finds its way into an Indian bill while it is still in committee, and is reported to the Senate with the rest. Even the members of the committee who have consented to the inclusion of the item may have nothing to say in its defence beyond the unadorned explanation that 'Senator Blank wished that amendment added, and of course we put it on.'"[51]

This practice controls much of Indian legislation today. Senator Slade Gorton of Washington developed a severe resentment of Indians when he was attorney general of that state. He initiated a number of suits against tribes, specifically on the treaty fishing rights, and was responsible for a long period of oppression of the Indian groups in Washington. Finally the United States filed suit to protect the Indians, and in 1974 a federal district court ruled in *United States v. Washington*[52] that the Indians were entitled to half of the fish caught in that state each year under the Isaac Stevens treaties of 1854–1856. Gorton apparently seethed about this loss for years, and unfortunately for the Washington state tribes in particular and all tribes in general, he became a senator and secured membership on the important Committee on Indian Affairs, which is the authorizing committee for programs of the Bureau of Indian Affairs, the Indian Health Service, the Administration for Native Americans in the Department of Health and Human Services, and the Office of Indian Education in the Department of Education.

The committee also has oversight responsibility for operation of programs in all other federal agencies with programs affecting Indians, including the Indian Housing Program of the Department of Housing and Urban Development. In addition, it is charged with dealing with matters relating to tribal and individual lands, the government's trust responsibilities, Indian claims, and natural resources, among other things.[53] In short, this committee (and the subcommittee in the House) is charged with an enormous task: the oversight of Congress's continuing historical, constitutional, and legislative obligations to over five hundred tribal and Alaska-native polities.

During his tenure on the committee, Gorton has sought to stymie tribes in their efforts to be self-governing. In 1995, for example, Senator Gorton introduced H.R. 1977 making amendments to the Department of the Interior's budget for the next year. Basically, Gorton wanted to take away certain fundamental rights of Indian tribes that had been undisputed since the beginning of the republic. His amendment reads:

Sec. 115 (a) Of the funds appropriated by this act or any subsequent act providing for appropriations in fiscal years 1996 and 1997, not more than 50 percent of any self-governance funds that would otherwise be allocated to each Indian tribe in the State of Washington shall actually be paid to the account of such Indian tribe from and after the time at which such tribe shall—

(1) take unilateral action that adversely impacts the existing rights and/or customary use of, nontribal member owners of the tribe's reservation to water, electricity, or any other similar utility or necessity for the nontribal members' residential use of such land; or

(2) restrict or threaten to restrict said owners' use of areas to publicly maintained rights of way necessary or desirable in carrying the utilities or necessities described above.

(b) Such penalty shall attach to the initiation of any legal action with respect to such rights or the enforcement of any final judgment, appeals from which has been exhausted, with respect thereto.[54]

In effect, Gorton sought to take away all property rights of the tribes and even punish them for filing a lawsuit with which a white person might disagree. Some tribes provided the utility services to non-Indians living on the reservations, and they would have been forbidden under this rider to raise normal sewer and garbage collection fees on white residents even if the same fee raises were imposed on tribal members receiving the services.

There was a deafening silence from constitutional law professors regarding the appropriateness or constitutionality of Gorton's actions. Had it not been for the Seattle newspapers that protested this amendment and the support of Senators Domenici, McCain, and Inouye, the amendment might have become law. In 1997 Gorton struck again. Once more using the Department of the Interior's appropriation bills, Gorton inserted a provision that tribes would have to waive sovereign immunity for lawsuits that would normally go to tribal courts, thus allowing anyone to sue the tribe in federal court, overturning over a century of tribal-court existence. Another provision would have forced tribes to account for all their income; the wealthier tribes would then be denied federal assistance, whether conditions on the reservations warranted it or not.

Clearly, the abuses described by former Commissioner Leupp had only increased since 1910. Gorton's provisions were withdrawn on the promise by other senators that hearings would be held in 1998 on his amendments.

Three hearings were held in 1998, but Gorton again went on the offensive, this time drafting a freestanding bill reprising his 1997 appropriation rider, ironically titled the "American Indian Equal Justice Act." As the *New York Times* put it in an editorial, "Senator Slade Gorton has once again declared war on the Indians."[55] As of this writing, a victor has not yet been declared. Gorton, however, has indicated that he will continue to use all his senatorial power in his quest to weaken if not eclipse tribal powers of economic self-determination. Gorton pushed ahead despite the fact that his political efforts violate the federal government's long-standing treaty and moral obligations to tribes. Because legislators and the legislative process are so inconsistent in fulfilling the constitutional mandate to tribal nations, it seems somewhat problematic that the federal courts would use the phrase "wisdom of Congress" and try to determine congressional intent when examining and interpreting federal statutes. Clearly a much higher sense of personal morality and ethics is required of Congress if the constitutional provisions are to work with any degree of justice at all. There were times in this century, however, when members of Congress actually visited Indian reservations, observed conditions, and initiated efforts for reform. Between 1928 and 1945, the Senate Indian Committee conducted an extensive investigation of Indian conditions.[56] Touring senators held hearings in most of the western states at reservation-agency headquarters, and extensive hearings were held in Washington, D.C. The prolonged exposure of the lawmakers to Indians was the first real effort by a formal committee of Congress to fulfill its constitutional mandate. Reports of the committee were influential in later legislative successes: the passage of the Indian Reorganization Act;[57] the Leavitt Act,[58] which cancelled irrigation charges against Indian allotments; the Johnson-O'Malley Act[59] for Indian education; and the Indian Claims Commission Act.[60]

In the 1960s Senator Sam Ervin's Subcommittee on Constitutional Rights held hearings for several years on Indian civil and criminal jurisdiction problems, resulting in the passage of the Indian Civil Rights Act.[61] The American Indian Policy Review Commission,[62] arising out of the occupation of Wounded Knee in 1973, was originally an effort to get people in Congress to investigate for themselves what was happening on the reservations. Unfortunately, the commission appointed eleven task forces to investigate and turn in reports. Again some positive legislation emerged from the conclusions of this commission, although no member of Congress actually toured the Indian areas as had the senators in 1928.

In 1987 Congress initiated a two-year bipartisan investigation of the alleged corruption, fraud, and mismanagement of the Bureau of Indian Affairs and several other agencies that dealt with tribes.[63] Congress's investigation had been prompted by a six-month investigative report by several journalists working for the *Arizona Republic* newspaper.

Other than these efforts, very little has been done in this century by Congress to develop expertise in Indian matters, which would enable members of the two houses to do their constitutionally mandated work.

Indians and the Judicial Branch

Although it was contemplated in *The Federalist Papers* that a supreme court was necessary to create a viable national government, the existence of a judicial branch has not materially aided Indians in seeking justice, nor has it provided much constitutional protection. One of the arguments for a supreme court and federal judiciary put forward by advocates of the Constitution was to avoid the possibility of having each state supreme court issue its own interpretation of federal treaties and laws. In spite of this hope, in Indian affairs, as well as in treaties and domestic legislation dealing with Japan and China and their citizens, state courts have often felt free to promote their own version of federal treaties and statutes to the detriment of these racial minorities.[64]

The most important thing to remember about the Supreme Court is that though the executive may make treaties, issue executive orders, and promulgate rules and regulations, and though Congress may pass statutes, conduct investigations, and pass resolutions, nothing that either branch does is regarded as law in the ultimate sense until the Supreme Court, reviewing a challenge to the actions of the two other branches, declares it constitutional. In spite of massive evidence supporting a particular interpretation of a statute, the Supreme Court may, and often does, substitute its own meaning and content to the actions of the other branches, attributing motives to both actors and branches that could not possibly have existed at the time the action was taken. Thus the Supreme Court in *San*

Mateo Co. v. Southern Pacific R.R. Co.[65] accepted the unreasonable argument made by Roscoe Conkling, former senator and lawyer for the railroad, that the Senate had been thinking primarily of corporations when it framed the Fourteenth Amendment. Chief Justice Waite in *Santa Clara Co. v. Southern Pacific R.R. Co.*[66] simply announced this doctrine, and corporations have been blessed and protected ever since.

Although some commentators believe the Supreme Court has been a stalwart protector of Indian rights,[67] this rather naive view comes from a limited perspective on the actions of the Court. Indeed, one can trace short periods of time when a court has ruled favorably in some Indian cases. On the whole, however, the Supreme Court has been inattentive, flippant, and disrespectful of Indian rights, and has seen its task as one of finding arguments that will make actions by the other two branches appear legal. Many "doctrines" have emerged over the course of 170 years of hearing Indian cases, but the various courts have felt no compulsion to follow precedent, nor have they paid much attention to the historical activities of the federal government toward Indians, often inventing their own version of history as they decided each case.[68]

In the pre–Civil War period, most litigation revolving around American Indians was heard in state courts and usually involved questions of citizenship for those Indians who had remained east of the Mississippi when their parent tribes moved west during the Indian removal period (1830s–1840s). A few cases that appear to involve Indians are in fact the result of whites' claiming land or privileges that ultimately derive from some treaty or statute involving Indians. Thus, the most popular articulation of the doctrine of discovery, *Johnson v. McIntosh*,[69] is a quarrel between two whites over title to lands that were once ceded by Indian tribes to the United States and under public sale by Great Britain. *Gaines v. Nicholson*,[70] another case of some note, did not have an Indian plaintiff or defendant, and *New Jersey v. Wilson*[71] was an effort by a white man to claim a tax exemption given the Delaware Nation and to determine whether that exemption applied to later holders of the land.

Beginning with the Cherokee cases in 1831–1832, the federal courts began to see Indian nations as occasional parties to lawsuits. Legal scholars have not dealt adequately or properly with the nature of the Cherokee cases, so that the relationship of Indian nations to the judicial branch remains unclear to this day, even though practice has made Indians regular visitors to the federal court system. The basic question of *Cherokee Nation v. Georgia* (1831) was whether or not the Cherokees could approach the Supreme Court as a court of original jurisdiction based on their treaty rights. Justice John Marshall's answer had to be a resounding "No" because he was faced with the prospect of watching a tidal wave of lawsuits filed by various Indian nations flood his court. Hence, contained in the decision is demeaning language hinting at a wardship status for Indians and declaring tribes to be "domestic-dependent nations." In *Worcester v. Georgia* (1832), however, the question was phrased squarely: did federal laws hold in territory under federal protection? The disparaging remarks of the earlier decision were now firmly recast as supportive of the federal treaty process and its validity.

In the abstract—the manner in which law professors think—the more appropriate action of the Cherokees would have been to send a delegation to see the president and demand action, supported by foreign nations with a concern for international legal principles. But because governments are operated by persons, whereas constitutions express ideals, such a course would have been disastrous because Andrew Jackson was committed to removing Indians from east of the Mississippi—if not from the face of the earth. Gradually during the nineteenth century and increasingly in this century, with little chance to negotiate changes and with Congress unilaterally passing statutes that radically changed their status and occasionally confiscated their property, the Indian nations were reduced to seeking what relief they could in the federal court system.

At first there were what could be called test cases, in which an Indian agreed to become a plaintiff in order to test the scope and application of federal law. *Elk v. Wilkins* (Indian citizenship),[72] *Lone Wolf v. Hitchcock* (legality of congressional change of agreement),[73] and *Quick Bear v. Leupp* (tribal funds for sectarian education)[74] quickly come to mind. And a number of cases involved Indian plaintiffs who understood the law and sought relief, such as *The Cherokee Tobacco*.[75] In some cases that went to the Supreme Court, the Indian was the complainant but hardly a knowledgeable party, such as *Ex parte Crow Dog*[76] and *United States v. Kagama*.[77] Finally, there were cases in which lower-level federal employees, zealous to bring some measure of justice to the Indians, moved a case through the courts to protect the tribes, such as *United States v. Winans*.[78] Congress even passed a statute allowing a member of the Five Civilized Tribes to seek relief in the Supreme Court, but he was turned aside in *United States v. Muskrat*[79] with the comment that Congress had authorized the Court to give an advisory opinion, which it could not do. Deprived of relief in the other two branches of government, the tribes began to see the federal courts as a possible source of support. Thus the Yankton Sioux, in negotiating the agreement of 1892, asked that one of the provisions be that any disputes between them and the United States be settled by the Supreme Court.[80] In 1863 Congress had prohibited cases involving treaties to go to the Supreme Court without its permission — ostensibly to block an effort by the French government to use American courts but in reality to turn aside the Five Civilized Tribes who were coming to understand American jurisprudence.[81] For a long while the Congress was expected to both interpret and remedy nebulous or unfulfilled provisions of treaty articles.[82] Although petitions continued to be addressed to Congress, a growing number of tribes sought special legislation to get their claims heard in the U.S. Court of Claims, with the hopes for appeal to the Supreme Court on a point of law. In this century it has simply become an automatic track of the federal court system that has moved a mass of Indian cases through the district and circuit courts to the Supreme Court with hopes of receiving certiorari.

   The Brethren by Bob Woodward and Scott Armstrong draws a less than flattering portrait of the justices' attitude toward Indian cases. Discussing the decision in *Tooahnippah v. Hickel*,[83] the authors note that the case was called a "peewee" by Justice Harlan, a term for an insignificant matter. Justice Brennan, a supposed liberal on the Court, rebelled at being assigned to write the opinion in *Antoine v. Washington*,[84] calling it a "chicken-shit case."[85] It may be that previous courts and justices did not relish hearing or deciding Indian cases, either, and felt uncomfortable when they were called upon to write the opinions. The flippancy and illogical reasoning of some decisions[86] would lead the impartial reader to conclude that the Supreme Court did not even try to reach a just conclusion, either for or against Indians — that the decisions may have been written during a fit of intellectual discomfort. How else can we account for the reasoning in the cases listed below:

The Cherokee Tobacco—Cherokee Indians are found liable to pay federal revenue taxes on their products even when it is admitted they do not live within a revenue district.

U.S. v. Kagama—The federal government has jurisdiction over criminal activity on a reservation in California not because of the commerce clause or treaty provisions but because it is the property owner of the land where the crime was committed.

Lone Wolf v. Hitchcock—Congress can override treaty provisions in an emergency; therefore it can override them as a normal procedure, and besides, it is a mere transformation of Indian property and therefore an administrative matter.

U.S. v. Sandoval—Congress cannot exercise its power over any community by "calling them an Indian tribe" but only over "distinctly Indian communities."

Incisive and tedious review of Supreme Court decisions would show that this tendency to write law without reference to any doctrines or precedents is more the rule than the exception.

At other times, justices simply let their prejudice run wild. In *U.S. v. Sioux Nation,*[87] Justice Rehnquist, filing a bitter dissent, remarked:

> There were undoubtedly greed, cupidity, and other less-than-honorable tactics employed by the Government during the Black Hills episode in the settlement of the West, *but the Indians did not lack their share of villainy either.* [Emphasis added]

In other words: Sure we committed a great many crimes when we took the Black Hills from the Sioux Indians, but they used to beat their wives, get drunk, and stampede cattle, so the scales are balanced—even though the purpose of the litigation is to secure just compensation for these admitted wrongs. Rehnquist continued, complaining that:

> It seems to me quite unfair to judge by the light of "revisionist" historians or the mores of another era actions that were taken under pressure of time more than a century ago. Different historians, not writing for the purpose of having their conclusions or observations inserted in the

reports of congressional committees, have taken different positions than those expressed in some of the materials referred to in the Court's opinion.[88]

Justice Blackmun, writing for the majority, gave a stinging rebuke to Rehnquist's dissent in a footnote that, though extensive, is worth reproducing:

> The dissenting opinion suggests, post, at 434–437, that the factual findings of the Indian Claims Commission, the Court of Claims, and now this Court, are based upon a "revisionist" view of history. The dissent fails to identify which materials quoted herein or relied upon by the Commission and the Court of Claims fit that description. The dissent's allusion to historians "writing for the purpose of having their conclusions or observations inserted in the reports of congressional committees," post, at 435, is also puzzling because, with respect to this case, we are unaware that any such historian exists. The primary sources for the story told in this opinion are the factual findings of the Indian Claims Commission and the Court of Claims. A reviewing court generally will not discard such findings because they raise the specter of creeping revisionism, as the dissent would have it, but will do so only when they are clearly erroneous and unsupported by the record. *No one, including the Government, has ever suggested that the factual findings of the Indian Claims Commission and the Court of Claims fail to meet that standard of review.* A further word seems to be in order. The dissenting opinion does not identify a single author, nonrevisionist, neorevisionist, or otherwise, who takes the view of history of the cession of the Black Hills that the dissent prefers to adopt, largely, one assumes, as an article of faith.[89] [Emphasis added]

Rehnquist's outburst was not in defense of anything the government had raised as a point of law or fact. It was his own personal bias — so intemperate that Rehnquist did not even try to disguise it beneath the rhetoric of legal principles. Rehnquist became chief justice in 1986, and during his term in this office Supreme Court decisions involving Indians have taken a radical turn for the worse.[90]

Two cases covering American Indian religious freedom, *Lyng v. Northwest Indian Cemetery Protective Association* (1988)[91] and *Employment Di-*

vision, Department of Human Resources of Oregon v. Smith (1990),[92] to be discussed in greater detail in Chapter 6, were decided by the Rehnquist Court, both of them denying any protection to traditional Indian religious practices. In the first case the Court insisted on deciding the issue even when it had been rendered moot by the passage of a wilderness act setting aside the area that Indians had been concerned to protect. The second case, involving the ceremonial use of peyote by two men who also worked in social services, overturned the long-standing compelling-interest test established in *Sherbert v. Verner,*[93] by which the state was required to justify any substantial burden on religious conduct by narrow means and by showing a compelling state interest.

The *Smith* case proved disastrous to every other religion in the country as well as to traditional Indian religions. Urban planners, state morticians, and all manner of professional people who had been inhibited from interfering with religious practices now found their way clear to enforce secular laws in spite of religious protests and beliefs. A coalition was formed to seek remedial legislation (from which Indians were excluded), and in 1993 the Religious Freedom Reformation Act[94] was passed by Congress. But the Court quickly found it to be unconstitutional in *City of Boerne v. Flores,*[95] leaving American religious bodies in a legal limbo, subject to the whims of state and local governments and secular laws.

In summary, while law professors and political scientists wax eloquent in their classroom lectures about the smooth and impartial functioning of the tripartite government, in reality much of the posture of government is dominated by the people who run it. The bottom line for American Indians is that ultimately the federal courts determine the federal relationship with Indians. In the chapters to come we will depend almost wholly on court decisions to interpret how the Constitution affects American Indians. And we will seek to find some consistency in spite of the grotesque historical record.

CHAPTER V

THE HISTORICAL DEVELOPMENT

OF CONSTITUTIONAL CLAUSES

A thorough analysis of the applicability of constitutional phrases and clauses to Indians and Indian affairs would require volumes of explanation and involve a discussion of hundreds of statutes and cases. The result of such a tour de force would be profound confusion, for it is not simply constitutional authority that must be discussed. The changing condition of American society creates a continuously evolving view of the Constitution, so that its applicability at any one time in American history may vary considerably from what has gone before and what will come. It is much better to take the major constitutional clauses and see how they have been applied over a period of time, examine at what point additional clauses and phrases have been mustered to bolster a novel or emerging view of the primary clauses and powers, and identify the several principles that refer to and affect Indian tribes that have appeared throughout American constitutional history.

For purposes of economy, and in order to establish a clear understanding of the major constitutional clauses and principles that have been cited as authority to justify the actions of the United States toward Indian tribes, we will confine our discussion to an examination of three clauses: the treaty-making clause, the commerce clause, and the property clause. Only these refer to relationships outside the domestic interest of the United States. When Indian tribes began their political relationship with the United States, they were considered to be outside the scope of the Constitution. And so it is in the context of the geographical incorporation of Indians within the boundaries and jurisdiction of the United States that these clauses prove most important for our understanding.

The constitutional clauses cited above do not form a critically important authority for the actions of the United States. They are more often seen as additional arguments raised as a means of giving direction and justification to a course of action that has been proposed. For example, a treaty may well require a tribe to agree to allow a road or series of roads to be built in or through its treaty-defined territory. The primary question is the exercise of treaty powers, but a peripheral consideration is the exercise of the federal responsibility to provide roads and post roads for its citizens. The argument may well run that the United States may use any of these three constitutional provisions to justify its actions, but in point of fact the treaty-making power is always cited because the clause authorizing the construction and maintenance of post roads is reasonably remote from the subject of Indians. Tradition, the familiarity of the treaty arguments, and the ease with which the treaty argument can be understood and assented to by Indians are all factors that mitigate in favor of using the treaty argument instead of another constitutional clause.

The constitutional authorities that provide the federal government with the power to deal with subjects foreign to or outside of the domestic sphere of activities—a power derived from and ceded by the states—are the clauses and powers that substantially affect the Indian tribes. This is the general rule for understanding the historical development of the relationship of the United States with Indians. Citation of other constitutional clauses and authorities, no matter how clearly and persuasively presented, have not been seen as sufficiently convincing to form an important part of federal Indian law or the federal relationship with Indians.

The Treaty-making Power

Without question the first generation of American statesmen believed the treaty-making power was the primary constitutional authority for dealing

with Indian tribes. But this clause was *always* considered in conjunction
with the power to regulate commerce. With the exception of the treaties
signed in 1815 as a requirement of the Treaty of Ghent,[1] and with the exception of the Indian-removal treaties of the 1820s and 1830s,[2] all treaties
signed with Indians prior to 1849 can be said to have expressed the concern for the regulation of commerce with the tribes. Beginning in 1849
with the Treaty of Cheille (Canyon de Chelly) with the Navajo[3] and continuing until 1865, again with some few exceptions, treaties made with Indian tribes are concerned with establishing the title to lands occupied by
Indians in the United States, thereby precluding the claims of Mexico and
Great Britain and confirming U.S. jurisdiction over lands that had been
incorporated into the United States as a result of these treaties.

From 1865 through 1868 Congress emphasized the establishment of
peace with the western plains tribes in order to restrict their activities and
occupancy to a considerably more limited geographical area. From 1871
until 1914 there were a series of agreements with Indian tribes, primarily
in the western states, that sought to gain large cessions of land and allot
the remaining lands to tribal members. The major difference between
agreements and treaties is that agreements are ratified in the form of regular congressional statutes, passed into law by both houses of Congress, and
signed by the president, whereas treaties only need the approval of the
Senate. Agreements are negotiated by special commissions or commissioners and so fall into the diplomatic format of negotiations.

With respect to allotment under the General Allotment Act,[4] Congress
authorized the president to proceed with the allotment of tribal lands
"whenever in his opinion any reservation or any part thereof of such Indians is advantageous for agricultural and grazing purposes."[5] But the executive branch is required by the same statute to negotiate for the purchase
and release of the Indians' remaining lands:

> That at any time after lands have been allotted to all the Indians of any
> tribe as herein provided, or sooner if in the opinion of the President
> it shall be for the best interest of said tribe, it shall be lawful for the
> Secretary of the Interior to negotiate with such Indian tribe for the
> purchase and release by said tribe, *in conformity with the treaty or
> statute under which such reservation is held,* of such portions of its
> reservation not allotted *as such tribe shall, from time to time, consent*

to sell, on such terms and conditions as shall be considered just and equitable between the United States and said tribe of Indians, *which purchase shall not be complete until ratified by Congress, and the form and manner of executing such release shall also be prescribed by Congress.*[6] [Emphasis added]

In these provisions we find the basic treaty format, containing at least three critical conditions necessary for a valid transfer of the Indian title to lands: the purchase must be in conformity with treaties or statutes already defining the rights of the tribe, it must secure Indian consent to the proposed action, and it must be ratified by the Congress in order to be regarded as legal and binding.

For the purposes of discussing the application of the treaty clause as it affects Indians, the principle involved is that laid down by Congress in the Northwest Ordinance of 1787. It declared: "The utmost good faith shall always be observed toward the Indians; their land and property shall never be taken from them unless in just and lawful wars authorized by Congress; but laws founded in justice and humanity shall from time to time be made, for preventing wrongs being done to them, and for preserving peace and friendship with them."[7] And since this ordinance is defined as the permanent policy of the United States in settling new territories and creating new states, presumably it is the standard by which the acts of the legislative and executive branches must be judged when they are dealing with Indians.

We have defined the period when the United States used the treaty format in dealing with Indians as 1778 to 1914 by including the agreement-making provisions as a thinly disguised form of the treaty-making power. Certainly it can be argued with powerful effect that the provisions of the General Allotment Act required negotiations with tribes, Indian consent, and the ratification of agreements by the Congress, all necessary and vital ingredients of the treaty-making process.

Within this period, however, there is a definite and profound discontinuity between the manner in which Indian treaties are seen by Congress and the manner in which agreements are understood. In 1871, after several years of controversy between the House and the Senate, a rider was attached to the 1871 Appropriation Act that stated:

Provided, That hereafter no Indian or tribe within the territory of the United States shall be acknowledged or recognized as an independent nation, tribe, or power with whom the United States may contract by treaty: Provided further, That nothing herein contained shall be construed to invalidate or impair the obligation of any treaty heretofore lawfully made and ratified with any such Indian nation or tribe.[8]

There is no question that the United States, or for that matter any other nation, can refuse to recognize another national entity for the purposes of making treaties or conducting other diplomatic relations. Following the Second World War the United States steadfastly refused to recognize the existence of Red China. And there are many instances in world history when existing nations refused to recognize another nation because it was under the control of a group of people distasteful to the family of nations. So the question here is not whether the United States may recognize Indian tribes or withdraw such recognition. To be precise, and if we include John Marshall's description of Indian tribes from *Cherokee Nation v. Georgia*,[9] Indian tribes had never been recognized as independent or separate from the United States. Rather, Indian tribes were believed to have the *capacity* to negotiate treaties and agreements with the United States, just as they had earlier negotiated with Great Britain.

A good question would be whether the United States felt so strongly about its primacy in native matters that it would have gone to war to prevent other nations from making treaties with the Indian tribes on its borders. Certainly the treaty-making powers and diplomatic horizons of the tribes were not exclusively focused on the United States. Chief Black Hawk continually traded with the British and considered himself a British subject regardless of how Congress looked at the Sac and Fox Indians. What Congress came to believe and what the Indians believed prior to the 1850s are radically different and cannot be reconciled.

The congressional debate in the Senate in the late 1860s and early 1870s gives us some insight into the nature of the controversy over the provision to end treaty making with Indians. Part of the difficulty lay in the fact that both houses of Congress were slack in performing their legislative duties. Instead of extensive floor debate over the provisions of proposed legislation, it was becoming standard practice to authorize a conference committee to work out all the miscellaneous riders attached to bills by each house of Congress to be considered by the other house. The committee's report was accepted as the final version of congressional thinking as if there had been full floor debate and deliberations by each house. Thus, on more than one occasion radically different changes of policy were effected by a few people sitting in the conference committee without consideration of the issue by both houses of Congress and without consultation or consent of the affected Indians.[10]

The original rider attached to the appropriation bill by the House of Representatives reads as follows: "That nothing in this act contained shall be construed to ratify any of the so-called treaties entered into with any tribe, band, or party of Indians since the 30th of July, 1867."[11] This provision is not difficult to understand. The act of July 20, 1867[12] had authorized a Peace Commission composed of three army officers, the commissioner of Indian affairs, the chairman of the Committee of Indian Affairs of the Senate, and two prominent civilians to negotiate treaties with the plains tribes in order to secure a permanent home for the Indians and guarantee security for a number of railroads then being constructed and contemplated that would cross Indian country. Some members of the House vigorously disagreed with the provisions of these treaties because they involved the expenditure of massive sums of money for prolonged periods of time. The rider was a means of protesting both the expense and the fact that House of Representatives had played no part in the commission.

Senator Eugene Casserly of California objected to the methods used by the House regarding the treaty provision. "I was speaking of a great and growing evil in our legislation admitted to be such by every person who had had occasion to consider it. . . . Because the Senate proposed a very proper provision guaranteeing the integrity of past treaties with the Indians, the House of Representatives, disagreeing in that and other amendments, as it would seem, obtained a conference. The result of that conference is that while that provision is retained we have this in addition: That hereafter no Indian nations or tribe within the territory of the United States shall be acknowledged or recognized as an independent tribe or power with whom the United States may contract by treaty."[13]

Casserly then reviewed the history of the treatment of the Indian tribes and cited approvingly the words of the Supreme Court in a recent case, *The Kansas Indians*,[14] which described the Indians as a "people distinct from others, capable of making treaties."[15] The objection, or sting, as Casserly described it,

> is not in the word "independent," so much as in the assertion that the Indians are not a people "with whom the United States may contract by treaty." I deny the right of either or both Houses of Congress to pass such a law. The Indians are not a part of the people of the United States; still less are they a portion of the citizens of the United States. I speak now of course of the Indians as tribes. It is not easy to define expressly their political relation to the United States, but I shall speak with sufficient accuracy when I say that their relations are those of a State having an existence of its own, having a certain independence of its own, but still under the protection and control of the United States according to treaty stipulations.[16]

Senator Casserly then adopted and clarified the statement of John Marshall in the *Cherokee Nation* case: "We find this amply recognized in the constitutional grant to Congress of the power 'to regulate commerce with foreign nations, and among the several States, and with the Indian tribes.' The tribes are something different from foreign nations or from the States, more independent than the States, less independent than foreign nations."[17]

In other words, Casserly understood the commerce clause as vesting a particular status in Indian tribes that could not constitutionally be denied by any subsequent congress. "It is more than doubtful whether Congress, dealing with a people like the Indians, whose relations with us are so well established by treaty after treaty, and the whole practice of the Government, can annul, as to them, the treaty-making power vested in the President and the Senate, *But the main objection is that the tribes are under the protection of the Constitution and the treaties and the laws made in accordance therewith. Of that protection they cannot be deprived but with their own consent"*[18] [emphasis added]. The Constitution, therefore, in mentioning Indians, extended its protection to the degree that acting outside the treaty-making power in dealing with them was believed to be unconstitutional. Casserly suggested an alternative course for Congress to take:

> Instead of attempting to abrogate the provisions express and implied, of the Constitution, and to override the unvarying current of authorities in our own courts and of practice in our Government, we should let

time solve it. Time will solve it if we have patience, either by the disap-
pearance of these dwindling races or by their own voluntary acceptance of the relations of citizenship. In my judgment, it is only in this
way that you can ever undertake to deal with these tribes. The United
States has no peaceful control over them for any purpose whatever except through treaties made with them. It is by treaties that you exercise
your authority. It is by treaties or by war that you regulate your relations with them; and yet here is a provision that we shall not again
make treaties with them.[19]

Other senators were more concerned about the effect on the treaty-
making powers of the Senate and president than about the effect of the
provision on Indians. Senator Samuel C. Pomeroy of Kansas argued that:
"it would be difficult by a law of Congress to limit the power of the President and Senate over treaties as provided in the Constitution. The Constitution of the United States defines and fixes the powers of the Executive
and the Senate in regard to treaties; they are the treaty-making power. Now,
you come in here on an appropriation bill, and by an act of Congress prohibit that power, contract it, limit it, when no law can have anything to
do with it."[20] Senator Garrett Davis of Kentucky was even more specific:
"Now, the principle is this: the whole treaty-making power is vested by the
Constitution in the President and the Senate. The House of Representatives have nothing to do with it except to pass appropriation bills that may
be necessary to execute treaties. Beyond this power of appropriation the
House has nothing to do with the subject of treaties either with foreign nations or with the Indian tribes."[21] Davis's argument is sound constitutional
law. Could the House of Representatives dictate to the president which foreign nations he could recognize for the purposes of making a treaty simply
on the basis that they would refuse to appropriate funds if the president
made a treaty with a country they did not like?

Davis said some prophetic words regarding the future course of Indian
affairs:

Is not the President of the United States competent to execute the
power, according to his discretion, of negotiating a treaty with an Indian nation? Do we not all know that there are about eighty thousand
Indians in the southwest part of the United States, who are civilized,
who are advancing in civilization and in all the developments of civi-

lization, where they have their own government, their own constitution, their own language, their own alphabet, their own literature, and where they are making rapid progress in human improvement? Well, what is the effect of this article in the report of the committee of conference in relation to them? That the President in the future shall not have the power to negotiate a treaty with those Indians, either as tribes or as a confederate nation?[22]

Davis concluded his speech dramatically: "I deny the power of the committee of conference to concede that great principle. I deny the power of the Senate to sacrifice it. I deny the power of the Congress of the United States to expunge it from the Constitution. *It is as deeply moored, as fixed and immutable in the foundations of the Constitution as any other power whatever or any other principle established by it*"[23] [emphasis added].

In view of these forceful arguments raised against the prohibition of recognizing Indian tribes as political entities capable of making treaties, it is indeed ironic that the General Allotment Act and other legislation later passed by Congress allow that the president should be given instructions and authority to negotiate with the tribes for the cession of their lands. The section of the General Allotment Act that gives the president the authority to negotiate with the tribes in fact *restores* to the chief executive a power previously limited by Congress.

It has become the practice of Congress to insist that the tribes agree, at least informally and in principle, to legislation that affects them. For example, during the termination hearings of the 1950s, the Joint Subcommittee on Indians was constantly assured by the Bureau of Indian Affairs that the tribes being terminated had agreed to the move. And when the tribes came to Congress to get their termination acts repealed, members of the congressional committees threw back at them the accusation that they had agreed to the termination legislation.[24]

The record of the United States in upholding the existing treaties with Indian tribes has been spotty at best. There has been no consistent approach to interpreting or enforcing treaty rights. The Congress generally was rigorous in abiding by the provisions of the treaties that did not require the expenditure of funds. In the early days of the Republic, Congress would carefully amend or interpret treaty provisions so as to abide by the spirit of the treaty. Thus the act of March 3, 1817,[25] made provisions for the location of lands reserved for the Creek chiefs in the Treaty of August 9, 1814; the Act of June 30, 1834,[26] carried into effect the fourth article of the Treaty of January 8, 1821, with the Creeks; the Act of June 17, 1844,[27] interpreted the treaty with the Chippewa of Saginaw of January 23, 1838. That practice continued into this century. Thus it was Congress, not the federal courts, who originally interpreted treaty provisions.

Congress generally abided by the provisions of the treaties, with some notable exceptions. In 1882–1883 the government negotiated an agreement with the Sioux to reduce the great Sioux reserve, but when the Congress discovered that it lacked the proper number of signatures, the act, although already negotiated, failed of passage.[28] Congress again passed the same basic agreement in 1888[29] but when the proper number of Sioux did not approve the act, even though it had been passed by Congress, it was regarded as inoperative.

Considering the wide variety of allotment agreements made with tribes, the exercise of power given to the executive by the General Allotment Act greatly resembled the latitude the president had enjoyed when vested with his full treaty-making powers. Agreements made under this provision were with tribes who did not have treaties and whose reservations had been set aside by executive order prior to the allotment act. Some reservations were inhabited by various Indian tribes who had been told simply to go and live there; the inhabitants had no previous tradition of having a government to represent them. Yet all Indians on all reservations who made the allotment agreements were asked to approve the terms of the agreements as if they were owners in fee simple. So frantic was the government to obtain permission of tribal members that federal employees even invaded the boarding schools in the east to obtain the signatures of the Indians. Thus Jim Thorpe, when but a young man, was asked to approve an agreement with the Sac and Fox as if he were a regular reservation resident and eligible adult tribal member.

In authorizing the construction of dams on the Missouri River in North and South Dakota, for instance, Congress instructed the army chief of engineers and the secretary of the interior to negotiate settlements with the Standing Rock and Cheyenne River Indians and required that "no such contract shall take effect until it shall have been ratified by Act of Congress and ratified in writing by three-quarters of the adult members of the two respective tribes."[30] This formula is the necessary number required by the Fort Laramie Treaty of 1868 with the Sioux.[31]

On some occasions the Supreme Court has rigorously examined the hearings of Indian legislation to determine whether or not the Congress has intended to violate an Indian treaty. For instance, the termination legislation of the Menominee Tribe in 1954 contained a provision that "all statutes of the United States which affect Indians because of their status as Indians shall no longer be applicable to the members of the tribe."[32] According to this language, the Menominee seemed to have lost even their hunting and fishing rights. But the Supreme Court in *Menominee Tribe of Indians v. United States* (1968)[33] ruled that the hunting and fishing rights granted or preserved by the Wolf River Treaty of 1854 survived the 1954 termination act. The Court was able to connect the termination act with another piece of legislation, Public Law 280,[34] which specifically preserved the hunting, trapping, and fishing rights to all tribes — clearly a law that affected the Menominee because of their status as Indians.

A tedious review of the case law would only serve to prove the utter inconsistency of the record. In the 1970 case *Choctaw Nation v. Oklahoma,*[35] for example, the Supreme Court held that the tribe was entitled to half the bed of the Arkansas River on the basis of a treaty provision; while in *Montana v. United States*[36] the Court held that the Crow tribe did not own the bed of the Big Horn River. In the *Choctaw* case the river formed a boundary for a reservation that had previously been abolished; in the Crow case, the river ran *through* the reservation, and the reservation was still intact.

There is presently no accurate way to predict or anticipate how the Supreme Court will interpret an Indian treaty, nor is there any way to determine whether or not the Congress will require a federal or state agency to follow the provisions of an Indian treaty. But the Court has held that Congress does not have to seek the consent of a tribe before a treaty provision can be disregarded by Congress.[37] In 1867 the Kiowa, Comanche, and Apache signed a treaty with the United States that contained the provision that no further land cessions would be regarded as valid unless three-quarters of the tribes' adult males agreed. In 1892 the three tribes were asked to sign an agreement allotting their lands and selling the surplus to the United States. The required three-fourths of adult males did not agree, and after much delay legislation approving a very changed version of the agreement was passed by Congress. Lone Wolf, a Kiowa chief, sued to prevent the secretary of the interior from enforcing the legislation.

The Supreme Court turned aside the argument of the Indians that the three-quarters provision prohibited the Congress from making material changes in the agreement and passing it into law. The Court ruled that "to uphold the claim would be to adjudge that the indirect operation of the treaty was to materially limit and qualify the controlling authority of Congress in respect to the care and protection of the Indians, *and* to deprive Congress, in a possible emergency, when the necessity might be urgent for a partition and disposal of the tribal lands, of all power to act, if the assent of the Indians could not be obtained." [38]

The reasoning of this decision is spurious and fictional, but because it is a Supreme Court decision, it is regarded as good law. First, the three-fourths provision was inserted in the treaty at the initiative of the United States as a pledge of good faith and assurance to the tribes that there would be some tangible protection of tribal lands in the future. Second, such a provision does not act indirectly. It is what is called a self-operating provision. That is to say, it does not need any further action by Congress to become effective. Finally, there was no emergency when the agreement was proposed to the tribes and no emergency arose during the consideration of the legislation that would require a hasty conclusion to the matter. Almost as if the Court were embarrassed at its rhetorical evasion of the protections the treaty offered the Indians, the justices added a final touch. Citing a case that had been decided that term wherein the Court had declared that Congress possessed full administrative power over Indian tribal property,[39] the Court characterized the actions of Congress as "an exercise of such power, a mere change in the form of investment of Indian tribal property."[40]

Finally, the Court simply gave up its effort to justify the decision and declared:

> We must presume that Congress acted in perfect good faith in the dealings with the Indians of which complaint is made, and that the legislative branch of the government exercised its best judgment in the premises. *In any event, as Congress possessed full power in the matter, the judiciary cannot question or inquire into the motives which prompted the enactment of this legislation. If injury was occasioned,*

which we do not wish to be understood as implying, by the use made by Congress of its power, relief must be sought by an appeal to that body for redress and not to the courts.[41] [Emphasis added]

The problem is that unless the treaty-making process is continued in some formal manner, the treaty-making clause does not apply and there is no protection under the Constitution for Indian tribes at all. Tribal rights of self-government predate the Constitution and derive not from the American people or the Constitution but from the inherent sovereignty of a given tribe. When a controversy involves the relationship of the federal government to the tribes, nothing compels the United States to deal justly with the tribe because the nature of the relationship is political; it is diplomatic and without appeal to the family of nations because Indians are now considered a domestic matter of the United States. So there are no checks and balances available that would prevent any branch of government from doing whatever it wanted with Indians and their lands and rights. The Constitution provided a form of protection for Indian tribes because it identified tribes as having a particular political status that demanded treaty (bilateral) relationships and not simply legislative (unilateral) deliberations. When Congress limited the president's ability to deal with Indians in the usual manner and instead assigned him the task of negotiating with tribes on a piecemeal basis under separate authorizing acts, it eliminated the flexibility of the chief executive to deal with Indians realistically according to the best discretionary authority of his office. Congress thereupon intruded upon the powers of the executive and in fact assumed those powers for itself.

After the disclaimer of treaty making in 1871, any previous constitutional protections for Indians were no longer recognized. The doctrine of discovery, which justified the claims of the United States, was at that time nullified. Indians were made subject to the powers of Congress as subjects of the country but had no rights and no standing to contest their change in status. Unfortunately there have been no corrective actions taken to remedy this situation. Indian tribes are still recognized as sovereigns by the United States, but they are deprived of the one power all sovereigns must have in order to function effectively—the power to say "no" to other sovereigns.

The Power to Regulate Commerce

The commerce clause is the heart and soul of the Constitution. Under its auspices the federal government has done almost anything it wanted. It has been expansively interpreted to provide benefits and services to the citizens, has become the vehicle for almost all civil rights legislation, and has allowed Congress a free hand in determining the fate and conditions of American Indians.

There are some spotty indications, at least from the Supreme Court's perspective, that Congress's days of wielding largely unrestricted power in regards to issues of federalism under the commerce clause may have run its course and that federal power to enact a cornucopia of legislation designed to regulate state and local activities is to be limited.[42] The result of this shift in emphasis is that federal legislation is now being interpreted so that it will favor state governments. Thus long-standing doctrines of interpretation are being turned upside-down. The Court no longer cares about hearing what the Indians understood was happening to them. The movement now is to strip the tribes of every possible right by developing novel doctrines of the "intent" of Congress in the face of overwhelming evidence to the contrary.

The liberal reading of the commerce clause in the field of Indian affairs preceded by half a century the expansion of the power of Congress in other areas of American life. Initially Congress saw its duty toward Indians as one of adjusting the commercial relationships between the United States and the tribes adjoining the settled areas of the eastern United States. The first three acts passed by Congress dealing with Indians demonstrated the manner in which the legislative branch understood its duties under the commerce clause. The first act, of August 7, 1789,[43] established the War Department and authorized that agency to assume whatever duties relative to Indians that the president should assign it. The second act,[44] passed the same day as the first, confirmed and adopted the Ordinance of 1787 and established policies for the settlement of new territories and for the treatment of Indians. We will deal with this ordinance when we discuss the part of the property clause that is directly on point. The third statute,[45] enacted August 20, 1789, appropriated a sum not exceeding $20,000 to defray the expenses of negotiating with Indian tribes and provided for the appointment of commissioners to negotiate the treaties. Taken together these acts indicate that Congress saw its task as one of arranging the internal authorities and institutions of the United States so that it could deal on a diplomatic basis with the Indian tribes and provide services promised in the treaties.

Beginning in 1790 and continuing until 1834, aside from the ratification of treaties Indian legislation reflected a goal of providing rules and regulations under which non-Indians could deal with Indian tribes. Traders were required to have licenses, provisions were enacted to punish non-Indians committing crimes against Indians, and a series of trading houses or factories were authorized to enable the federal government to make an effort to dominate Indian trade and set the standards against which private ventures would be measured.[46] Congress well understood that the United States was competing for both trading privileges and political loyalty against Great Britain and Spain, whose colonies encompassed the new republic just beyond the Indian lands to the north, west, and south.

Federal legislation might have remained a wholly commercial venture had it not been for the humanitarian impulse of the United States. In 1819, at the urging of many people concerned about the precipitous population decline of the frontier tribes, Congress passed an act "making provision for the civilization of the Indian tribes adjoining the frontier settlements."[47] The first section of this statute stated:

> That for the purpose of providing against the further decline and final extinction of the Indian tribes, adjoining the frontier settlements of the United States, and for introducing among them the habits and arts of civilization, the President of the United States shall be, and he is hereby authorized, in every case where he shall judge improvement in the habits and condition of such Indians practicable, and that the means of instruction can be introduced with their consent, to employ capable persons of good moral character, to instruct them in the mode of agriculture suited to their situation.[48]

The importance of this provision cannot be underestimated. It meant that Congress had adopted a policy of civilization instead of a policy of extermination and that the task of Congress divided into two basic responsibilities: first, to consider and pass laws that were necessary to carry out the provisions of treaties made with the Indians, and second, to pursue a policy of civilization, assimilation, and eventually absorption of the Indians into the body politic of the United States. The first responsibility derives from the constitutional provisions for treaty making and the power to regulate commerce, but the second mission is a wholly gratuitous task that Congress voluntarily assumes. Later, of course, these so-called gratuitous expenditures would be credited to the United States' "offsets" against land claims filed by Indian tribes under the provisions of the Indian Claims Commission.[49] Allowance of these expenses freely made as a policy of the government in effect meant that Indians were made to pay for their own cultural destruction. But the first congresses could not have foreseen this development. Their efforts can even be characterized as good-faith attempts to assume responsibility for the aboriginal inhabitants under the requirements of the doctrine of discovery, although at no time did Congress cite this responsibility as a motive for its actions.

The desire to civilize cannot be logically and clearly tied to the exercise of power under the commerce clause. Nevertheless, since it was framed with a benevolent purpose, few people questioned the actions of Congress in this regard. Basically the philosophical framework involved in this decision was one that regarded culture as a function of commerce rather than the reverse. Ironically, the tribes to whom this policy was first applied were among the best organized and most sedentary peoples the United States would encounter in its history, with the possible exception of the Pueblo groups of New Mexico. These Indian nations were the Five Civilized Tribes, the Indian confederacies of the Ohio Valley, and the Six Nations of New York. The primary difference between the Indian settlements and the non-Indian settlements insofar as civilization and agriculture were concerned were two: non-Indian agriculturists looked forward to achieving commercial status whereas Indian agriculturists were predominantly concerned with subsistence, and Indian land tenure was by assignments that were unalienable rather than by the division of lands into plots regarded as private property and disposable at the will of the owner. Ultimately, then, it is the presence or possibility of the profit motive that distinguished Indian from non-Indian agriculture and settlement.

The difficulty facing Congress once its motives and goals had been complicated by the introduction of its self-imposed responsibility to civilize the Indians can be seen in the Committee of Indian Affairs' report that accompanied the 1834 acts of regulating trade and organizing the Department of Indian Affairs:

> The committee are aware of the intrinsic difficulties of the subject — of providing a system of laws and of administration, simple and economical, and, at the same time, efficient and liberal — that shall be suited to the various conditions and relations of those for whose benefit it is intended; and that shall, with a due regard to the rights of our own citizens, meet the just expectations of the country in the fulfillment of its proper and assumed obligations to the Indian tribes. . . . The Indians, for whose protection these laws are proposed, consist of numerous tribes, scattered over an immense extent of country, of different languages, and partaking of all the forms of society in the progression from the savage to an approximation to the civilized. With the emigrant tribes we have treaties, imposing duties of a mixed character, recognizing them in some sort as dependent tribes, and yet obligating ourselves to protect them, even against domestic strife, and necessarily retaining the power to do so. With other tribes we have general treaties of amity; and with a considerable number we have no treaties whatever.[50]

In looking at the larger picture of Indian affairs, Congress could not determine a consistent policy regarding Indians because the condition of Indian tribes varied so significantly. The two acts passed in 1834[51] are both well within the scope of the commerce clause because the first act creates a more universal set of rules for conducting trade with the tribes while the second establishes an institutional framework within which treaty services can be properly delivered. Yet this report and these acts project an image of confusion over the scope of congressional responsibility. We see no determination to cease treaty making but instead find in the congressional intent and legislation a genuine puzzlement over how to deal with the broad spectrum of Indian conditions.

Subsequent events in American history demonstrate that as Indian trade declined in importance, the task of the institutional bureaucracy increased. Because the department of Indian affairs was supported primarily by gratuitous expenditures, as time passed there would be an increasing cry for a reduction of the cost of funding Indian services and programs, leading eventually to a final termination of the responsibilities of the national government toward tribes. This conflict can be seen as early as the 1830s' removal treaties, when provisions were made for tribal members to reject tribal membership, take allotments, and remain in the South as private citizens. By 1854 the full weight of the government was being placed on the idea of allotting Indian lands and bringing individual Indian families into the small town/family farm way of life.[52] Thereafter, if the debates in Congress are any measure, almost all policy decisions were driven by the budget. In 1868 Indian Commissioner Nathaniel G. Taylor estimated that it would cost $1 million for each Indian killed by the army, that it would take $6 billion to kill all the Indians, and that in the process 7.5 million whites would be killed.[53] Thus the Peace Commission was formed.

Beginning with the Reagan administration and continuing through the Clinton years, we have seen a reenactment of this basic dilemma. The government, in seeking to end or at least dramatically reduce Indian dependence on federal largesse, has stressed the unbridled development of reservations' natural resources — in effect, the reinstitution of Indian trade. And the contemporary recognition of Indian tribes as sovereigns under the banner of Indian self-determination may well be regarded as a step toward restoring the original balance between commercial relations and gratuitous expenditures encouraging the civilization of the Indians. But restoring this balance requires a concomitant move to recognize, respect, and protect the self-governing aspects of tribal life and, particularly, to provide a mechanism whereby tribes can reject (or at least insist that the government recast) the overtures of the United States. This kind of protection, as we have seen from our discussion of the treaty-making power, has not been restored.

After 1834 it was merely a matter of time before the Congress usurped the self-governing powers of Indian tribes and substituted a large and cumbersome administrative agency to direct the lives of Indians. Gratuitous expenditures to encourage civilization soon became coercive measures to force assimilation. Indians were given no relief from this pressure, and by the 1880s almost everything that happened on Indian reservations was under the control of the federal government. Then two Supreme Court decisions and a federal statute created havoc in the placid waters of the commerce clause.

In 1883 the Supreme Court heard the case of *Ex parte Crow Dog*,[54] in which Crow Dog, a Brule Sioux, had been convicted by a territorial court of murdering Spotted Tail, chief of the tribe. Crow Dog's relatives had settled the incident according to traditional Sioux custom by compensating Spotted Tail's relatives. The Court relied upon two sections of the Revised Statutes of the United States—2145 and 2146, the latter of which allowed an Indian tribe to preserve certain subjects from federal jurisdiction through treaty provisions—to free Crow Dog and overturn his conviction. The Bureau of Indian Affairs, which had been planning to test these sections of the Revised Statutes for several years, promptly worked to stir up public outrage at the decision, interpreting it as allowing a murderer "to pay money instead of suffering punishment." [55] Pressure from the public, Christian reform organizations, and the ever insistent calls by the BIA that lawlessness reigned in Indian country convinced Congress to pass the Seven Major Crimes Act in 1885.[56] This act purported to extend federal jurisdiction over several enumerated crimes—murder, manslaughter, rape, assault with intent to kill, arson, burglary, and larceny—on all Indian reservations. Although worded to apply universally, strangely this act was not believed to be applicable to the Five Civilized Tribes because of their treaties—the exact situation in which the Sioux had found themselves.

The first test of this statute came in the fall of 1885, when the Supreme Court heard the case of *United States v. Kagama,*[57] involving a convicted Hoopa Indian who had killed another Indian on the Hoopa reservation in California and was questioning the basis for federal jurisdiction. *Kagama* is a stunning rejection of the commerce clause and a confused rendering of a combination of the property clause, the treaty-making power, and a smattering of natural-law philosophy. Because the case is so important to the understanding of the commerce clause and because it has proven remarkably noncontroversial in spite of its reasoning, it is important that we examine the decision carefully.

The opinion reads:

> The mention of Indians in the Constitution which has received most attention is that found in the clause which gives Congress 'power to regulate commerce with foreign nations, and among the several States, and with the Indian tribes.' This clause is relied on in the argument in the present case, the proposition being that the statute under consideration is a regulation of commerce with the Indian tribes. *But we think*

it would be a very strained construction of this clause, that a system of criminal laws for Indians living peaceably in their reservations, which left out the entire code of trade and intercourse laws justly enacted under that provision, and established punishments for the common-law crimes of murder, manslaughter, arson, burglary, larceny, and the like, without any reference to their relation to any kind of commerce, was authorized by the grant of power to regulate commerce with the Indian tribes." [58]
[Emphasis added]

In view of the extensive body of federal law dealing with Indian tribes and the unbroken tradition of congressional legislation dealing with Indians and commerce, the rejection of the commerce clause by the Supreme Court was nothing short of astounding. Possibly the Court was criticizing the abrupt insertion of such a far-reaching provision in an appropriation act, but it does not specifically cite the misuse of an appropriation statute for a major policy change. About the best that can be made of this rejection is that had the Congress established a strong code for trade and intercourse prior to dealing with criminal law, the criminal code would naturally follow from the commercial definitions. In fact, as we look at the two 1834 statutes dealing with Indian trade, there is no reason to suppose that Congress had not already more than fulfilled the Court's expectations in that respect.

The Court then turned to its own reasons for upholding the Seven Major Crimes Act, and here the justices' logic is confusing at best:

But these Indians are within the geographical limits of the United States. The soil and the people within these limits are under the political control of the Government of the United States, or of the States of the Union. . . . What authority the State governments may have to enact criminal laws for the Indians will be presently considered. *But this power of Congress to organize territorial governments, and make laws for their inhabitants, arises not so much from the clause in the Constitution in regard to disposing of and making rules and regulations concerning the Territory and other property of the United States, as from the ownership of the country in which the Territories are, and the right of exclusive sovereignty which must exist in the National Government, and can be found nowhere else."* [59] [Emphasis added]

Proprietorship, then, carries with it all necessary powers and attributes that the Constitution itself would otherwise have vested in the national government.

The property clause, however, is not the source of federal power either, according to the Court:

> These Indian tribes *are* wards of the nation. They are communities dependent on the United States. Dependent largely for their daily food. Dependent for their political rights. They owe no allegiance to the States, and receive from them no protection. Because of the local ill feeling, the people of the States where they are found are often their deadliest enemies. *From their very weakness and helplessness, so largely due to the course of dealings of the Federal Government with them and the treaties in which it has been promised, there arises a duty of protection, and with it the power.* This has always been recognized by the Executive and by Congress, and by this Court, whenever the question has arisen.[60] [Emphasis added]

The property clause and the treaty-making clause seem to be peripheral elements of constitutionality in this case; they give the decision a superficial veneer of legality. The commerce clause is rejected in its entirety, and the power to pass a criminal code applicable to reservation Indians seems to originate in the fact that the United States throughout its history possessed the power to pass laws dealing with Indians and Indian affairs because it was, through its relationship with the Indians, creating a dependency among them. Conceivably this is an equity argument in which the United States must accept responsibility for Indians because they are helpless — rendered helpless by federal policies. But why that responsibility would accrue to a property owner is never explained by the Court.

The Seven Major Crimes Act is regarded generally as a substantial intrusion on the rights of Indians on reservations to govern themselves, hence a drastic deterioration of the sovereign right to self-government. If the Court here implies that a kind of tort or equitable liability accrues to the United States for its actions toward Indians, it does not follow that this history justifies further intrusion and disruption. If the reference to treaties is to be taken seriously, then the application of the Seven Major Crimes Act must be subject to the consent, through negotiations, of the Indians affected.

The final analysis of the *Kagama* case, a conclusion that most lawyers and federal officials are reluctant to draw, is that somehow the Supreme Court held a federal statute applying to Indians to be constitutional while rejecting every possible constitutional clause and phrase that would render it so. How a judicial forum can step outside the Constitution to hold a law constitutional is yet to be explained. The fact remains that, as with the treaty-making clause, Indians stand outside the Constitution insofar as that document limits any branch or agency of government from legally doing what it wishes with Indian lives and properties. The allusions to land ownership are certainly subject to the paramount doctrine of discovery, but that doctrine is nowhere admitted in *Kagama* to be worthy of consideration or mention.

The mixture of motives detected in the two 1834 acts becomes the Gordian knot the Court cannot or will not unravel. At its best reading, the Court seems to be saying that because the United States voluntarily undertakes a mission of humanitarian concern on behalf of Indians, there is no limit to the powers the government can exercise over them, whether the Indians wish to receive such humanitarian aid or not. The Constitution, and its powers of specific authorization, are naught in comparison to this long history of benignly intended involvement of the United States with Indian tribes. It remains, then, to examine the property clause to determine if and how the Constitution actually empowers the federal government to deal with Indians and under what conditions and auspices.

There should be no question, however, that in the mainstream of American legal thinking, easily identifiable in the acts of Congress, there is a substantial body of law dealing with Indians and passed by the Congress as an exercise of its powers under the commerce clause. In general, when these laws are carefully examined, it is apparent that the most precise use of the commerce clause occurs when the Congress acts to fulfill the provision of treaties and agreements. The further from this function Congress strays, the more peripheral and extraneous become arguments in Supreme Court decisions attempting to find constitutional validity in congressional acts. There must be, therefore, a limit to the exercise of powers under the commerce clause, but it is yet to be articulated clearly and unequivocally.

The current trend of the Rehnquist Court to curtail Congress's exercise of commerce power vis-à-vis states and to a lesser extent tribes might be interpreted in a positive light as an effort by the Court to reign in congressional plenary power. However, while this clearly seems to be the case regarding the expanding idea of state sovereignty, in various cases the Court has expressed a much narrower view of tribal sovereignty and continues to maintain that Congress may wield extraordinary power over tribes while at the same time legitimizing state efforts to exercise an increased amount of jurisdictional authority over tribes and their resources.[61]

The Property Clause

Although it never seems to play a prominent role in the deliberations of either Congress or the federal courts when they deal with Indian matters, an analysis of critical decisions of the Supreme Court seems to suggest that the property clause, and/or the fact of American claims to legal title to lands in North America under the doctrine of discovery, plays an important part in determining the posture and actions of the United States toward Indians. Much of the impact of this clause originates, as does the treaty-making power, from the general background within which the constitutional fathers lived and acted. The property clause itself, contained in Article 4, section 3, paragraph 2, is a model of restraint:

> The Congress shall have Power to dispose of and make all needful Rules and Regulation respecting the Territory or other Property belonging to the United States; and nothing in this Constitution shall be so construed as to Prejudice any Claims of the United States, or of any particular State. Within the context of post–Revolutionary War political thought this paragraph asserts a national rather than a state claim to property while promoting a compromise between the federal government and specific state claims.

One of the most critical problems encountered at the Constitutional convention concerned the relationship between the larger states, such as Virginia, Pennsylvania, New York, and Massachusetts, and the smaller states. A political compromise was reached wherein the legislative body was divided into two parts, one to represent state sovereignty and therefore to testify to the basic equality of the states, the other to reflect the actual disposition of the population, thereby recognizing the people as such.

The national government agreed to assume the debts of the respective states which had been incurred during the Revolutionary War; Alexander Hamilton saw in the sale of public lands to the west the financial solution to this burden. Consequently, a good deal of negotiations between the federal government and the various states began with the adoption of the Constitution, with the goal that the federal government would become the eventual owner of lands and/or land claims the states possessed under their original colonial charters. These charters naively and benevolently bestowed on individual colonies the title to lands to the South seas, not realizing that the continent was considerably larger than anyone had suspected. As early as 1780, in order to maintain the allegiance of the smaller colonies who had no expansive land pretensions, New York and Connecticut ceded their claims to the United States as a means of settling the question. After the adoption of the Constitution, only Georgia and North Carolina maintained the fiction that they possessed western lands to the exclusion of the United States. Finally in 1802, under special articles of agreement and cession, Georgia surrendered her dubious claims to the west to the federal government,[62] but only after extracting a pledge from Congress that it would oversee the extinguishment of Creek and Cherokee title to land Georgia wanted for her own citizens, land that the federal government had guaranteed to the Indians in prior treaties.[63]

With the cession to the national government of land claims assumed to be valid under the old colonial charters, the United States consolidated its position with respect to England and Spain, its two competitors east of the Mississippi, and with respect to the Indian tribes who inhabited the area east of the Mississippi and south of Canada. Land titles within this area were presumed to be valid only if they were derived from patents issued by the states or colonies prior to the time of cession to the United States or issued since then by a land office or officer of the United States.

In 1823 in the case of *Johnson v. McIntosh*,[64] the Supreme Court received its first clear opportunity to articulate the position of the United States on its claim to legal land titles. At issue was the question of whether a land title given by the Indians under British supervision at an open public sale was superior to a title derived from the United States through a sale by designated federal land officers. The opinion is long and to some degree incoherent because the Indian land title was in fact transferred under the supervision of the British at a time when England was the dominant sovereign on the continent. The land was conveyed using the regular process that all colonial deeds used prior to the establishment of the United States. The Court therefore had no valid reason for calling the transaction into question—indeed, *all* deeds given under the Crown would have to have been questioned.

A selective citation of the salient points of Justice Marshall's argument is enlightening in that it clarifies the understanding of the United States, insofar as its proprietary rights to land and the ensuing privileges this ownership entailed are concerned:

> On the discovery of this immense continent, the great nations of Europe were eager to appropriate to themselves so much of it as they could respectively acquire. Its vast extent offered an ample field to the ambition and enterprise of all; *and the character and religion of its inhabitants afforded an apology for considering them as a people over whom the superior genius of Europe might claim an ascendancy.* The potentates of the old world found no difficulty in convincing themselves that *they made ample compensation to the inhabitants of the new, by bestowing on them civilization and Christianity* in exchange for unlimited independence. But, as they were all in pursuit of nearly the same object, it was necessary, in order to avoid conflicting settlements, and consequent war with each other, to establish a principle which all should acknowledge as the law by which the right of acquisition, which they all asserted, should be regulated as between themselves. *This principle was that discovery gave title to the government by whose subjects, or by whose authority, it was made, against all other European governments*, which title might be consummated by possession.[65] [Emphasis added]

Marshall continued:

> In the establishment of these relations, the rights of the original inhabitants were, in no instance, entirely disregarded; but were necessarily, to a considerable extent, impaired. *They were admitted to be the rightful occupants of the soil, with a legal as well as just claim to retain possession of it, and to use it according to their own discretion; but their rights to complete sovereignty, as independent nations were necessarily diminished*, and their power to dispose of the soil at their own will, to whom-

soever they pleased, was denied by the original fundamental principle that discovery gave exclusive title to those who made it.[66] [Emphasis added]

The basic outlines of the doctrine of discovery have been emphasized in the quotations above. They seem to fall easily into a strangely logical sequence: the culture and religion of indigenous peoples was judged inferior to that of Europeans, civilization and Christianity were offered them as compensation for their lands, discovery gave title to a government against other Europeans, the Indians were still the rightful owners of the land, but their sovereignty was reduced by the European agreement to restrict the sale of land to the discovering country. Here, sovereignty and land proprietorship are regarded as the same thing, an idea that certainly originates in the feudal system of land tenure in Europe.

Marshall connects the American claim to the European doctrine as follows:

> By the treaty which concluded the war of our revolution, Great Britain relinquished all claim, not only to the government, but to the 'propriety and territorial rights of the United States,' whose boundaries were fixed in the second article. By this treaty, the powers of government, and the right to soil, which had previously been in Great Britain, passed definitively to these states. We had before taken possession of them, by declaring independence; but neither the declaration of independence, nor the treaty confirming it, could give us more than that which we before possessed, or to which Great Britain was before entitled.[67]

Here is the incoherence: under Marshall's own reasoning this deed had to be valid. The Indians had transferred their land at public auction under the supervision of British officers *prior to* the Revolution.

Although the decision in *McIntosh* was politically dependent upon the fact that all land titles were premised upon this reasoning, the fact remains that Marshall felt that to overturn it at that point would have wreaked untold havoc on the American political system:

> However extravagant the pretension of converting the discovery of an inhabited country into conquest may appear, if the principle has been

asserted in the first instance, and afterwards sustained; if a country has been acquired and held under it; if the property of the great mass of the community originates in it, it becomes the law of the land, and cannot be questioned. So, too, with respect to the concomitant principle, that the Indian inhabitants are to be considered merely as occupants, to be protected, indeed, while in peace, in the possession of their lands, but to be deemed incapable of transferring the absolute title to others. *However this restriction may be opposed to natural right, and to the usages of civilized nations, yet, if it be indispensable to that system under which the country has been settled, and be adapted to the actual condition of the two people, it may, perhaps, be supported by reason, and certainly cannot be rejected by courts of justice.*[68] [Emphasis added]

Whatever the pretensions of English-speaking colonists against the Indian nations, once it was accepted that colonial- and imperial-supervised land sales in all other instances had given good title — not from the Indians but from the Crown or colonial governor — it seems incontrovertible that when the United States assumed the claims of Great Britain it also assumed the responsibility for bringing civilization and Christianity to the natives. It also seems true that this responsibility accrues prior to the claim to legal title to the lands. Further, it appears that the Court is saying that political and legal sovereignty are a function of land ownership and that both the Indian tribes and the United States are sovereign to the degree that they are possessors of land. But if sovereignty of the tribes is dependent upon ownership of land, then each loss of land entails an irretrievable loss of status.

Marshall's analysis lacks a certain crispness and precision that is often missing in Supreme Court decisions. If the doctrine of discovery is acceptable as a legal concept, how do European nations purchase the equitable titles from non-Christian peoples with whom they have dealings? In North America this question was settled through the treaty-making process in which France, England, Spain, and Russia all engaged with tribes. Once sovereignty of the Indians is admitted — and this admission would be made by the purchase agreement — the transaction should end without additional burden of preaching Christianity or civilization. We are not, after all, asked to subscribe to new ways of living when we purchase lands, houses, automobiles, or any other form of property. In giving the land purchase a thin coating of morality—i.e., religion and culture—Marshall completely confused the argument for subsequent generations reading his opinion.[69]

In *Cherokee Nation v. Georgia*,[70] Chief Justice Marshall struggled with a definition of the tribe that would justify denying its motion for an injunction against Georgia, tediously examining the treaty provisions for signs of political vulnerability. Justice William Johnson in a concurring opinion went straight to the point. He described the status of the Cherokees by using a biblical analogy:

> Their condition is something like that of the Israelites, when inhabiting the deserts. Though without land that they can call theirs in the sense of property, their right of personal self-government has never been taken from them; and such a form of government may exist though the land occupied be in fact that of another. The right to expel them may exist in that other, but the alternative of departing and retaining the right of self-government may exist in them. And such they certainly do possess; it has never been questioned, nor any attempt made at subjugating them as a people, or restraining their personal liberty except as to their land and trade.[71]

It is not simply the fact that the Cherokees did not hold good title to their lands in the eyes of the Americans that made this situation complicated. Rather it was the location of these lands that made all the difference. They were now inside the territorial confines of what had become the United States. John Marshall observed that "the Indian territory is admitted to compose a part of the United States. In all our maps, geographical treatises, histories, and laws, it is so considered. In all our intercourse with foreign nations, in our commercial regulations, in any attempt at intercourse between Indians and foreign nations, they are considered as within the jurisdictional limits of the United States, subject to many of those restraints which are imposed upon our own citizens."[72]

Consequently it was the fact that the Cherokee lands were contiguous to the American lands that made the Cherokees a dependent people. Had the Cherokees occupied Cuba, with an intervening body of water between them and the United States, the case would almost certainly have reached a much different conclusion. But it is a characteristic of human societies to regard natural features as the limiting factors in their definition of themselves, their lands, and their governments.

Faced with Marshall's geographical realities, Justice Smith Thompson in dissent made the only argument possible: that the Cherokees were foreign in the political sense. Citing Emmerich de Vattel copiously, he contended that:

> Every nation that governs itself, under what form so ever, without any dependence on a foreign power, is a sovereign state. Its rights are naturally the same as those of any other state. Such are moral persons who live together in a natural society, under the law of nations. It is sufficient if it be really sovereign and independent: that is, it must govern itself by its own authority and laws. We ought, therefore, to reckon in the number of sovereigns those states that have bound themselves to another more powerful, although by an unequal alliance. The conditions of these unequal alliances may be infinitely varied; but whatever they are, provided the inferior ally reserves to itself the sovereignty or the right to govern its own body, it ought to be considered an independent state.[73]

Although we have been taught to regard the *Cherokee Nation* case as settling the question of the status of Indian tribes, in fact this interpretation makes law out of fictional reasoning. The real substance of the case is in its application of the idea of property and proprietorship earlier articulated in *Johnson v. McIntosh*.[74] Subsequent American political history demonstrates that the ideas of Justices Johnson and Thompson fluctuate back and forth as definitions of the status of Indian tribes. Inchoate nationhood and the foreign nature of jurisdiction when it involves the exercise of self-government by Indian tribes remain with us today. Instead of the constitutional system defining the rights of Indian tribes through treaty or commercial relations, the feudal system of holding land, adapted to fit the North American social setting, actually controls the manner in which people think about Indians and their relationship to the United States. As the recognition and exercise of the proprietary functions increase and decrease, so does everything else relating to Indian tribes.

Although not articulated clearly, and perhaps not even part of the conscious motivation of congressional actions regarding Indian tribes, the propensity to appropriate funds for the civilization of Indians is a substantial part of the old doctrine of discovery. Until the Constitution can recognize and offer significant protections for Indian property, there can be no resolution to the problem of the relationship between Indian tribes and the United States.

A case pitting the treaty-making power against the property clause occurred at the beginning of this century—*Lone Wolf v. Hitchcock*.[75] The Kiowas and Comanches had made a treaty with the United States in 1867 as part of the work of the Peace Commission. As with all treaties made by this group, it contained provisions and promises that the United States would never thereafter consider a land cession valid against the tribes unless it were approved by three-quarters of the Indians involved. In the 1890s the Jerome Commission made another agreement with these tribes but was still not able to get the required number of signatures. At least part of the reason for failure was the inability of the Indian agent to count the Indians and figure a percentage. Seeking to stop the allotment of their lands, several chiefs filed a suit to enjoin the secretary of the interior from carrying out the provisions of the statute ratifying the amended agreement, which had changed the original agreement so substantially that, they argued, it was no longer what they had bargained for.

The Court ruled against the tribes, arguing that in a time of emergency the United States could not be held to a previous treaty agreement. This reasoning sounds logical to the layperson, although treaty case law indicates that foreign governments and their citizens do not lose their property rights even in times of war. The only limitation that appears to be placed on alien governments' property is that property that would aid in the prosecution of war cannot be used by them. The Court cited no pressing emergency that would have justified the division of lands and distribution of the tribal property estate. As if to add insult to injury, the Court gratuitously concluded that the Indians had not lost anything, anyway, because the transaction was merely a change of investment and therefore basically an administrative action to benefit the tribes. Had this rationale been accepted from the beginning of colonization, Indian tribes might have provided the capital for the Industrial Revolution in Europe by a simple distribution of their homelands. Here the treaty does not hold against an

arbitrary power to transform wealth by the national government—wealth
that it did not own but for which it merely acted as a trustee.

Another, earlier case illustrates the power the concept of property has
when measured against the treaty provisions. In *The Cherokee Tobacco*,[76]
the Supreme Court faced the question of whether a section of the revenue laws, passed two years after an Indian treaty, acted to repeal or abrogate a treaty provision. Section 107 of the 1868 Revenue Act imposed taxes
on distilled spirits, fermented liquors, tobacco, snuff, and cigars that were
produced anywhere within the exterior boundaries of the United States.
Article 10 of the 1866 Cherokee Treaty, however, provided that "Every
Cherokee Indian and freed person residing in the Cherokee nation shall
have the right to sell any products of his farm, including his or her live-
stock, or any merchandise or manufactured products, and to ship and
drive the same to market without restraint, paying any tax thereon which is
now or may be levied by the United States on the quantity sold outside the
Indian territory."[77]

The Cherokees contended that the Revenue Act did not extend to Indian territory and that consequently the Internal Revenue Service could
not levy the tax. Not surprisingly, the Court found that the Cherokees
were within the exterior boundaries of the United States—even though
the treaty clearly delineated lines between the United States and Indian
territory and even though it was demonstrated that there *was no revenue
collection district that included the Cherokee lands,* making it impossible
to purchase revenue stamps for the tobacco and whiskey the Indians produced. The Court ruled that the treaty had been repealed by the succeeding statute, not because Congress intended to do so—for there was
no language to that effect, a point noted by the dissent—but because the
Cherokees were within the lands and jurisdiction of the United States.

The application of the property clause is not always detrimental to Indians, however. It continues to form a significant, though no longer unas-
sailable, protective barrier for the tribes against state taxation because the
states cannot tax federal property; as long as Indian lands are held by the
United States in trust for the Indian tribes, there is no way that the states
can intrude into the situation with their taxing power.[78] Cessions of civil
and criminal jurisdiction over the same lands, however, are fraught with
controversy because the exercise of tribal sovereignty over the reservations

involves the recognition of an additional political entity, the tribal government, which does not assert ultimate and absolute title to its lands.

In concluding our discussion of the three major constitutional clauses that have affected the rights and status of American Indians, we can make the following observations. First, the commerce clause has two aspects: regulation of the manner in which the tribes and American citizens, states, and federal agencies will have political and economic relationships, and the gratuitous policy of Congress's providing civilization and Christianity to the Indians. Second, the substance and meaning of both the treaty-making power and the property clause depend upon ideas and assumptions about the world once prevalent in European political circles. If there was no question in the minds of the constitutional fathers that Indian tribes should be dealt with by treaties, there was also no doubt in their minds that the United States owned the lands it claimed at the end of the Revolutionary War and that subsequent purchases of land from either the Indians or European colonial powers would vest absolute title in the United States.

The principle of Indian consent is highly visible in the treaty-making process, and even identifiable in the exercise of the commerce clause, but is nowhere to be seen in the application of the property clause. Consent by Indians is necessary under the doctrine of discovery, and presumably the Constitution is based upon the principle of the consent of the governed. But absolute proprietorship precludes the consent of anyone except the owner in selling property, and although Indians were regarded as having equitable title to their lands, the United States consistently used every tactic available to force tribes to sell their lands. When American political history is understood in the light of the property clause, the importance of the commerce and treaty-making powers diminishes considerably.

Miscellaneous Constitutional Clauses

Initially we listed the constitutional clauses that had a measure of applicability to Indians, excluding for the moment the general-welfare and war-making powers. The original list of constitutional powers contained some obvious clauses, such as the power to make all necessary laws for executing the other powers. The power to make post roads can be seen in the background of consideration in several treaties, and it is often mentioned but never invoked today when the federal government wishes to build a road through a reservation. Basically it is much easier to simply use the power of condemnation of the sovereign — better known as eminent domain — than to go through the tortuous procedure of justifying a proposed action by using the post-road power.

The presidential power to grant reprieves and pardons has been used once to benefit Indians. In 1862 the Sioux of Minnesota, after suffering much abuse from their agent, attacked the settlements in that state. Overwhelmed by whites after a few weeks of conflict, the Sioux found themselves imprisoned at Fort Snelling and other military outposts where they were given the semblance of a military trial. Some 303 Sioux were found guilty of murder and sentenced to death. President Abraham Lincoln insisted on seeing the trial record, and he assigned two men to go over the proceedings with care to determine which of the Indians might actually be guilty of a crime and which were only responding to the general confusion and defending themselves, their homes, or their families. Lincoln pardoned all but 40 of the Indians.[79]

The power to make new states and the power to protect states from domestic violence can probably be discussed together. There is no question that in stationing army troops near Indian reservations as late as the First World War, the president was exercising this power to protect both the settlers against the Indians and the Indians against the land-hungry Boomers and Sooners, who always loafed near the fringes of reservations clamoring for land cessions. Since everyone knew that Indians were a wholly federal matter, there was no need to invoke this power as separate and distinct from the larger plenary power that had been exercised from the beginning of the republic. It is noteworthy, however, that the protest at Wounded Knee II in 1973 was exclusively a federal matter, although surely the State of South Dakota had an interest in the outcome.

The power to admit new states took a deliberate turn when states from the midcontinent were considered for admission to the union. The fact that they possessed sparse populations and had large Indian tribes within their borders meant that the new states would quickly look to the Indian lands for sources of revenue and wealth in order to keep themselves and their institutions viable. Thus it was that Congress, in admitting new states to the union, exempted Indians and Indian property from the application of state laws. In the enabling acts for a number of western states, including North Dakota, South Dakota, Montana, and Wyoming;[80] Washington;[81] Oklahoma;[82] and Arizona and New Mexico[83] are provisions often termed "disclaimer clauses" that specify what the state may not do inside Indian country. Article 26 of Washington State's constitution is typical:

> That the people inhabiting this state do agree and declare that they forever disclaim all right and title to the unappropriated public lands lying within the boundaries of this state, and to all lands lying within said limits owned or held by any Indian or Indian tribes; and that until the title thereto shall have been extinguished by the United States, the same shall be and remain subject to the disposition of the United States, and said Indian lands shall remain under the absolute jurisdiction and control of the Congress of the United States and that the lands belong to citizens of the United States . . . and that no taxes shall be imposed by the state on lands or property therein, belonging to or which may be hereafter purchased by the United States or reserved for use: Provided, That nothing in this ordinance shall preclude that state from taxing as other lands are taxed any lands owned or held by an Indian who has severed his tribal relations, and has obtained from the United States or from any person a title thereto by patent or other grant, save and except such lands as have been or may be granted to any Indian or Indians under any act of Congress containing a provision exempting the lands thus granted from taxation, which exemption shall continue so long and to such an extent as such act of Congress may prescribe.[84]

The federal government made the disclaimer clauses a requirement for state admission to the union. States have argued, with only sporadic success, that these limitations placed them on a less than equal status with existing states of the union.[85] Yet a combination of the commerce and treaty-making clauses with the power to admit new states has prevailed in the courts until the present time. In 1953, when Congress passed PL-280,[86] it gave permission for the states to amend their constitutions to omit the exclusionary disclaimer clause and to assume jurisdiction over Indian reservations within their borders if they so desired. In 1968, in the Indian Civil Rights Act,[87] the provisions of PL-280 were amended to provide for Indian consent before states could assume such jurisdictional control.

Another important though little-discussed constitutional power, one that even Felix Cohen did not cite in the section of *Handbook of Federal Indian Law* entitled "Sources of Federal Power Over Indian Affairs," is the appointment power vested in the president under Article 2, section 2. This gives the president the power to: "nominate, and by and with the advice and consent of the Senate, shall appoint ambassadors, other public ministers and consuls, judges of the supreme court, and all other officers of the United States, whose Appointments are not herein otherwise provided for, and which shall be established by Law: but the Congress may by Law vest the appointment of such inferior officers, as they may think proper, in the president alone, in the Courts of Law, or in the Heads of Departments." He also has the power to make "recess appointments" when the Senate is not in session. These appointees can hold office through the next session even without Senate confirmation. In fact, the major concern of the appointments clause is to ensure that executive power remain independent, free from congressional encroachment.[88]

Theoretically, the nomination of government officials is the "sole act of the President," as Chief Justice John Marshall stated in *Marbury v. Madison* in 1803.[89] And these are important acts indeed, for, excepting the president and vice-president, all persons in the civil service of the federal government are appointed, including the top administrative officials who carry out the bulk of U.S. treaty and trust obligations to tribes—the secretary of the interior and the assistant secretary of Indian affairs (formerly the commissioner of Indian affairs).

Such Indian policy appointees, the Supreme Court has held, act on behalf of the president, and their actions are presumed to be those of the president.[90] Administrative powers of the secretary of the interior, under direction or delegation of the president, include enforcing Indian preference hiring policies; establishing superintendencies, agencies, and subagencies; appointing the Indian Arts and Crafts Board; appointing various Indian Bureau employees; and discontinuing services of agents, interpreters, and the like.[91]

In *Confederated Tribes of Siletz Indians v. U.S.*[92], the Confederated Tribes contested the denial (after an initial approval) by the secretary of the interior of their application to have lands taken in trust for their benefit for the purpose of setting up a gaming facility when Oregon's governor refused to concur with the plan. The secretary's rejection of the tribes' application was based on his interpretation of a key provision of the 1988 Indian Gaming Regulatory Act (IGRA), which required that gaming on newly acquired trust lands have the concurrence of the governor of the state where the trust land is located.

The U.S. District Court held that the governor's concurrence provision violated both the appointments clause and the separation-of-powers doctrine, but the court still granted summary judgement for the United States and upheld the secretary's rejection of the Indians' application. Cross appeals were taken. The ninth circuit court of appeals, however, held that the governor's-concurrence provision was a valid delegation of congressional legislative authority and did not violate the appointments clause or the separation-of-powers doctrine.

"The Governor's authority," said Chief Judge Hug, "under IGRA extends only to making a single determination—which is unlikely to arise often in a particular state. This narrow concurrence function does not impermissibly undermine Executive Branch authority, when exercised by the Governor as a state officer, in the performance of a state function, under an express delegation of congressional power to control Indian lands."[93] This is a situation in which the separation-of-powers doctrine holds true at the national level, but where the doctrine of federalism is defined in such a way as to allow states' veto power over a clearly defined congressional authority.

The two clauses granting the power of judicial review and the power to constitute interior tribunals should also be taken together. They constitute a mixed blessing for Indians. Judicial review is the only avenue open to Indians since the foreclosure of treaty and agreement making, but, as we have seen in the discussion of the Cherokee cases, it is hazardous to predict how the courts will view Indian plaintiffs. In 1855 Congress established the U.S. Court of Claims[94] as a means of eliminating the hundreds of requests from private citizens for redress from real and imagined wrongs visited upon them by the United States. In 1863, however, Congress changed the jurisdiction of the court by prohibiting it from hearing any claims based upon treaties, thus effectively closing this forum to Indian tribes who might have used it as a means of enforcing their treaty rights.[95] Thereafter, Indian tribes could file suit only with the legislative permission of Congress in a special jurisdictional act that clearly laid down what was to be the subject of litigation and the conditions under which the case would be heard. Indians generally fared very badly in these cases because the court of claims interpreted the jurisdictional basis for Congress's granting admission very narrowly, eliminating many causes of action.

In 1891, after processing numerous claims made against the Indian tribes as the result of the final wars on the plains and in the southwestern United States, Congress decided to allow the court of claims to hear all cases brought against the tribes for alleged violation of treaties in what was known as the Indian Depredation Act.[96] While Indian tribes were barred from any judicial relief except that which was carefully crafted by legislative deliberations, the court of claims allowed even the most frivolous suits to be filed against the Indians.[97]

Throughout the first part of this century, an increasing number of Indian tribes went to Congress seeking legislation that would open the court of claims to them. Fundamental to any successful effort to settle their claims was the demand by the government that Indians admit that the United States had taken their lands and that they were seeking only a monetary compensation; the lands could not be returned to them. In 1928 the *Meriam Report*[98] advised that Indian claims should be settled as quickly as possible, so throughout the 1930s efforts were made to pass legislation establishing an Indian Claims Commission. In 1946 the commission was finally authorized.[99] Although designed to be a commission, not a court, and to handle the claims with a fair degree of flexibility, the prevalence of attorneys accustomed to dealing with the court of claims' procedures made it inevitable that the commission would adopt regular courtroom procedures. Finally, in 1978, Congress let authorization for the Indian Claims Commission lapse and sent all remaining claims to the court of claims, later reconstituted as the U.S. Claims Court.[100]

These "inferior tribunals" substantially altered the idea of land cession and materially changed the interpretation of American history. In order to file a claim a tribe would have to agree to hire an attorney approved by the Department of the Interior, and since all attorney contracts were approved by the United States, the government ensured that it would have cooperative attorneys to represent the Indian plaintiffs. Attorneys received a minimum 10 percent of recoveries, and so they were inclined to settle cases as quickly as possible. Consequently, many important facts and points of law were stipulated in an effort to make the cases simpler. Attorneys had almost complete control over the course of litigation, informing their Indian clients only when it was felt they had a need to know or when they wanted the tribal government to approve a major step in the litigation. The net result of the Indian Claims Commission was to set to rest long-standing problems of land cession in which, after the tribe had agreed to accept the commission's award, *res judicata* would preclude the tribe from raising the issue again in a federal court. The process had been a denial rather than an affirmation of justice.

The two remaining clauses mentioned in our original list are the power to lay and collect taxes and the power to establish a rule for naturalization of citizens. Both of these clauses, insofar as they affect American Indians, were later the topic of constitutional amendments, and we will discuss them later in that context. In summary, we can conclude that the record looks mixed when we examine how miscellaneous constitutional phrases and clauses have been applied to American Indians. In some instances the outcomes were beneficial, in others they were detrimental. In no case was there a sufficiently significant development of power as it was applied to American Indians. Rather the overwhelming presence of the three major clauses—treaty-making, commerce, and property—precluded any development of other constitutional powers in the treatment of American Indians.

CHAPTER VI

THE CONSTITUTIONAL

AMENDMENTS

T H E application of the constitutional amendments to American Indians requires an in-depth discussion. The Bill of Rights was added to the Constitution shortly after its ratification, at a time when the Indian nations were seen as separate political entities who might suddenly align themselves with the European nations still seeking colonies in North America. Not all amendments dealt with subjects that would one day affect Indians. The Thirteenth Amendment was passed just before the great treaty-making period of the 1860s, the Fourteenth when the government was undecided about how to deal with Indians and Congress was about to terminate treaty making, and the Fifteenth came when Indians were still protected by treaty provisions and were not regarded as American citizens.

The Sixteenth, Eighteenth, and Twenty-first Amendments were ratified long after the end of the treaty-making period and, in fact, after the *Lone Wolf* decision in 1903, when the Bureau of Indian Affairs concluded that Indian affairs were now a matter of proper administration. After 1924, when American Indians were made citizens of the United States, insofar as they enjoyed the status of citizens, provisions of later amendments applied if and when they were raised in litigation. However, the preemptory role that the federal government enjoyed with regard to Indians was never seriously challenged by state or local governments, so that virtually nothing in the way of case law developed regarding the later amendments and Indians. They were simply presumed to be a part of the body politic. This chapter addresses the amendments of the Bill of Rights that have some application to Indians; Chapter 7 addresses the later amendments.

The Bill of Rights

The Bill of Rights, born largely through the work of George Mason, Thomas Jefferson, and James Madison, was a necessary addition to the Constitution that made ratification a reality. These ten amendments are a combination of prohibitions against the exercise by the federal government of certain powers and functions that when previously exercised in Europe by despotic monarchs had caused the colonists to flee to America. The thrust of these protections is a guarantee to the citizens that their national government will not act in an arbitrary manner against their personal freedoms. The Constitution, being a federal document, did not describe the possible arbitrary actions of state governments against their own citizens. This kind of protection did not concern the authors of the Bill of Rights because most of the states' constitutions had the same or similar provisions regarding state governmental actions.

Because Indians were not officially recognized as a racial, ethnic, or political group whose individual members were citizens until the Indian Citizenship Act of 1924,[1] we have not been as a rule interested in the application of these rights to American Indians until after that date. Since these federal constitutional rights exist only when Indians are living off the reservation as American citizens, their application is not unlike that given to any other citizen. This unique and ongoing extraconstitutional status of Indians was clearly described by Senator Frank Church (Democrat, Idaho), chairman of the Senate Subcommittee on Indian Affairs, during initial congressional hearings on the constitutional rights of American Indians in 1961. In his testimony, Senator Church noted that:

> We gave the Indian citizenship, true, but for lack of anything else to call it, we gave him full citizenship, with a major geographic excep-

tion. By this I mean on the one hand we said "you are now a full American citizen." And on the other hand we took no action to change the existing situation, which was, and is now, that the Indian tribes are not subject to Federal constitutional limitations in the Bill of Rights. What did this mean to the Indian citizen? It meant he had all the constitutional rights of other citizens, except at one place. The one place where he lived. In effect, we said, "move away from home and you can have the protections of the Constitution too."

The stark reality of Church's testimony appeared to surprise several of the committee members who presumed that U.S. citizenship implied the derogation of Indian citizenship. Then there was this interesting exchange between Senator Kenneth B. Keating (New York) and Senator Church:

SENATOR KEATING: "May I interrupt you, Senator Church?"

SENATOR CHURCH: "Yes, indeed."

SENATOR KEATING: "So I am sure I understand your line of reasoning? What you say is that an Indian, if he is on the reservation, is not protected by the U.S. Constitution unless there is also in his tribal constitution or laws a complementary protection form?"

SENATOR CHURCH: "Yes. And in this case his protection would derive from the provision in the tribal constitution, and in the absence of such provision there would be no restriction upon the tribal action that could be taken against him. So the normal, universal, application of constitutional restrictions that apply elsewhere do not necessarily apply in Indian reservations."[2]

Unfortunately, senators and congressmen always describe this situation in negative terms, and because the membership of Congress changes every two years, there are always many scenarios wherein a senator or congressman who has not had any previous experience with Indians properly expresses his or her horror at this condition. The implication is always that lack of application of the Bill of Rights produces a lawless territory where almost anything can occur. In fact, the preservation of tribal jurisdiction was a major point of contention in many treaties because the tribes did not wish to forsake their traditional ways. Many tribal justice systems are far more mature than the rigid application of Anglo-Saxon, Old Testament, eye-for-an-eye justice, and many Indians did not want their codes of law and order to be based upon the principle of revenge. Over the decades, particularly since 1934, tribal nations have been encouraged to adopt western-style constitutions and governments. The gap between justice and the actions of tribal governments has widened greatly now that tribal constitutions resemble those of non-Indian states and municipalities.

Our major interest, then, is to examine the prohibitions against federal action and to determine whether or not these prohibitions extended to the treatment of Indians by the federal government. The amendments within the Bill of Rights that have relevance to our study are the First Amendment, which prohibits Congress from making any law "respecting the establishment of religion, or prohibiting the free exercise thereof" and guaranteeing the freedoms of speech, assembly, and the press, and the right to petition the government for redress; the Fourth Amendment, which protects individuals from unreasonable searches and seizures; that part of the Fifth Amendment that prohibits double jeopardy[3] and provides just compensation for property taken for a public use; the Sixth Amendment section that guarantees persons accused of criminal offenses legal counsel; and, arguably, the Tenth Amendment, which reserves to the states and the people respectively powers not delegated to the United States by the Constitution. Of these amendments in the Bill of Rights, the religious restrictions contained in the First Amendment are most significant and require careful discussion.

The First Amendment: The Establishment of Religion

The first section of the First Amendment prohibits Congress from making any law "respecting an establishment of religion," and this clause, with respect to American Indians, has been honored far more in its breach than in its enforcement. And while constitutional law experts agree that the establishment clause of the First Amendment forbids the creation of a single "official" religion in the United States, there is no doubt that for much of this nation's history most federal policy makers and non-Indian reform organizations made a concerted effort to establish Christianity as the official religion among tribal nations.

Historical practices originally determined the interplay of religious groups and federal Indian policy. On the frontier it was more often than not the missionary who represented civilization, and quite frequently missionaries were among the first people to have contact with an Indian tribe on a continuing basis. By the time of the American Revolution, it was already an established practice that missions and missionaries would be provided for tribes if they desired them. French, Spanish, and English missionaries had already visited tribes on the frontier and converted large numbers of people. Among the Iroquois and the tribes of the Michigan-Ohio-Indiana-Illinois country, the predominant denomination was Roman Catholic. In New England, as might be expected, various Protestant denominations were well represented among the tribes. In general, we can describe the situation as one in which the United States inherited a colonial practice that, if it had rigorously enforced a separation of church and state, would have been considered unconstitutional by its courts and regarded as a hostile act by the Indians involved.

The missionaries at this time functioned as interpreters of European civilization, advocates for Indian rights, and avenues for helping Indians gain the necessary skills to deal with the white men rushing into the territories of the tribes. Missionaries commanded some respect from the whites on the frontier. And in spite of their zealous and rigid behavior in attacking the traditional tribal customs and ceremonies, they were often seen as allies of the tribes when crises threatened. Most active missionaries had sought permission of the chiefs of the tribes when they entered Indian country, and some tribes even decreed when and where missionary activities could take place. This condition existed until quite late in the nineteenth century.[4]

With the expansion of programs for civilizing the Indians in the early 1800s (e.g., the 1819 Civilization Fund Act), the federal government naturally turned to the missionaries for assistance. Promises to provide education for the children of the tribe, or on occasion health services, generally involved the federal intent to use existing facilities and personnel, which meant that missionaries were provided with funds from the treaties to carry out these activities. This use of federal funds probably cannot be described as the establishment of a religion because the missions were usually in place prior to the signing of treaties. Additionally, the funds promised were derived from the sale of tribal lands and therefore could possibly be characterized as tribal funds, the services being simply purchased from the churches under government supervision.

Evidence supporting this interpretation can be seen in various treaty provisions, such as Article 3 of the December 2, 1794, treaty with the Oneida,[5] in which $1,000 was provided to build a church; and Article 16 of the September 29, 1817, treaty with the Wyandots, Ottawas, and Chippewas,[6] which granted the rector of St. Anne's Catholic Church in Detroit a considerable tract of land in exchange for the promise to provide a Catholic education for the children of the tribes. Even if the missionaries used undue influence in securing these benefits, the fact remains that the treaty specifically established a contract between the tribes and the churches, with the federal government acting as the administrator of funds in the transaction.

Missionaries occupied a critically important role in relations with the Cherokee tribe during its problems with Georgia in the early 1800s. Samuel Worcester and several other missionaries entered the Cherokee lands under the provisions of the Cherokee treaties and the federal laws passed to carry the treaties into effect. In *Worcester v. Georgia*,[7] the Supreme Court upheld the federal laws and Indian treaties, although to no avail because of Andrew Jackson's refusal to take action. Worcester *and the other missionaries* do not appear here as intruders into Cherokee life but as willing defendants in a test case supporting Cherokee rights, and there is no question about the establishment of religion in their actions.

The peace policy of President Ulysses S. Grant, initiated in 1869 with a meeting with the Society of Friends and a subsequent congressional act establishing the Board of Indian Commissioners,[8] is probably the first example of the federal government's overstepping the bounds of constitutional prohibitions and overtly acting to establish a religion among Indian tribes. Although the first Board of Indian Commissioners did not directly represent church bodies, it was composed of aggressive laymen of the Protestant denominations. And early in 1869, the president asked the churches to nominate agents for the various agencies. In exchange for providing good Christian men to lead the Indians to civilization, the churches received an almost exclusive right to proselytize the tribes at the agencies to which they had been assigned.

As of 1872, the following churches had exclusive or near-exclusive control of the following Indian agencies:

American Board of Commissioners of Foreign Missions:	Sisseton Sioux
Baptist:	Cherokee, Creek, Walker River Paiute
Catholic:	Tulalip, Colville, Grande Ronde, Umatilla, Flathead, Grande River, Devils Lake
Christian:	Pueblo Agency, Makah
Congregational:	Green Bay, Chippewa of Lake Superior, Chippewa of the Mississippi
Episcopal:	Whetstone Agency, Ponca, Upper Missouri Agency, Fort Berthold, Cheyenne River, Yankton, Red Cloud, Shoshone
Friends (Hicksite):	Great Nemaha, Omaha, Winnebago, Pawnee, Oto, Santee Sioux
Friends (Orthodox):	Potawatomi of Kansas, Kaw, Kickapoo, Quapaw, Osage, Sac and Fox, Shawnee, Wichita, Kiowa, Upper Arkansas
Lutheran:	Sac and Fox of Iowa
Methodist:	Hoopa Valley, Round Valley, Tule River, Yakima, Siletz, Skokomish, Quinault, Warm Springs, Klamath, Blackfeet, Crow, Mild River, Fort Hall, Michigan Agency
Presbyterian:	Choctaw, Seminole, Abiquiu Agency Navajo, Mescalero Apache, Southern Apache, Hopi, Nez Perce, Uintah Valley Agency
Reformed Dutch:	Colorado River, Pima and Maricopa, Camp Grant, Camp Verde, White Mountain Apache
Unitarian:	Los Pinos Agency, White River Agency[9]

Francis Paul Prucha noted that "What the government wanted from the churches was a total transformation of the agencies from political sine-cures to missionary outposts."[10] And he noted that "maintaining a position against a conflicting group was . . . often a more powerful motivation than concern for the welfare of the Indians."[11] There is no question, then, that the peace policy was a violation of the First Amendment, at least in respect to the establishment clause.

Not only was concern about the establishment clause suppressed to al-low the churches to gain a foothold over the Indian tribes, the actions of the missionaries when they had control of the agencies were hardly in ac-cord with the free-exercise prohibition of the First Amendment. "What was more serious," according to Prucha, "was the complete disregard for the religious views and the religious rights of the Indians themselves. Quakers, Methodists, Episcopalians, and all the other Protestants, fighting for the religious liberty of their own groups on the reservations, made no move to grant so much as a hearing to the Indian religions."[12] The record of the Catholics is no better. They criticized Protestant bigotry and called for freedom of conscience, but they did not believe that this freedom ex-tended to native religions, which were universally condemned. The mis-sionaries were not interested in the Indians' right to maintain and defend their own religions: *"By religious freedom they meant liberty of action on the reservations for their own missionary activities"*[13] [emphasis added]. And because the missionaries were acting as direct federal agents in this instance, the effect was the establishment of denominational religious freedom and denial of traditional Indian religion—a clear violation of both prohibitions on establishment and free-exercise guarantees. For ex-ample, Congress passed an act on March 1, 1889, to establish a federal court in Indian territory.[14] Section 22 of that law made it a criminal offense punishable by fine and imprisonment for any person to "maliciously or contemptuously disturb or disquiet any congregation or private family as-sembled in any church or other place for religious worship . . . by pro-foundly swearing or using indecent gestures, threatening language, or committing any violence of any kind. . . ."[15] There was no corresponding protection of traditional Indian religious practices.

For all practical purposes, the allocation of agencies to the churches on a relatively exclusive basis ended during the tenure of Columbus Delano as secretary of the interior in the early 1870s. He argued that the secretary

always had preserved the right to appoint agents and saw the church recommendations as simply recommendations, not as requirements. But the
conflict among the Christian churches continued and reached a fever
pitch in the quarrel over the continuance of sectarian school funds. The
churches provided educational facilities and programs for many of the
tribes because the Bureau of Indian Affairs was unable to operate an extensive school system. In addition to their own funds, many of the church
schools received federal funds for this purpose. When the Catholic schools
continued to expand, the Protestants felt they had an unfair advantage,
and so, beginning in 1895, the Protestants started to work for the abolition of funds for sectarian schools, hoping to hamper Catholic progress on
the reservations. In 1897 Congress passed a prohibition against the use of
funds for sectarian education in the contract schools,[16] and the prohibition was included in appropriation acts several more times in the succeeding years.

The Catholics, however, had supported the Democrats and had sufficient political influence to devise a way to continue to receive funds for
their schools. They simply had the Bureau of Indian Affairs give them
tribal monies for this purpose. The practice was justified on the basis that
Indian funds were treaty and trust funds (from land sales) and therefore
not publicly appropriated moneys, which Congress had prohibited. The
Indians whose children attended Catholic schools were designated as petitioners who had asked for their share of tribal funds for use in the education of their children. So the bureau divided the tribal funds into a per-
capita share and took the shares of the petitioning Indians each year and
used them for the Catholic schools.

In 1908 this practice was challenged in the Supreme Court in the case
Quick Bear v. Leupp.[17] Quick Bear, a Protestant Sioux Indian who lived
on the Rosebud Reservation in South Dakota, objected to the use of tribal
funds for Catholic schools. The Court, in one of the most ironic decisions
ever written, declared that:

> it would be unjust to withhold from an Indian or community of In-
> dians the right, within reasonable limits, in good faith, and under the
> safeguards provided by the President's instructions, to choose their own
> school and to choose it frankly because the education therein is under
> the influence of the religious faith in which they believe and to which

they are attached, and to have the use of their proportion of tribal funds applied under the control of the Secretary's discretion to maintain such schools. *Any other view of the case perverts the supposed general spirit of the constitutional provision into a means of prohibiting the free exercise of religion.*[18] [Emphasis added]

In effect, the Court reached through the tribal entity in order to grant free exercise of religion to Indians by taking their funds to support a particular church that had once received an exclusive franchise to proselytize them. So one clause of the First Amendment was used to justify the violation of another one. Actually, the so-called petitioning Indians received considerably more than their pro-rata share of tribal assets because the funds in the treasury each year represented both the remaining shares of the nonpetitioning Indians and the yearly income of the tribe. So that after the first year of sectarian school support, the shares reflected an additional draw by the petitioners against tribal funds to which they had no claims. In other instances, when an Indian individual took his or her share of tribal assets in cash, that Indian was no longer regarded as a tribal member and was not entitled to any further distribution of tribal assets. In fact, an act the previous year, on March 2, 1907,[19] allowed the secretary of the interior to designate Indians deemed capable of managing their own affairs and to issue them pro-rata shares of tribal funds, allowing them to withdraw from the tribe.

There is no question that the prohibition against the establishment of a religion contained in the First Amendment did not apply to laws and practices of the United States, by both the Congress and the executive branch, and that the violation of this prohibition was excused on the justification that the United States was allowing the free exercise of religion—at least of the Christian religion—which was presumed to be the free choice of the Indians.

Another question needs to be addressed when discussing the establishment clause. In its dealings with Indians, does the United States, either deliberately or unwittingly, establish the Christian religion? In the 1890s Congress granted a right-of-way through Osage Indian lands to the Missouri, Kansas and Texas Railway Company. The Indians loudly protested, and the controversy landed in the Supreme Court in *Missouri, Kansas and Texas Railway Co. v. Roberts.*[20] In upholding the expansive powers of Congress to deal with Indian property, the Court declared that "though the law as stated with reference to the power of the government to determine the right of occupancy of the Indians to their lands has always been recognized, it is to be presumed, as stated by this court in the *Buttz* case, that *in its exercise the United States will be governed by such considerations of justice as will control a Christian people in their treatment of an ignorant and dependent race . . . "*[21] [emphasis added].

If Christian doctrine, morality, or concepts of justice are the criteria for judging the propriety of federal actions toward Indians, has the United States established the Christian religion and abandoned a position of neutrality with regard to religion? Certainly the justification for granting the Indian lands is that this exercise of congressional power is the Christian, and therefore proper, thing to do. An apocryphal tale about President Dwight D. Eisenhower further illustrates this point: he was said to remark while signing Public Law 280, which extended civil and criminal jurisdiction over Indians without their consent, "this is a most un-Christian thing to do." He nevertheless signed the bill and wistfully commented that he hoped that the Congress would amend the law later to provide for the consent of the Indians.[22]

One of the problems in establishing Christianity as a moral or perhaps even legal criterion for dealing with Indians is determining exactly *what* tenets of Christianity serve as the standard of behavior. Citation of the golden rule would seem to call for the utmost concern for Indians — if we do not want someone taking away our property and homes, we should not take the Indians'. On the other hand, if domination of the earth is a divine command, then actions even worse than originally contemplated might be in order. Further, we must ask, *which* interpretation of these alternatives would be permissible? The golden rule as defined by Roman Catholic, Baptist, or Presbyterian leaders might vary radically, and the idea that the natural world must be subdued could range from the preservation-conservation ethic of St. Francis of Assisi to the commitment to asphalt all the holdings of a Methodist land baron.

Former Indian Commissioner Francis Leupp gave an eloquent and humorous example of the difficulties arising when Christians interfered with Indian culture and religion. Remembering the sly question of an old Indian man, Leupp recounted:

One missionary, he told us, — referring to a visit from a Mormon
apostle several years before — had four wives, and said it was good in
the sight of the white man's god; the missionary who preached at the
agency school had only one wife, and said that that was all right, but
it would be wicked for him to marry any more; but the priest who
came once in a while to bless the children had no wife at all, and
said that the white man's god would be displeased with him if he took
even one.[23]

The mixture of Christianity, then, in the affairs of the state can lead to
utter confusion and chaos. Similar contradictions could be found everywhere this intrusion exists.

Perhaps the best argument to be made is that dealing with tribes is an
external affair of the United States and that the establishment clause extends only to the affairs of the citizens in a domestic setting. Therefore, the
citation of Christian doctrine and behavior as a justification for congressional action and as the standard by which federal action is judged is
proper because it testifies to the essential civilized state of the nation. If
this argument is an acceptable definition of the status of the United States
vis-à-vis Indian tribes, this must then mean that Indian tribes — notwithstanding the citizenship status of individual Indians — remain outside the
scope of the Constitution and that the original protections they enjoyed,
based on treaty making through informed consent, must be honored when
the United States deals with these nations.

The First Amendment: The Free Exercise Clause

There can be no question that Indians, until very recently, have not enjoyed the protection of the First Amendment insofar as the free-exercise-
of-religion clause is concerned. With the final settling of Indians on the
reservations in the West, with enforced hair cutting, education, and general supervisory functions of the Bureau of Indian Affairs over the lives of
Indians, there was a determined effort to eradicate Indian religion and culture. The primary event in this dreary history is the Wounded Knee mas-
sacre of 1890, when Indians doing the Ghost Dance were brutally massa-

cred by the Seventh Cavalry. Prohibitions on the practice of some Indian customs, because these customs were integral to the practice of the tribal religion, also fall into this broad category of denial of rights.

As late as the 1920s there was severe repression of Indian religion on the reservations. The Office of Indian Affairs Circular No. 1665, dated April 26, 1921, reads as follows:

> The sun-dance, and all other similar dances and so-called religious ceremonies are considered "Indian Offences" under existing regulations, and corrective penalties are provided. I regard such restrictions as applicable to any dance which . . . involves the reckless giving away of property . . . frequent or prolonged periods of celebration . . . in fact any disorderly or plainly excessive performance that promotes superstitious cruelty, licentiousness, idleness, danger to health, and shiftless indifference to family welfare.[24]

Two years later, on February 14, 1923, Commissioner of Indian Affairs Charles H. Burke supplemented this circular, directing that:

> . . . the Indian dances be limited to one in each month in the daylight hours of one day in the midweek, and at one center in each district: the months of March and April, June, July, and August being excepted. That none take part in the dances or be present who are under 50 years of age. That a careful propaganda be undertaken to educate public opinion against the dance.[25]

It is not difficult to see the violation of the free-exercise clause in these administrative directives. One need only substitute "the Mass" for "the dance" to understand the degree of oppression involved. Prohibitions on dances and ceremonies were halted in 1933, when newly appointed Commissioner of Indian Affairs John Collier issued Circular No. 2970, "Indian Religious Freedom and Indian Culture," which stated that Indian religious practices would no longer be prohibited.[26] This memo and other important changes in federal Indian policy were legislatively articulated the following year with congressional enactment of the Indian Reorganization Act.[27] But this statute, insofar as religion was concerned, only laid the groundwork for the exercise of religious freedom on reservations.

Not only were tribal dances forbidden for a long period of time, but with the spread of the peyote religion, attacks were made on sacramental substances, in this instance the use of the peyote cactus button. By 1914 the use of peyote had come to the attention of the federal government and church groups. Plans were made for its suppression. In 1916 the first anti-peyote bill was introduced in Congress, and finally in 1918 Congressman Carl Hayden of Arizona introduced a bill that would have classified peyote among the intoxicants and outlawed its use by any Indian over whom the Bureau of Indian Affairs had jurisdiction. After extensive and heated congressional hearings, in which a great deal of prejudice and misinformation about the peyote religion was placed on the record, the bill passed the House of Representatives but was defeated in the Senate.[28]

Following the hearings members of the peyote religion gathered together to organize their constituency in a manner similar to the church organizations of the Christian denominations so that, if attacked again, they would be able to present to Congress and to state and federal courts an organizational structure that reasonably paralleled accepted religious institutions. From that time forward, with varying degrees of efficiency and suffering sporadic attacks by state and federal governments, the Native American Church has continued to exist as a religious body. It is important to note here that to the degree that Indians have been willing to change their customs and conform their practices to the kinds of behaviors similar to those of the Christian churches, they generally have been protected in the practice of religion. We say generally, however, because the 1990 *Smith* case,[29] to be discussed below, was a powerful affront to this trend. But as we will show, there was a political response to this decision that once again placed the peyote religion and its adherents in a protected status. To the degree that the behavior of the peyote people has followed traditional Indian spontaneity, however, the religion has remained suspect.

Everything we have discussed has been generally applicable to Indians living on the reservations under the strict control of the Bureau of Indian Affairs. It might be argued that if the tribes are completely separate from the United States in a political and constitutional sense, the First Amendment protections should not and cannot apply to them. But the repression of religion is constitutionally prohibited regardless of who the practitioners are unless the government can show a compelling reason and provide a rational basis for why it wants to restrict a given religious practice — because the government is without authority to punish any persons for their religious beliefs. And it has been the executive branch, encouraged

and supported by the Congress, that has been the oppressor in this practice. Once Indians are off the reservation and outside both tribal and federal jurisdiction, they theoretically assume the constitutional rights of all
other American citizens, or have done so since the Indian Citizenship Act
of 1924. So the discussion must turn to the conditions Indians have faced
when living off the reservation and how their religious beliefs and practices have been treated. We shall see below that in some cases even off-
reservation Indians have discovered that U.S. citizenship is insufficient to
protect their religious liberties.

Two areas of conflict come immediately to the fore. During the period
of establishing reservations, most tribes were placed on greatly reduced
land holdings. Since many tribes were not only migratory but migrated
according to religious directions, holding their important ceremonies at
specific locations within their original occupancy area, tribes were denied
entrance to and use of important religious shrines in lands under the control of the federal government, state governments, or private owners. Thus,
access to and use of holy places has been a major point of conflict in the
practice of traditional religions.[30]

Ceremonies frequently require the use of bird and animal parts and
special individual pledges of piety, the most important of which is the care
of hair. We can use the secular word "outfits" to convey the extensive instances this area represents, and wearing long hair and the use of bird and
animal parts in the outfits has become a subject of bitter controversy. Indians have had great difficulties with school and prison authorities over
the length of hair, while state and federal game and wildlife agencies have
devoted considerable time and energy to harassing Indians about the number and kinds of feathers in their headpieces and medicine bundles. Many
Indians have been arrested by federal agents for allegedly possessing eagle
feathers without a permit, which they are required by the U.S. Fish &
Wildlife Service to have. Yet it is a fact that a number of American politicians want to be adopted into Indian tribes and expect to receive a war
bonnet in token of their admission, and then use their eagle feathers in a
wholly secular manner as office decorations. To date, not a single American politician has inquired how the Indians were able to get the eagle
feathers for their decorative war bonnets, and no American politicians
have been prosecuted for having eagle feathers without a permit; whereas
in parts of the United States eagle feathers are presently being confiscated

from Indians unless the Indian possessing them can prove his title to them by showing a valid permit.

This state of affairs was the subject of congressional action when in 1978 the American Indian Religious Freedom Act (AIRFA) was passed.[31] The act, though technically a joint resolution, was designed to answer many of the problems that had arisen with respect to traditional Indian religious practices. According to the House report that accompanied the measure, the intent of Congress was "to insure that the policies and procedures of various federal agencies, as they may impact upon the exercise of traditional Indian religious practices, are brought into compliance with the constitutional injunction that Congress shall make no laws abridging the free exercise of religion."[32] There was great hope among Indians that this act would finally provide some basic protections for them against unwarranted and intrusive federal actions.

The result of AIRFA, however, was to focus the attention of federal agencies on Indians, and it produced a torrent of conflict. Non-Indians conceived religion as a matter of creedal and intellectual preference, not as a way of life that required continuing devotional acts. Considerable litigation followed, including *Sequoyah v. Tennessee Valley Authority*,[33] *Badoni v. Higginson*,[34] *Fools Crow v. Gullet*,[35] *Wilson V. Block*,[36] *Inupiat Community of the Arctic Slope v. United States*,[37] *Bowen v. Roy*,[38] *Lyng v. Northwest Indian Cemetery Protective Association*,[39] *United States v. Means*,[40] and *Employment Division Department of Human Resources v. Smith*.[41] In all these cases, except *Bowen*[42] and *Smith*,[43] the issue concerned the right of Indians to practice their religions on land under federal control. In each of the land-related cases, except for the federal district court's ruling in *Northwest Cemetery*,[44] the Indians lost because the federal courts insisted on devising a balancing test whereby they weighed the relative worth of the practice of Indian religion against the construction of dams, roads, and recreation developments. It is clear that AIRFA only confused the matter of Indian religious freedom. The Supreme Court's recent cases, *Lyng* and *Smith*, wherein the Court finally considered the issue of Indian religious freedom and powerfully denied that freedom to individual Indians and to tribal nations, indicate that from the Supreme Court's perspective religious freedom remains an elusive goal for American Indians and is still a controversial subject.

Though all the above decisions are important, for purposes of this analysis some greater attention must be paid to *Lyng* and *Smith*. These two Supreme Court cases, coming in the wake of all the prior litigation, when read together wrought a great revolution in both federal Indian law (*Lyng*) and constitutional law (*Smith*). Because of these two opinions, American Indians were basically stripped of whatever protection they might have expected from the federal courts and the American Constitution regarding the practice of traditional tribal religions.[45] We will discuss these in chronological order.

The *Lyng* Decision

Lyng is typical of much contemporary litigation over the subject of how federal lands may be used. The U.S. Forest Service, which manages most of the nation's forests, proposed to construct a six-mile paved road in the Six Rivers National Forest that would link two existing roads leading to the towns of Gasquet and Orleans in northern California.[46] The proposed road was to run through the Chimney Rock section of the forest. It and the accompanying forest management plan providing for the harvesting of timber would disrupt the sanctity and solitude of a remote area in the forest considered sacred to the Yurok, Karok, and Tolowa Indians, who had used the area for untold generations as a ceremonial place to engage in vision quests, sacred dances, the training of medicine people, and the gathering of medicinal plants and roots.[47]

The tribes were not alone in their quest to stop construction of the road. A host of non-Indian conservation, environmental, and governmental organizations, along with several interested individuals, were eager to protect the area from logging and wanted it designated as wilderness. This grouping included the Sierra Club, the Wilderness Society, California Trout, Siskiyou Mountain's Resource Council, Redwood Region Audubon Society, North Coast Environmental Center, and the state of California — acting through the Native American Heritage Commission. This impressive assemblage, along with an Indian coalition representing the tribes' interest called the Northwest Indian Cemetery Protective Association, and several individual plaintiffs were now allied against the U.S. Forest Service and that agency's home unit, the Department of Agriculture.[48]

The Indians and their allies first tried administrative appeals to stop the proposed road construction, which proved unsuccessful. They then filed two suits in the U.S. District Court for the Northern District of California, which were consolidated for the trial. The plaintiffs claimed that the Forest Service's decisions violated the First Amendment, the AIRFA of 1978, the National Environmental Policy Act and the Wilderness Act, the Federal Water Pollution Control Act, the water and fishing rights reserved to the Hoopa Valley Indian Reservation members, the federal trust responsibility for Indians, and several other federal statutes.

Under then-prevailing case law,[49] the Forest Service was required to show a compelling reason for the construction of the road that would justify the substantial religious burden that was to be placed on the plaintiffs. The Forest Service's asserted interests were the following: that the G-O road would increase the quantity of timber accessible for harvest in the Blue Creek Unit, stimulate employment in the region's timber industry, provide recreational access to the area, improve efficient administration of the National Forest lands, and increase the price of bids on future timber sales by decreasing the cost of hauling the timber.[50] Additionally, the Forest Service contended that implementation of the management plan would increase timber production in the disputed area, which, in turn, would stimulate the area's timber industry, thus increasing Forest Service revenue.[51]

During the trial, however, Judge Stanley A. Weigel meticulously dismantled the government's arguments by showing that some of the alleged reasons for the road lacked merit. In fact, the Forest Service itself conceded that construction of the G-O road "would not improve access to timber resources in the Blue Creek Unit";[52] that, in fact, "timber could be harvested without building the Chimney Rock Section."[53] Moreover, it was determined that road completion would not result in increased jobs and that increased recreational access to the area was an insufficient rationale to justify infringing the Indians' First Amendment rights. Judge Weigel also cited as without merit the government's argument that prevention of road construction because of the Indians' free-exercise claim would constitute establishment of a government-managed "religious shrine in violation of the Establishment Clause of the First Amendment." As the judge noted, "actions compelled by the Free Exercise Clause do not violate the Establishment Clause."[54]

The district court upheld the First Amendment rights of the Indians and the federal government's trust responsibility to protect the Indians' fishing and water rights, and it found that the Forest Service's decision violated several environmental laws. Judge Weigel, accordingly, granted the permanent injunction the Indians and other plaintiffs had sought in order to prevent the G-O road's construction. The issue, however, was far from resolved. The court still provided the Forest Service with an opportunity to construct the road in the Blue Creek roadless area if and when it prepared and circulated a supplemental environmental impact statement that identified specific measures to mitigate the negative impact of the proposed logging activity on water quality and fish habitat. Thus the larger issues of the life of an ancient forest, the national heritage, the spiritual traditions of three tribes, and the environmental concerns of a number of groups were now captives of a process of simple technical readjustments to an environmental impact statement that was to be written by the very agency intent on constructing the road in the first place.

The Forest Service appealed the district court's ruling to the ninth circuit court of appeals in July 1984. Judge William C. Canby Jr.[55] issued the court's opinion on June 24, 1985. The circuit court affirmed all of the district court's decree except for the portion of the ruling that had precluded timber harvesting or road construction until the Forest Service had prepared an environmental impact statement regarding the wilderness potential of the Blue Creek unit. This portion was vacated because on September 28, 1984, Congress had enacted the California Wilderness Act,[56] which placed in wilderness status a large chunk of the Blue Creek area. Because no logging is allowed on federal lands designated as wilderness, such status had rendered moot the need for an environmental statement.[57] However, this act included a provision of frightening dimensions to Indians and environmentalists because it preserved the corridor in which the proposed logging road was to be located until other decisions were made regarding construction. In other words, Congress was saying that there would be a wilderness designation but that there still could be a logging road.

The Forest Service appealed the ninth circuit's ruling, and the case went to the Supreme Court, where it was decided on April 19, 1988.[58] Sandra Day O'Connor, writing for a five-to-three majority (Justice Anthony Kennedy did not participate), dramatically reversed the lower court's rulings and rejected the application of a balancing test to local management decisions by the federal government. The High Court held that unless there was specific governmental intent to infringe upon a religion or the government's actions coerced individuals to act contrary to their spiritual beliefs, then the First Amendment provided no protection for Indian peoples to practice traditional religions even against federal action that potentially could destroy Indian sacred sites. The thrust of O'Connor's opinion was aimed directly at the previous holding in *Sherbert v. Verner*,[59] in which the Court declared that the government could burden a fundamental right like the free exercise of religion only if it was protecting a compelling interest by the least intrusive means possible. As O'Connor noted:

> Whatever may be the exact line between unconstitutional prohibitions on the free exercise of religion and the legitimate conduct by government of its own affairs, the location of the line cannot depend on *measuring the effects of a governmental action on a religious objector's spiritual development*. The government does not dispute, and we have no reason to doubt, that the logging and road building projects at issue in this case could have devastating effects on traditional Indian religious practices . . . even if we assume that . . . the Constitution simply does not provide a principle that could justify upholding respondents' legal claims.[60] [Emphasis added]

The measuring test, however, was precisely the line that should have been drawn. So that when O'Connor then admitted that the Forest Service's proposed projects would devastate the Indians' ability to practice their religion, the issue should have been resolved. Instead, the Court, mimicking the deregulation mood of an increasingly conservative government, asserted that the federal government as landowner had certain rights that could not be infringed upon by either its wards or its citizens.[61]

Lyng, besides holding that there was no constitutional First Amendment protection for Indian religions, also declared definitively that the statutory mechanism outlined in the AIRFA of 1978 was unavailable to Indians as a substitute measure that could protect their religious liberties. O'Connor found the Indians' reliance on AIRFA to be without merit, and she stated in emphatic terms that "nowhere in the law is there so much as a hint of any intent to create a cause of action or any judicially enforceable individual rights."[62]

Distilled to its essence, the core of the matter before the court was to weigh the government's trust responsibility toward the Indians against its right to manage its own affairs. Clearly, an integral part of those affairs was proper execution of the trust responsibility itself. Thus, the question should have been academic. However, the context in which trust responsibility was conceived to be important was at the local level as spelled out in the Theodoratus Report. The report, prepared by a research team headed by Dr. Dorothea Theodoratus, had been commissioned by the U.S. Forest Service. This comprehensive ecological, historical, and archaeological study of the Chimney rock area was intended to gauge the effect the road would have on the lands in question. The study concluded that the construction of the road would cause irreparable damage to the area. The team recommended that the G-O road not be completed.[63] When the Forest Service made the decision to proceed with its plans notwithstanding the Indians' religious concerns and its own acknowledged role in fulfilling its trust obligations to the tribes, then the integrity and independence of federal-agency decision-making powers became the issue, and the Supreme Court felt impelled to protect one of its federal partners.

Once the federal trust responsibility was negated — and this neutralization could only occur by conceiving of Indians as private parties petitioning the government rather than as several tribal nations to whom a trust responsibility was owed — it became necessary to attack the practice of religion itself. Thus, the Court had to destroy the religious issue in order to deny the Indians.

The minority opinion, written by Justice William Brennan with Thurgood Marshall and Harry Blackmun, assailed the majority holding. Brennan began his vigorous dissent by stating that:

'The Free Exercise Clause,' the Court explains today, is written in terms of what the government cannot do to the individual, not in terms of what the individual can exact from the government. . . . Pledging fidelity to this unremarkable constitutional principle, the Court nevertheless concludes that even where the Government uses federal land in a manner that threatens the very existence of a Native American religion, the Government is simply not 'doing' anything to the practitioners of that faith. Instead, the Court believes that Native Americans who request that the Government refrain from destroying their religion effectively seek to exact from the Government *de facto* beneficial ownership of federal property. These two astounding conclusions follow naturally from the Court's determination that federal land-use decisions that render the practice of a given religion impossible do not burden that religion in a manner cognizable under the Free Exercise Clause. . . .[64]

Recall that O'Connor had developed a coercion test, which meant that unless the government's actions had actively coerced individuals to act contrary to their religious beliefs then the First Amendment offered no protection against governmental action that adversely affected or even might destroy the sacred sites of Indians. But Brennan countered by arguing that "the Court's coercion test turns on a distinction between governmental actions that compel affirmative conduct inconsistent with religious beliefs, and those governmental actions that prevent conduct consistent with religious beliefs."[65]

Although Brennan found such a distinction to lack any "constitutional significance," the distinction was important as precedent. Armed with this new test, governments — federal, state, or municipal — could deliberately oppress minority religions as long as it was not apparent in the legislative record that there was an overt attempt to do so. *Lyng* thus leads directly to *Smith*, which placed all religious groups under the auspices of the state.

The *Smith* Decision

Unlike *Lyng*, which dealt specifically with the AIRFA and the unenforceability of the federal Indian trust doctrine, the *Smith* case, though involving two individual Indians (Alfred Smith and Galen Black) and an Indian religion (the Native American Church), deals more broadly with the larger constitutional question of the relationship of religion and the state and powerfully evidences the reality that the First Amendment is practically without value as a constitutional amendment that can protect the religious beliefs of American Indians.

The case arose in the early 1980s in Douglas County in the state of Oregon. It had a most interesting procedural history[66] before it culminated in the final 1990 decree written by Associate Justice Antonin Scalia for a majority Court.[67] In *Employment Division v. Smith*,[68] Justice Scalia abandoned the compelling-interest doctrine created in *Sherbert v. Verner*[69] and expanded in *Wisconsin v. Yoder*[70] and simultaneously resuscitated the so-called belief-action doctrine laid out in the nineteenth-century case *Reynolds v. United States*.[71] Under the *Reynolds* doctrine, government lacks constitutional authority to punish people for their religious *beliefs*, but has authority to regulate religious *actions* so long as it can show a rational basis for doing so.[72]

Expressing the view that the denial of unemployment compensation in *Sherbert* was not based on the plaintiff's perpetuation of an illegal act, Scalia maintained that the state's interest in maintaining the integrity of the unemployment insurance fund was of sufficient importance to justify its refusal to pay benefits to Smith and Black, who were deemed guilty of unlawful conduct because of their use of peyote. With apparent ease, Scalia circumvented, or reformulated, the previous precedent generated by the Court, which specifically involved the free-exercise clause. Without expressly overruling the previous case law, which had provided vast protection for First Amendment free exercise rights, Scalia dramatically confined cases like *Sherbert* and their progeny to their facts or recast the holdings of decisions like *Yoder* from free-exercise opinions that protected religious freedom into due-process opinions that shielded family rights.[73]

Notwithstanding the Oregon court's several opinions, the state's unenforceability of the law that criminalized peyote, the federal government's exemption of peyote from drug control laws when used for religious purposes, and Congress's AIRFA, Scalia gave great weight to the fact that peyote was "prohibited by law."[74] Having abandoned the findings of both Congress and the state courts and focusing solely on the state law that criminalized peyote in the abstract, the argument was then easily made by Scalia that "we have never held that an individual's religious beliefs excuse him from compliance with an otherwise valid law prohibiting conduct that the State is free to regulate."[75]

In other words, the majority held that the only independent protection offered by the free-exercise clause was in its prohibition of laws animated by a desire to disadvantage religion, on the theory that such laws impose an intentional burden, instead of a merely incidental or unanticipated burden, on religious exercise. In Scalia's words: "There being no contention that Oregon's drug law represents an attempt to regulate religious beliefs, the communication of religious beliefs, or the raising of one's children in those beliefs, the rule to which we have adhered ever since *Reynolds* plainly controls."[76] Scalia closed his opinion by stating that the disfavoring of minority religions was nothing more than a logical consequence of democratic government, and he encouraged disadvantaged religious individuals and groups to use the political process—that is, to approach Congress and seek legislative religious exemptions. But by having declared that there are no longer any constitutionally compelled religious exemptions under the free-exercise clause, Scalia sent a stunning message to all religious groups—one that was especially unnerving to Indians and practitioners of other minority religions because these individuals and groups typically lack the political clout necessary to effectively lobby Congress or state legislatures for exemptions that would allow their particular religious practices. And for members of the Native American Church who had already secured just such an exemption in many states and from the federal government, the blow was even harder to fathom. This decision vividly showed that as the last decade of the twentieth century began, American Indians—even those living off the reservation and practicing a federally incorporated religion—were still without fundamental religious liberties.

Even more strange, however, was Scalia's identification of the kinds of religion that the Constitution would protect. In a casual and potentially controversial sentence, Scalia announced that the Court would be bound to respect "making graven images" or "worshipping a golden calf." The thrust of his decision, then, was to protect ancient religions long ago abandoned and unknown to the vast majority of Americans. Living religions, in his view, could not be practiced absent permission from the state.

Because the AIRFA was intended to clarify the status of Indian religious rights, it must be supposed that Congress did not believe that the wording of the First Amendment was sufficient to protect Indian religions. The two cases just discussed bear this out in dramatic fashion. The ensuing controversies and the refusal of both federal agencies and courts to give real protection to Indian religions demonstrate adequately the constitutional no-man's-land in which Indians live.[77] In spite of congressional directions such as AIRFA, there is presently only partial protection for the practice of traditional Indian religions.[78] They are seen as simply another kind of activity, lacking the sacred attributes the Christian and Jewish religions possess.

Even the most sacred Indian religious shrines must be used in conjunction with skiers, hikers, campers, and hunters and, on occasion, can be nearly destroyed by the exploitation of natural resources by federal agencies. For example, on June 8, 1996, less than a month after President Clinton issued an executive order to allow Indians greater access to sacred sites, a federal district judge in *Bear Lodge Multiple Use Association v. Babbitt*[79] ruled that the National Park Service had violated the First Amendment rights of a nonprofit corporation in its development of a comprehensive management plan that was sensitive to the spiritual needs of Indians who consider the ironically named Devil's Tower in Wyoming a sacred site. The Park Service's plan had simply asked that recreational rock climbers voluntarily refrain from climbing Devil's Tower during the culturally significant month of June, when various Indians use the area for religious ceremonies.

According to Judge William Downes, the voluntary closure of Devil's Tower to commercial and recreational climbing violated the First Amendment's establishment clause because this action advocated Indian religious practices. This decision draws attention to the significant difficulties Indians have in attempting to exercise their religious rights. Why, for instance, is recreational rock climbing considered a constitutionally protected First Amendment right, while having access to sacred land in the peace and quiet required to practice living spiritual traditions, such as vision quests, sweat lodges, and individual meditation, is not?

The *Bear Lodge* case went to a full hearing in April 1997, and, fortunately, the Indians' attorneys had done their homework. When they cited a wide variety of practices by federal agencies wherein the government had given *exclusive* use to a number of denominations of the Christian religion when they wished to hold religious services at different sites on federal lands, the evidence so overwhelmingly showed a decided preference for Christian activities that the federal judge finally had to uphold the Park Service's voluntary ban at Devil's Tower. Easter services, prayer vigils, baptisms, marriages, and just about every activity imaginable were occurring with the full support and blessing of federal officials. As it was, the judge took almost a year to finally, reluctantly, write his opinion, knowing that it would be controversial for the simple reason that he was upholding the Indians' right to practice their traditional religion at a sacred location.

Thus American Indians, because they are Indians and even though they are American citizens, are largely deprived of the freedom of religion guaranteed by the First Amendment insofar as the practice of their traditional religions is concerned, with the exception of the statutory protection recently afforded members of the Native American Church. There is no good, present way to bring Indians within the confines of First Amendment protections. Efforts to clarify the situation only seem to produce additional conflicts between Indians and federal agencies. Conflicts with state agencies and private organizations are only now being explored,[80] and there will certainly be additional conflicts with these entities as well.

The conflicts basically center on the *nature* of religion. Traditionally in the United States religion is seen as the creedal affirmation of a set of religious beliefs about the world. Religion is, therefore, for the purposes of American domestic law, a thing of the mind and not of the complete person; it is an abstract belief, not a way of life that requires moral actions. This proposition in all its ramifications was set down in a series of cases involving the Mormons and polygamy, an integral part of the original Mormon belief and practices. In the 1878 case *Reynolds v. United States*,[81] the Supreme Court asked: "Can a man excuse his practices to the contrary because of his religious belief? To permit this would be to make the professed doctrines of religious belief superior to the law of the land, and in effect permit every citizen to become a law unto himself. Government could exist only in name under such circumstances."[82] The *Reynolds* precedent was restated and reinvigorated in the 1990 *Smith* decision. And in *Davis v. Beason*,[83] the Court further elaborated on this idea:

> The First Amendment to the Constitution, in declaring that Congress shall make no law respecting the establishment of religion, or forbidding the free exercise thereof, was intended to allow everyone under the jurisdiction of the United States *to entertain such notions* respecting his relations to his Maker and the duties they impose as may be approved by his judgment and conscience, and to exhibit his sentiments in such form of worship as he may think proper, not injurious to the equal rights of others, and to prohibit legislation for the support of any religious tenets, or the modes of worship of any sect. The oppressive measures adopted, and the cruelties and punishments inflicted by the governments of Europe for many ages, *to compel parties to conform, in their religious beliefs and modes of worship, to the view of the most nu-*

merous sect, and the folly of attempting in that way to control the mental operations of persons, and enforce an outward conformity to a prescribed standard, led to the adoption of the amendment in question. *It was never intended or supposed that* the amendment could be invoked as a protection against legislation for the punishment of acts inimical to the peace, good order and morals of society.[84] [Emphasis added]

Clearly the situation described by the Court, in which Mormon polygamy was defined as "conduct" outside the purview of First Amendment protection rather than as a constitutionally protected religious belief, is comparable to the conditions under which American Indians have suffered when they have been informed that their beliefs in the sanctity of the land are defensible but that religious practices required to exercise those beliefs will not be protected. And when Indians have sought redress under the AIRFA, as they did in *Lyng* and *Bear Lodge,* the opposing argument has been that to uphold the Indian claims would be to establish a religion, since recognition is thought to be equivalent to preference. This situation can only be resolved if and when American society gains a more sophisticated understanding of both religion and American Indians.

The First Amendment: Freedoms of Speech and Assembly

The First Amendment also guarantees the freedom of speech and peaceful assembly. We have already discussed how the government prohibited the performance of Indian religious ceremonials. So there is no question that Indians have not received the protection of the First Amendment insofar as the right of peaceful assembly is concerned. During the early reservation days and until the shift in federal policy in the New Deal, almost any meeting of Indians that did not have the sanction of an agent or a missionary station was suspect, and through the courts of Indian offences,[85] established during the 1880s on most of the western reservations, an agent was able to suppress assemblies of Indians according to his own dictates. Today tribal governments have replaced agents as the authority on reservations, and freedom of assembly is a subject for tribal government concerns under the Indian Civil Rights Act.[86] Important for our discussion here is the fact that Indians were not believed to possess the freedom of assembly until the middle of this century.

Freedom of speech on the reservations has a similar history to that of the freedom of assembly, with some notable statutory exceptions. During the first several decades of the republic, when it was surrounded on three sides by the colonies of European powers, Congress passed a number of statutes that dealt with free speech. In order to forestall European agents from stirring up enmity among the tribes toward the United States, Congress prohibited the sending or carrying of seditious messages to Indians and correspondence with foreign nations intended to incite Indians to war.[87] At the time, this provision was not unreasonable; British and Spanish agents were frequent visitors among the frontier tribes.

The Trade and Intercourse Act of 1834[88] greatly expanded the powers of the United States to take actions in Indian country regarding disruptive persons and activities there. Section 6 required foreigners to obtain passports in order to enter Indian country. Section 10 empowered the superintendent of Indian affairs to remove persons illegally in Indian country. Sections 21 and 23 gave the president great leeway in employing military force in arresting Indians. In 1858 Congress expanded these powers by authorizing the commissioner of Indian affairs to remove any person from a reservation whose presence in his judgment seemed detrimental to the peace and welfare of the Indians.[89]

A critical review of the conditions existing in Indian country in 1834 shows no impending conflict with European powers that would require such measures to be authorized. Additionally, the sweeping authority of the 1858 act seems to have been designed to meet no other problem than the simple control of the Indians on the reservations. All these statutes were carried forward in the revised statutes of 1872, were made part of the United States code, and were not repealed until the Act of May 21, 1934,[90] as part of the New Deal reforms. In the interim period agents could arrest any Indian for almost any cause imaginable without fear of having the arrest reversed by a state or federal court. Many agents used these laws to suppress dissent on the reservations; Felix Cohen's *Handbook of Federal Indian Law* freely admitted that these laws were used to suppress free speech on the reservations.[91]

Cohen cited a description of the status of Indians as detailed in a claims case involving the Cheyenne of Montana. This statement is worth repeating because it helps explain why the protections of the Constitution, particularly the Bill of Rights, had no relevance in the Indian situation until very recently.

> These Indians, indeed, in 1878 occupied an anomalous position, unknown to the common or civil law or to any system of municipal law. They were neither citizens nor aliens; they were neither free persons nor slaves; they were wards of the nation, and yet, on a reservation under a military guard, were little else than prisoners of war while war did not exist. Dull Knife and his daughters could be invited guests at the table of officers and gentlemen, behaving with dignity and propriety, and yet could be confined for life on a reservation, which was to them little better than a dungeon, on the mere order of an executive officer.[92]

As recently as 1950, when the Oglala Sioux Nation criticized the Bureau of Indian Affairs' extension-service program in South Dakota by asking Congress to stop what it considered wasteful expenditures to the bureau, the tribal government was told that $140,000 of credit funds that had previously been allocated would be withheld until the tribe withdrew its criticisms.[93]

And in 1965, after the tribal chairman of the Pyramid Lake Paiute criticized the bureau, the superintendent of the Nevada Indian Agency told the chairman to recant or resign. The chair resigned. The tribe lobbied Washington and eventually succeeded in having the superintendent removed from his position. But rather than fading quietly away, the superintendent was officially cited "for outstanding performance with the 26 tribal groups throughout Nevada" and was promoted to a new post that gave him administrative control over most of the tribes in the neighboring states of Washington, Oregon, and Idaho.[94]

It is not difficult to understand that when Congress refused to recognize the national status of the tribes, they had no status at all within the constitutional framework. Since there was no appeal to an international forum, Indians were simply people without status, a country, or rights of any kind. In this situation it was not difficult to suppress any kind of activity that the government disliked. It is noteworthy that these practices could continue for exactly a century without anyone inquiring into the situation or asking whether or not some constitutional protection was being violated.

The Fourth Amendment: Search and Seizure

It goes without saying, in light of the discussion above, that the protections offered against unreasonable searches and seizures by the Fourth Amendment had no application to Indians on a reservation until federal policy was changed in 1934.[95] Since a good many of the seizures of Indian property involved religious objects such as medicine bundles, the activities that violated the Fourth Amendment were generally those that also violated the protections of the First Amendment. In addition, when the Indians went to the reservations they were deprived of their pony herds, weapons, household goods, and other possessions. A few tribes eventually received some compensation for some of these losses through court-of-claims decisions, but on the whole a substantial amount of property was simply seized and confiscated.

A strange practice that may be regarded as a corollary of the seizure question concerns the disposal of personal clothing worn by Indian children on the trip east to attend government boarding schools such as Hampton and Carlisle. When these students arrived they were deprived of their traditional clothing and made to wear army uniforms and specially designed dresses that emphasized the new life they were being trained to live. In many instances the clothing that was the best and most resplendent their parents could afford was simply regarded as the property of the school. Some of this clothing is now displayed in museum exhibits in the eastern United States, even though the original owners and their heirs can easily be traced. Confiscation is surely an integral part of seizure, but again, this confiscation does not seem to be prohibited by any constitutional provision.

Once again, the 1950s, known as the termination era, provide a vivid example of the fragility of Indian personal liberties. Commissioner of Indian Affairs Dillon Meyer spearheaded a federal campaign to restrict Indian civil liberties while strangely preparing them for termination and ultimate absorption into the American mainstream. On January 15, 1952, as part of that campaign, Representative Emanuel Celler introduced a bill, H.R. 6035, that would have authorized law enforcement officers of the Bureau of Indian Affairs to carry arms, make arrests, and engage in searches and seizures of Indians for alleged violations of bureau regulations regardless of whether the alleged offenses had occurred on or off an Indian reservation.[96]

Specifically, the bill, which had the full support of the BIA, would have authorized those bureau employees to make arrests of Indians "without warrant for any violation of such laws or regulations that have been committed in their presence or for any felony cognizable under such law if they have reasonable grounds to believe that the person to be arrested has committed or is committing such felony. . . ."[97] That the administration could sponsor such legislation is prima facie evidence that insofar as Fourth Amendment search-and-seizure rights are concerned, Indians had a tenuous claim to constitutional protections. Fortunately, after several hearings the judiciary committee terminated this measure.

In the 1960s, the Navajo Nation had a similar experience with federal officials. Norman M. Littell, then general counsel for the Navajo Tribe, and J. Maurice McCabe, executive secretary of the tribe's Department of Administration, recalled in testimony to Congress in 1965 that Secretary of the Interior Stewart Udall, in an effort to terminate Littell's contract with the tribe as general counsel, "launched a search and seizure of tribal files in three different offices . . . hoping to find evidence to sustain charges already made."[98] Littell recalled how Secretary Udall had created a special task force, headed by Stanley Zimmerman, that was charged with conducting the operation. In Littell's sworn testimony, he vividly described how "with the truck at the door of the tribal administration building, the task force, including the [BIA] area director and superintendent, entered the office of the executive secretary of the Navajo Tribe . . . and bodily carried out of his office a locked desk, locked file cabinet, and locked safe. Incidentally, my personal income-tax returns, titles also to my vehicles, my home, my mortgage papers, my bank statements, my financial affairs, were all included in the locked file cabinet."[99] Littell, it should be noted, was not an Indian but merely the attorney for the Navajo Nation, but the perceived lack of constitutional rights was applied to him because of his contract with the tribe.

The Fifth Amendment: Double Jeopardy

Until very recently it was presumed that all serious criminal activity on the reservations was the exclusive responsibility of the federal government. With the recognition of tribal governments as viable functioning governments, a new situation came into being. The federal government, state governments, and tribal governments could all promulgate a criminal code and describe the crimes that fell within its province. Each code, in theory, has integrity unto itself and is to be enforced in the appropriate courts. However, a situation can occur when one act falls within the purview of the respective jurisdictions, which have all defined the act in different ways, thus creating three separate crimes. While this situation is not precisely the same as double jeopardy, which involves prosecution by the same political entity for the same crime more than once when a decision has been made respecting the crime, it has sufficient potential for misuse that it should be discussed in this context.

Such a case arose on the Navajo reservation in 1974 when a Navajo, Anthony Robert Wheeler, was arrested at a reservation high school at Many Farms, Arizona, and charged with disorderly conduct. He pled guilty to two charges, disorderly conduct and contributing to the delinquency of a minor, and was sentenced to 15 days in jail and a fine of $30, or 60 days in jail or a fine of $120. A year later an indictment charging statutory rape was returned against him by a grand jury in the Federal District Court of Arizona. The district court dismissed the proceedings, and the court of appeals for the ninth circuit affirmed the judgment of dismissal on the grounds that since "Indian tribal courts and United States district courts are not arms of separate sovereigns," [100] the double-jeopardy clause barred the federal trial.

In deciding the case the Supreme Court raised an important question regarding the source of the power of the tribe to punish offenders of its criminal laws: "Is it a part of inherent tribal sovereignty, or an aspect of the sovereignty of the federal government which has been delegated to the tribes by Congress?" [101] The Court concluded that the Navajo Tribe possessed inherent powers of sovereignty: "That the Navajo Tribe's power to punish offenses against tribal law committed by its members is an aspect of its retained sovereignty is further supported by the absence of any federal grant of such power. If Navajo self-government were merely the exercise of delegated federal sovereignty, such a delegation should logically appear somewhere." [102] In the absence of any delegation of power, then, there was no double jeopardy because Wheeler was prosecuted by two different sovereigns.

In point of fact, tribal courts and tribal governments are so heavily supervised and subsidized by the federal government that they can be described as the same sovereign in a practical though not a political sense. In fact, this conclusion was drawn by another federal district court in 1965 in *Colliflower v. Garland*,[103] a case involving the status of a tribal court. Madeline Colliflower, a tribal member, refused to obey a tribal court order to remove her cattle from land she formerly leased but that was then being leased by the tribe to another tribal member. She was given a choice between a fine and five days in jail and chose the jail sentence because she had no money. She then sued out on a writ of habeas corpus to the federal district court in Montana.

The court of appeals for the ninth circuit, in reviewing the case, had to resolve the same question as the Supreme Court in *Wheeler*: the status of the tribal court system and whether or not it was a functional part of a separate sovereign. Here the court recognized the practical facts of reservation life that the *Wheeler* decision conveniently neglected to mention:

> While there is apparently still no Act of Congress providing for the establishment of tribal courts, the Congress, as well as the executive, has assumed considerable responsibility for these courts. Thus, the Bureau of Indian Affairs is now authorized to direct, supervise, and expend such moneys as Congress may from time to time appropriate for the benefit, care and assistance of the Indians for various purposes, including the employment of Indian police and judges (25 U.S.C. § 13). 25 U.S.C.§ 200 requires that whenever an Indian is incarcerated, a report or record of the offense is to be immediately submitted to the superintendent of the reservation and made a part of the records of the agency office.[104]

Consequently, the appeals court concluded,

> in spite of the theory that for some purposes an Indian tribe is an independent sovereignty, we think that, in the light of their history, *it is pure fiction to say that the Indian courts functioning in the Fort Belknap Indian community are not in part, at least, arms of the federal government. Originally they were created by the federal executive and imposed upon the Indian community, and to this day the federal government still maintains a partial control over them.*[105] [Emphasis added]

The importance of this kind of manipulation of the character of tribal courts for the protections of the Fifth Amendment are obvious. If the federal government has the kind of control that is described in the *Colliflower* case, and if the separate-sovereign idea of *Wheeler* is really fictional, then criminal codes can be manipulated at will to avoid the double-jeopardy prohibition when it comes to American Indians. The promise of the prohibition against double jeopardy for the criminal defendant is that it provides a sense of security and predictability that the judicial system will not be used for vendettas and persecution by zealous governments. By manipulating the status of tribal courts to fit its own purposes, the federal government is able to create a climate of uncertainty since no defendant in either tribal or federal court can ascertain when and under what circumstances a tribal court will be characterized as a separate entity and when it will appear as an arm of the federal government. If this situation does not violate the letter of the double-jeopardy prohibition, it certainly violates the spirit of it.

The Fifth Amendment: Due Process

The due-process clause of the Fifth Amendment reads in pertinent part that "no person shall . . . be deprived of life, liberty, or property without due process of law. . . ." This amendment on its face imposes restraints only on the federal government. And as several federal court rulings have held,[106] it is well established that Indian tribes are not subject to the Fifth Amendment when they are engaged in exercising local powers of self-government. But what of the federal government's actions toward tribes?

The best argument for securing for the Indian tribes a measure of protection under the due-process clause has never been made clearly: What steps must Congress take in its consideration of Indian legislation to demonstrate beyond a shadow of a doubt that it has given the most serious consideration to the rights of the Indians? Since *Lone Wolf v. Hitchcock*,[107] which we discussed earlier, the Kiowa, Comanche, and Apache tribes have claimed that their property rights vested with the ratification of the 1867 treaty, which required approval of three-quarters of the adult males in order to cede tribal lands. The Supreme Court sidestepped this issue by hypothesizing a possible future situation in which it might be imperative that Congress override the treaty for the best interests of the country and, more importantly, for the best interest of the Indians.

The three-quarters provision was not an issue about which the Indians felt strongly, and they did not insist upon its inclusion in the treaty. The initiative came wholly from the United States as a means of convincing the tribes that the country would ensure that the informed consent of the Indians first be obtained before it sought more land cessions. Thus the provision did not so much bind future congresses as it described the conditions under which future provisions for land cessions would be recognized as valid and binding upon the Indians. That the government went to extensive lengths during negotiations with the Jerome Commission to satisfy the treaty requirements seems sufficient evidence of the self-executing nature of the provision; it should have been considered valid federal law. Due process, therefore, would be the requirement that future representatives of the executive branch and future congresses abide by this process in regard to securing Indian consent.

In rejecting the Indian argument and weakly characterizing the actions of Congress as a mere change in the form of Indian property investment, the Supreme Court in *Lone Wolf* stripped away any pretense of Fifth Amendment protection for the tribes. The treaty, duly ratified by the Senate as part of its responsibility under the Constitution, thereupon became empty promises; not only empty, but deliberately deceptive and fictional. The same characterization can also be made about all Indian legislation, for no congress can bind a future congress and, retroactively, no existing congress need pay attention to the deliberations of any previous congress.

Fifth Amendment due process would require the Congress to announce, after the proper hearings, deliberations, and debates, the basis on which it had reached its conclusions. We have already seen, in the passage in 1871 of the prohibition against further treaty making, that the decision to prohibit treaties with Indian tribes was not the product of intelligent, mature, and considered debate, which might have been expected of a nation that had stepped into the shoes of Great Britain and accepted a role of protector for the original inhabitants of the continent. Rather, the treaty-making prohibition was the result of a committee-conference compromise and was accepted by representatives of each house as a means of securing a bill both found palatable.

At the present time there is a tendency within the federal courts to pretend that Congress has given serious consideration to the rights of Indians when considering legislation, with the corresponding result that conflicting provisions of legislation are said to be intentional acts of Congress to override existing treaty provisions and rights.[108] The most disastrous interpretation of this kind is the so-called McCarran Amendment in the field of Indian water rights. In 1952, as part of the Department of Justice's Appropriation Act, and as a means of simplifying water-rights adjudication, Congress waived on a limited basis the sovereign immunity of the United States for state court litigation involving water.[109]

This statute did not affect Indian water rights until 1971, when in two cases, *United States v. District Court for the County of Eagle*[110] and *United States v. District Court for Water Division No. 5*,[111] the Supreme Court announced that the McCarran Amendment applied to all water rights the United States then had or might in the future acquire. Because the United States holds Indian water rights in its own name under the Winters Doctrine[112] and Indian rights are an equitable-use, not a legal, title, then it followed, according to most commentators, that Indian rights were subject to state-court adjudication. Certainly Congress had no intention of placing a trust corpus in such a hazardous situation, for it would then become liable for damages if the trust were violated. But there is no mention of Indian rights in the McCarran Amendment. One can thus argue from the absence of Indians either that if Congress had intended Indians to be included, it would have so noted, or if Congress had wanted Indians excluded, it would have so noted.

Interestingly, McCarran's own actions in the Senate seem to suggest that his amendment was not intended to cover Indian rights. As termination began in 1953, McCarran made an abortive effort simply to strike out that part of the commerce clause that mentions Indians, as if by doing so all the problems with tribes could be resolved. He proposed a joint resolution, S.J. Res. 4, which proposed a constitutional amendment designed to bestow upon the Indian tribes "the same rights . . . which are enjoyed by all citizens of the United States." The proposed article read thus: "The Congress shall have the power to regulate commerce with foreign nations and among the several states."[113] It was the singular good fortune of Indians that Congress at the time knew so little about either Indians or constitutional law that the resolution died in the judiciary committee.

In view of how the McCarran Amendment interpretation developed, finally involving Indian water rights almost two full decades after its passage, what is due process under the Fifth Amendment in this instance? It cannot be that the fact of litigation of federal water rights in the Colorado court and the appeal to the U.S. Supreme Court has given the Indians due-process protection because Indians are not even mentioned in the decisions. Indian rights are a unique branch of rights, in certain ways inherent and in other ways intimately connected to federal rights via treaties, the trust doctrine, and specific or general legislation, and are supposed to be regarded as "sacred as fee simple," to quote a much used and abused phrase.[114] There is no requirement here that evidence of congressional deliberation specifically with respect to Indians be considered. Indians are simply victims, outside the Constitution and its amendments, with no possible way of finding shelter under its provisions.

All federal Indian legislation should be subjected to a minimal test that would guarantee some kind of due process before it could become applicable to Indian tribes. In order for either the federal courts or the executive branch to determine if a statute applies to Indians, there should be a requirement to show evidence that the Congress has deliberately and purposefully considered its treaty and trust responsibilities to Indians and clearly established the conditions under which the law would apply to them. Absent some kind of specific procedure easily and clearly identified, Indians will remain outside the protection of the Constitution.

The Fifth Amendment: Just Compensation

There is no question that no Indian tribe ever received anything approaching just compensation for its lands from the United States. Even the most carefully negotiated treaty only returned to the tribes pennies on the dollar, and some treaties had terms so outrageous as to shock the conscience of even the hardest cynic. Consequently, when the Indian Claims Commission was established in 1946,[115] it was a foregone conclusion that Indian tribes would not receive payment for the real value of their lands. However, the fact that claims would be heard and efforts would be made to settle long-standing grievances that could not be dealt with in any other forum made the commission a positive step forward in federal-Indian relations.[116]

In the course of settling Indian claims, a strange doctrine of law involving the Fifth Amendment and the concept of just compensation evolved. It is in every respect a jerry-rigged apparatus that has no logical consistency and no application outside the field of Indian claims. But since it appears to be an effort to apply the Fifth Amendment protections to Indians, it must be included in our discussion.

Under the doctrine of discovery, there was no opportunity for a European sovereign to acquire the complete title to lands of the aboriginal inhabitants without securing their consent or waging just and lawful wars against them. The Spanish solved this dilemma by converting the Indians and gathering them into small villages, thereupon declaring the lands they once occupied as vacant and abandoned and therefore belonging to the king. The English and Americans did not, as a rule, use this subterfuge to gain title to Indian lands, and as a consequence nearly all the lands in the United States have been purchased, for however slight a sum, from the Indian tribes by the government. But with the authorization of the Indian Claims Commission came a number of exceptions to this general rule, and these exceptions were created by a manipulation of the just-compensation clause of the Fifth Amendment.

The Fifth Amendment requires that any exercise of sovereign powers — primarily eminent domain, in which property is taken for public use — must be compensated for by payment of the fair market value of the property as determined by a court. First there is the question, rarely raised in the discussion of Indian lands, of the nature of the purpose for which the lands are taken. The Fifth Amendment speaks of taking land for a public purpose, and in this context it clearly refers to those occasions when the sovereign takes private land for a road, bridge, wharf, or some other specific purpose in order to fulfill the sovereign's duty to the people. Thus the purpose is not a general purpose, nor is it to accomplish a general policy — nor, incidentally, is it directed at a specific group of people.

When the United States and its courts have characterized the taking of Indian lands as having a public purpose, they have engaged in some shadowy rhetoric. The precise justification for taking Indian lands is public policy, not public purpose. Therefore, to require Fifth Amendment due process before tribes' claims could be justly determined and compensation paid and to pretend the confiscation of Indian lands was an exercise in eminent domain are illogical, ahistorical, and unconstitutional actions. When Indian lands were taken by the government, they were taken with the avowed purpose of transferring them to railroads, states, settlers, corporations, and so forth. While this action may conform to a general policy of settling the country, it cannot conceivably compare to the taking of a tract of land for a road, bridge, or government installation that must necessarily serve the entire public without discrimination or favoritism among groups within the citizenry. So the basic idea of applying the Fifth Amendment to the process of taking Indian lands is in itself perplexing.

Nevertheless, while attempting to settle Indian claims, the federal courts devised a means of applying the Fifth Amendment. In 1955 in *Tee-Hit-Ton Indians v. United States*,[117] the Supreme Court held that the taking of the Tee-Hit-Ton lands was not compensable under the Fifth Amendment because it was not "property" in the sense that recognized, titled land was property. In other words, in order to be compensated under the Fifth Amendment, a tribe had to have some prior acknowledgement by the United States in a treaty, a statute, or an executive order that the tribe owned its lands. This doctrine was certainly helpful in turning aside the claims of the Tee-Hit-Ton, but it left much to be desired when placed in the *Lone Wolf* context because the Kiowa, Comanche, and Apache certainly had a treaty-recognized title and therefore had a compensable Fifth Amendment claim against the United States. And this reasoning in turn posed the question of whether the Fifth Amendment did in fact limit the plenary power of Congress. It would have been a simple matter to have returned to the Fifth Amendment argument of the three tribes and reverse *Lone Wolf* as to congressional powers over Indians. So the Supreme Court was nearly hoisted on its own rhetorical petard.

In 1968 the court of claims came to the rescue of the Supreme Court in *Fort Berthold Reservation v. United States*,[118] when it tried to reconcile *Lone Wolf* and *Tee-Hit-Ton*. The court devised a method of determining the actual role of the government in dealing with Indians and in suggesting a test to determine in what capacity the government was acting in any particular situation. "It is obvious," the court declared, "that Congress cannot simultaneously act as a trustee for the benefit of the Indians, exercising its plenary powers over the Indian and their property, as it thinks is in their best interests, and exercise its sovereign power of eminent domain, taking the Indians' property within the meaning of the Fifth Amendment to the Constitution. In any given situation in which Congress has acted with regard to Indian people, it must have acted either in one capacity or the other. Congress can own two hats, but it cannot wear them both at the same time." [119] The ultimate test, according to the Court, is that the Congress must act in good faith when taking Indian property. So there must be a reasonable effort to transmute Indian property from land to money. [120] If there is no reasonable effort, then the courts can decide that Congress simply took the land for its own purposes and the Fifth Amendment applies to the confiscation.

Though it appeared that the *Fort Berthold* case established some reasonable tests that courts could use to determine the application of the Fifth Amendment, in fact the Court only placed the federal judiciary into deeper water; in order to determine good faith, the courts would have to examine congressional motives. Citing the political-question doctrine, which holds that it is not the province of the courts to address questions deemed essentially political in nature or to make inquiries into the motives of political actors since those are best left to the executive and legislative branches, the federal judiciary has nearly always defined this task as one beyond its constitutional powers. As luck would have it, the good-faith test was invoked in *United States v. Sioux Nation*, [121] and, of course, not a shred of evidence exists that the United States ever had anything approaching good faith in its dealings with this tribe. The import of the *Sioux Nation* case was the requirement that an Indian tribe must overcome the presumption of good faith in order to receive Fifth Amendment compensation. The situation is still unsettled with respect to the proper interpretation of this test, and because Indian claims cases are almost a matter of historical record now, it may be that no resolution of the Fifth Amendment application will ever occur.

The Sixth Amendment: Legal Counsel

Until the passage of the Seven Major Crimes Act in 1885, [122] jurisdiction over crimes was clearly divided between two separate sovereigns. By treaty, some Indian nations had preserved to themselves criminal prosecutions for crimes committed between tribal members on the reservations or within their occupancy areas. It was this right that was upheld in the *Crow Dog* decision. All crimes committed outside the boundaries of Indian country were presumed to be within the purview of the federal government. Any Indian charged in federal court was likely to be subject to the standard criminal procedures used against wrongdoers—with the added handicap of racial prejudice, exclusion from juries, and a basic ignorance of the degrees of crime for which they could be punished.

In 1862 the Santee Sioux attacked settlers in Minnesota and, after a brief struggle, were defeated when the frontier army was brought full-force against them. Numerous Indians surrendered or were captured, and a military court-martial was established to try them for acts committed during the war. Except for the brief Modoc War in northern California, in no other Indian-white conflict did the government regard the acts committed during hostilities as crimes for which the losers could be punished.

The court-martial could hardly be said to represent either the Sixth Amendment provisions or even regular military judicial process. General Sibley, who was determined to drive the Sioux out of Minnesota or exterminate them altogether, chose five officers to form a military court—men who weeks before had fought against the Indians. No defense counsel was allowed for the unfortunate men. The military officers used the testimony of a mulatto who had at first been implicated in the attack against the settlers, but who then turned military witness against the Santee. The Santee were simply paraded in front of the court, which allowed hearsay, rumor, innuendo, and falsehoods to be recorded as evidence of Santee wrongdoing. Some 319 men were convicted of a wide variety of crimes, 16 receiving long prison terms and the remainder being condemned to death. General Pope, who had recently been discredited in Virginia as leader of the Union forces and now was placed in command of troops on the western frontier, forwarded the trial papers to President Abraham Lincoln expecting that he would quickly approve the executions. He also passed along the warning that if things were not concluded with some haste, the territorial officials and militia leaders would probably proceed with the executions anyway.

President Lincoln assigned two lawyers to examine the files of the convicted Indians, charging his examiners with approving only those cases wherein there was abundant evidence of guilt — as opposed to the general rumors that constituted the majority of the documents. Lincoln pardoned all but thirty-nine of the Santees, causing a considerable stir in Minnesota, where people wanted them all killed. As the warriors were being led to the gallows, one Indian was spared at the last moment, leaving thirty-eight men to die. Later it was discovered that two of the men executed were not on Lincoln's final list, one of them having saved the life of a white woman during the conflict.

At no time during this unhappy process was there even the slightest indication that the Sixth Amendment guarantees had any application to the Santees, and no form of legal defense, let alone legal counsel, was offered to them. Indians were regarded as citizens of their own nations, and therefore it was natural that they would be excluded from constitutional protections. But because they were regarded as foreign citizens, the court-martial itself was illegal and unconstitutional since no forum could legally exist that would permit trial and execution of the fighting men of an enemy for acts committed during hostilities.

After the passage of the Seven Major Crimes Act, the prosecution of Indians followed the general trend of justice in the territories, with test cases generally ensuring that the Indian had significant legal representation so that the verdict would be respected. The Appropriations Act of 1893 [123] created a confusing situation that has never been satisfactorily resolved. It authorized the secretary of the interior to pay the legal expenses incurred by Indians in contests initiated by or against them. The concluding sentence of the paragraph stated: "In all states and Territories where there are reservations or allotted Indians the United States District Attorney shall represent them in all suits at law and in equity." [124]

It seems that this broad provision would require federal attorneys to represent Indians in all matters legal, which would impose a crushing burden on the federal government. However, no legal opinions or court decisions have attempted to define (or even narrow) the words to suggest a reasonable interpretation of the sentence, which must have meant something in the minds of Congress. Federal attorneys have represented Indian tribes in many areas of litigation as part of their treaty or trust obligations, but there has been virtually no effort to link the Justice Department's activities with Sixth Amendment guarantees.

In summary, the Bill of Rights has not been applied to tribal nations in their relationship to the federal government and has only partial application to Indians as individual citizens. Not only have the federal courts studiously avoided pursuing the matter, but Congress and the executive branch have consistently acted as if there were no limitation at all to their power to deal with Indians and Indian matters. It remains, then, to examine the later amendments to determine their applicability to American Indians.

CHAPTER VII

THE LATER

CONSTITUTIONAL AMENDMENTS

T HE later amendments with some peripheral application to Indians — the Thirteenth (1865), which abolished slavery and involuntary servitude; the Fourteenth (1868), which defined national citizenship; The Fifteenth (1870), which defined voting rights; the Sixteenth (1913), which established the federal income tax; the Eighteenth (1919), which dealt with the prohibition of liquor; the Twenty-first (1933), which repealed that prohibition; and the Twenty-sixth (1971), which lowered the voting age to eighteen years — were adopted at the end of the treaty-making period and more recently, when Indians lived on reservations and were therefore viewed as wards of the government rather than independent and separate political entities. Consequently, if American Indians had been considered a part of American society and if the intent to assimilate Indians into the American system had been a major consideration of federal policy, there should have been some specific mention of Indians or at least an intent to include them under the auspices of these amendments. Even peripheral relationships between Indian matters and these amendments are important in providing evidence for understanding the present relationship between the tribes and the Constitution.

The Thirteenth Amendment

The Thirteenth Amendment prohibited slavery and involuntary servitude within the United States or any place subject to their jurisdiction, except as a punishment for crime. This amendment theoretically placed the freedom of African Americans beyond the reach of succeeding congresses and administrations and represented a major change in American politics. For the first time, federal law imposed a significant constraint on the power of states to define the status of their own residents.

But it is not exactly clear how this amendment was understood in the Indian context. If the Thirteenth Amendment in fact freed the slaves everywhere in the United States, did it have the same effect in the Indian territory? Presumably because the Cherokee Nation, to take one example, was regarded as being within the exterior boundaries of the United States, the amendment would have full force there. But the abolition of slavery among the Five Civilized Tribes was settled by a treaty provision rather than the constitutional amendment, evidence of the fact that the Thirteenth Amendment did not apply to the Indian nations.

The treaty of March 21, 1866, with the Seminole,[1] for example, dealt with black slavery in Article 2: "The Seminole Nation covenant that henceforth in said nation slavery shall not exist, nor involuntary servitude, except for and in punishment of crime, whereof the offending party shall first have been duly convicted in accordance with law, applicable to all the members of said nation."[2] Almost identical articles were inserted in the treaties with the Choctaw and Chickasaw of April 28, 1866,[3] the Creek of June 14, 1866,[4] and the Cherokee of July 19, 1866.[5] The Cherokee, in fact, had already abolished slavery by act of their council in February 1863,[6] so this treaty provision was merely a confirmation of a tribal act previously taken.

Application of the Thirteenth Amendment, however, seems to have been a haphazard affair outside of Indian territory. An 1886 case in Alaska, *In re Sah Quah*,[7] prohibited customary slavery in that territory. A territorial court recognized that the slavery practice existed among Alaskan natives but refused to admit its validity because it conflicted with the Thirteenth Amendment, even while admitting that Alaskan natives "are not citizens within the full meaning of that term."[8] Interestingly, the federal district court went to great lengths to differentiate the legal status of Alaskan natives who lacked treaty rights from tribes in the lower forty-eight states who possessed treaty rights, implying that the Thirteenth Amendment would not apply to tribes in the states because they "have been treated as free and independent within their respective territories, governed by their tribal laws and custom, in all matters pertaining to internal affairs. . . ."[9]

Three years after the ratification of the amendment, however, Congress found it necessary to pass Joint Resolution Number 83,[10] which prohibited the peonage of women and children in the Navajo Tribe. This resolution was believed necessary in order to stop the profitable slave trade in the Southwest, for which Navajos were being captured and transported to Mexico, where they were sold as household servants.

There is also a question about the nature of involuntary servitude as experienced by reservation Indians. Annuities and rations were a part of the payment Indians received for their land cessions, and yet it quickly became the policy of the government to require Indians to work at the agency or for the tribe in order to receive these goods. The Act of June 22, 1874,[11] forced all "able-bodied male Indians to perform labor" before they could receive their treaty entitlements. Felix Cohen wryly commented that "The popular outcry that would have followed the application of a similar rule to white holders of Government bonds or pensions may well be imagined."[12] This provision was repeated in the Appropriation Act of 1875.[13] Commissioner of Indian Affairs Edward Smith commented in his annual report of 1875 on the effect of this indentured servitude on Indians: "Congress, at its last session, recognizing the propriety that Indians, like other people, should till for what they have, directed that all annuities should hereafter be paid only in return for some form of labor. . . . This eminently wise legislation has been of great avail to the Bureau during the year in enforcing industry. . . ."[14]

This practice became a matter of course at many agencies in the years that followed. If this requirement is not involuntary servitude, it comes so close to it that the distinction is meaningless.

The Fourteenth Amendment: Citizenship and Due Process

Of all the constitutional phrases and all the amendments, only the Fourteenth—which made all persons born within the nation citizens both of the United States and of the states where they lived, prohibited states from abridging the privileges or immunities of its citizens and from depriving all persons of due process of law or equal protection of the laws, among other things—has a supporting record showing that the United States seriously considered the role and status of Indian tribes. Though the amendment itself, adopted in 1868, reflected Republican determination that southern states should not be readmitted to the Union and Congress without guarantees that freed slaves would have their basic civil rights and liberties protected, it was not until April of 1870 that Congress had any concerns about the effect of the amendment on tribes. At that time Congress directed the Senate Judiciary Committee to inquire into what effect, if any, the amendment had on Indian tribes.[15] Did the Fourteenth Amendment make Indians citizens, or did it annul the treaties that had been made with the tribes? Since the question of ending treaty making was foremost in the congressional mindset at that time, the committee could easily have returned a report stating that the amendment had accomplished what Congress later did in prohibiting further treaty making. Indeed, the federal judiciary might well have decided that the amendment assimilated Indians into American society had the Senate committee not clearly spoken on the subject.

The judiciary committee concentrated its attention on the phrase, "and subject to the jurisdiction thereof," arguing that the answer could only be determined by examining the status of the tribes at the time the amendment was adopted. This approach represented a model of legislative reasoning because it was apparent that Congress did not have Indians in mind when it considered the amendment. Therefore, to imply that the amendment had an unanticipated effect on the tribes would have established the precedent that Indians were covered by legislation or constitutional amendment as a matter of course and not as the result of deliberate consideration by Congress.

The bulk of the pithy report examined various treaty and constitutional provisions, reviewed the Cherokee cases and Chief Justice John Marshall's discussion of the status of Indian tribes vis-à-vis the United States, and cited some of the jurisdictional acts wherein Congress had preserved the right of Indian tribes to exercise self-government. The committee succinctly noted that "volumes of treaties, acts of Congress almost without number, the solemn adjudications of the highest judicial tribunal of the republic, and the universal opinion of our statesmen and people, have united to exempt the Indian, being a member of a tribe recognized by, and having treaty relations with, the United States from the operation of our laws, and the jurisdiction of our courts." [16] Consequently, the report continued, the phrase dealing with jurisdiction specifically intended to exempt Indians. Thus the second section of the amendment, which had the words "excluding Indians not taxed," was deliberately repetitive of the original words of the Constitution, where this phrase was included in the clause dealing with representation in Congress and direct taxation.

The Fourteenth Amendment, the committee declared, was intended to eliminate the original constitutional phrase, "three-fifths of all other persons," which had described the status of slaves. "The inference," the report concluded, "is irresistible that the amendment was intended to recognize the change in the status of the former slave which had been effected during the war, while it recognizes no change in the status of the Indians." [17] The committee used unequivocal language in stating its conclusion:

> To maintain that the United States intended, by a change of its fundamental law, *which was not ratified by these tribes, and to which they were neither requested nor permitted to assent,* to annul treaties then existing between the United States as one party, and the Indian tribes as the other parties respectively, would be to charge upon the United States repudiation of national obligations, repudiation doubly infamous from the fact that the parties whose claims were thus annulled are too weak to enforce their just rights, and were enjoying the voluntarily assumed guardianship and protection of this Government. [18] [Emphasis added]

Of equal importance to the question of whether or not the Fourteenth Amendment applied to Indian tribes was the effort made by the Senate to link its report to the existing controversy regarding treaty making. In conclusion the committee stated:

> Although your committee have not regarded the questions proposed for their consideration by this resolution of the Senate as at all difficult to answer, yet respect for the Senate which ordered the investigation, and the existence of some loose popular notions of modern date in regard to the power of the President and Senate to exercise the treaty-making power in dealing with the Indian tribes, have induced your

committee to examine the question thus at length, and present extracts from treaties, laws, and judicial decisions; and your committee indulge the hope that a reference to these sources of information may tend to fix more clearly in the minds of Congress and the people the true theory of our relations to these unfortunate tribes. It is pertinent to say, in concluding this report, that treaty relations can properly exist with Indian tribes or nations only, and that, *when the members of a tribe are scattered, they are merged in the mass of our people, and become equally subject to the jurisdiction of the United States.* It is believed that some treaties have been concluded and ratified with fragmentary, straggling bands of Indians who had lost all just pretensions to the tribal character; and *this ought to admonish the treaty-making power to use greater circumspection hereafter.*[19] [Emphasis added]

It would not be difficult to imply that the Senate Judiciary Committee saw the continuance of the treaty-making power as necessary until the tribes became so dispersed that there was no longer a pretension that they maintained a form of self-government and could be considered a political entity. Clearly the suggestion here is that the treaty-making power should be exercised with more restraint and discretion, not that it should be abolished; the Fourteenth Amendment, in the eyes of the committee, anticipated the continued political exclusion of even individualized Indians as long as they remained in tribal relations.

Further, the committee suggested that it would be abhorrent for the United States to make any changes in its fundamental organic laws that would affect Indians without seeking their consent or ratification. This argument implies that not only are Indians outside the constitutional framework but that in all legislation that affects them their consent should be secured. The principle at issue here is the informed consent of the governed, and the committee did not want to be on record suggesting that the federal government could arbitrarily change the nature of the treaty relationship without making substantive overtures to the Indians regarding the nature of the change. Less than a year later the federal courts stepped in and gave judicial legitimacy to the extraconstitutional standing of Indians expressed by the Senate committee. In *McKay v. Campbell,*[20] the federal district court for Oregon held that "Indian tribes within the limits of the United States have always been held to be distinct and independent political communities, retaining the right of self-government, though subject to the protecting power of the United States."[21] Regarding the citizenship status of a mixed-blood Indian, the court held that because the plaintiff had been born a member of a tribe, he was not subject to the jurisdiction of the United States.

In an 1880 case, *United States v. Osborn*,[22] the applicability of the Fourteenth Amendment to Indians was directly tested. The court pointedly observed that Indians are not a portion of the political community called the people of the United States, and though not exactly foreign nations or persons, they had always been treated as distinct and independent communities. Even in the case wherein an individual Indian had voluntarily sought to become a U.S. citizen, the court held that this could not transpire without the direct consent and cooperation of the government. "The fact," said the court, "that he has abandoned his nomadic life or tribal relations, and adopted the habits and manners of civilized people, may be a good reason why he should be made a citizen of the United States, but does not of itself make him one. To be a citizen of the United States is a political privilege, which no one not born to can assume without its consent in some form."[23]

A few years later the question of the effect of the Fourteenth Amendment on individual Indians arrived at the Supreme Court in *Elk v. Wilkins*.[24] The case was brought by the same attorneys who had successfully handled *United States ex. rel. Standing Bear v. Crook*,[25] in which a writ of habeas corpus was issued on behalf of a band of Ponca Indians who had expatriated themselves from the rest of the tribe and sought refuge among the Indians of another tribe. Thus it was to be anticipated that in the case of John Elk—who had left the jurisdiction of his tribe, moved to Omaha, Nebraska, purchased a home, become a member of the state militia, and paid taxes—that the recognition of his American citizenship would most likely follow. Under then-existing Nebraska law, state voting privileges were allowed to individuals who intended to become citizens, hence Elk should have easily qualified because his expatriation from his tribe was a deliberate act demonstrating his intention to become an ordinary citizen of Nebraska.

The Supreme Court, however, followed previous court rulings and adopted the interpretation of the earlier Senate Judiciary Committee report, even in the face of a ringing dissent by Justice John Harlan. Harlan quoted the Senate debate that allowed Indians who were taxed to become citizens under the Fourteenth Amendment and also the veto message of President Johnson, who specifically mentioned "Indians subject to taxation" among the groups to whom the amendment would apply. But the majority in *Elk* insisted that absent a specific naturalization law, naturalization provision in a treaty, or action in a federal court, an individual Indian could not expatriate himself from a tribe and adopt the habits of civilized life and thereby become a citizen of the United States. He needed a specific act of the United States admitting him to membership and citizenship.

With a perversity frequently displayed by Congress during the succeeding decades, the question of Indian citizenship, and by extension the application of the Fourteenth Amendment, were horribly confused by occasional vague authorizations of citizenship inserted in Indian legislation. An example is the citizenship provision of the 1887 General Allotment Act[26]:

> And every Indian born within the territorial limits of the United States to whom allotments shall have been made under the provision of this act, or under any law or treaty, and *every Indian born within the territorial limits of the United States who has voluntarily taken up, within said limits, his residence separate and apart from any tribe of Indians therein, and has adopted the habits of civilized life, is hereby declared to be a citizen of the United States. . . .*[27] [Emphasis added]

This provision, it should be noted, is in direct contradiction to both the Senate Judiciary Committee's report and *Elk v. Wilkins.* And succeeding allotment acts and agreements only served to confuse the issue further. Finally, in 1924, Congress passed the Indian Citizenship Act, which succinctly stated: "That all noncitizen Indians born within the territorial limits of the United States be, and they are hereby, declared to be citizens of the United States."[28] But the brief act concluded with this enigmatic statement: "Provided, That the granting of such citizenship shall not in any manner impair or otherwise affect the right of any Indian to tribal or other property."

Indians thus became American citizens while retaining their own tribal citizenship and rights. Two questions emerge from this congressional act that substantially affect the manner in which citizenship is enjoyed. First, Elk could not become an American citizen of his own initiative — even if he had followed the provisions of a treaty that clearly spelled out the steps he had to take to become a citizen — without the concurrence through a specific act by the United States. Because Indians were in a treaty relationship with the United States and because the Senate Judiciary Committee's report firmly announced that the Fourteenth Amendment would not and could not be applied to Indians without their consent and ratification, is the bestowing of citizenship through the Indian Citizenship Act, *without the consent of the Indians*, applicable to Indians without some additional and specific act on their part indicating consent?

Consent is an important part of citizenship because the Senate Judiciary Committee, in its examination of the application of the Fourteenth Amendment, specifically denounced any unilateral action on the part of the United States to admit Indians to its citizenship. Additionally, a report of the Bureau of Municipal Research, submitted to a joint commission of Congress in 1915—a report specifically commissioned by Congress— stated that "the Indian (except in rare individual cases) does not desire citizenship."[29] Because federal administrators assumed that the 1924 citizenship act was applicable to all Indians, the subject has never received serious attention by either the courts or the Congress. If there is any consistency in the understanding of the Constitution in Congress, then the application of the Indian Citizenship Act should be on the basis of formal tribal acceptance of the act by the individual tribes affected. Where a tribe or tribal group has clearly indicated its rejection of such citizenship, it would seem that the United States has no alternative but to accept that answer and act accordingly.

The second aspect of citizenship that should be addressed here is the actual impact and implications of receiving or accepting citizenship. Apparently, according to the Supreme Court, the conferring of citizenship does not in any way affect the so-called wardship/guardianship status the Indians experienced prior to becoming citizens. This interpretation has come about through two cases dealing with the sale of liquor to Indians: *Matter of Heff*[30] (1905), which held that Congress could not regulate the sale of liquor to Indians who were citizens as a result of their having received allotments of land, and *United States v. Nice*[31] (1916), which expressly overruled the *Heff* decision, stating that "Citizenship is not incompatible with tribal existence or continued guardianship, and so may be conferred without completely emancipating the Indians or placing them beyond the reach of congressional regulations adopted for their protection."[32]

If citizenship does not enter into any consideration of the role of Congress in Indian affairs or restrict the powers of Congress with respect to Indians, the only apparent benefit to the Indians from citizenship would appear to be the power to vote in federal and state elections. Of course, because states had the power to set the eligibility criteria for voting, many Indians who wanted to exercise the franchise were denied this right until as recently as the 1950s.[33] In practical terms, the Indian Citizenship Act qualifies Indians to exercise rights under the Fifteenth Amendment but does not provide them with the due-process and equal-protection rights of the Fourteenth Amendment. As the tenth circuit court of appeals noted in the 1971 case *Groundhog v. Keeler*,[34] the Fourteenth Amendment's due-process clause is not embraced by the Indian Civil Rights Act of 1968, and, importantly, there is also no limitation on the power of Congress to enact legislation with respect to tribal nations.[35] There is, therefore, a considerable amount of clarification to be done respecting the actual relationship of American Indians to the United States in terms of the Fourteenth Amendment.

The Fifteenth Amendment

Once Indians had been granted citizenship in 1924, it should have forthwith made them eligible to vote in state and federal elections. But racial discrimination, ignorance of the law by state officials, and memory of Indians' past legal status worked against them. Many barriers were placed in the way of Indians assuming the full responsibilities of citizenship, primarily in the conservative western states. In 1937 Nathan Margold wrote a Solicitor's Opinion entitled "Suffrage—Discrimination Against Indians," in which he surveyed the state of Indian voting.[36]

At that time, seven states denied Indians the right to vote in spite of the citizenship act. Idaho, New Mexico, and Washington relied on the Fourteenth Amendment phrase "Indians not taxed" in Article 1. Colorado's state attorney general had simply written an opinion to the effect that Indians were not citizens. In answer to Margold's inquiry he wrote: "It is our opinion that until Congress enfranchises the Indian, he will not have the right to vote." Apparently word had not reached Colorado of the 1924 act.[37]

Utah's state attorney general had written an opinion to the effect that

Indians living on reservations were not actually residents of Utah but rather of their own nations, a view at least consistent with many Indian activists' today. North Carolina was excluding Indians under its general practice of denying African Americans the vote—with the claim that the applicants were illiterate. Superintendent Foght of the Cherokee Agency reported that "We have had Indian graduates of Carlisle, Haskell and other schools in instances much better educated than the registrar himself, turned down because they did not read or write to his *satisfaction*."[38] The Arizona Supreme Court ruled in 1928 that Indians were "wards of the government" and therefore "persons under guardianship" who were clearly prohibited from voting by the state constitution.[39] Idaho combined guardianship with the Indians-not-taxed burden. Maine also denied Indian voters on the same basis, though the state did not reply to Margold's survey.[40] Margold concluded that the citizenship act had made Indians, including those living on reservations, eligible to vote in state and federal elections. But there was no movement to include Indians in the election rolls.

Frederic Kirgis of the interior solicitor's office wrote another opinion on January 26, 1938, which reported on the legal opinions rendered by various states' attorneys general.[41] South Dakota adopted the provision that Indians who maintained their tribal relationships could not vote in that state, though Kirgis did not cite a specific law explaining the measure.[42] Idaho then claimed that same excuse as the basis for their denial of Indian voting. Kirgis's conclusion followed that of Margold's in declaring such laws and prohibitions as violating the Fifteenth Amendment.

Strangely, the Bureau of Indian Affairs, which had never been very aggressive in protecting or defending Indian rights, began to work actively to promote unrestricted Indian voting in the western states. Margold returned to the conflict in 1940, writing another opinion, entitled "Method of Determining 'Indians not taxed',"[43] undoubtedly written to provide a federal interpretation of constitutional phrases to compete with the many opinions being given by state officials. Placing a heavy emphasis on the federal right to determine citizenship and to tax, Margold found that there were no Indians who qualified for the old status of "Indians not taxed," and he did not question the exemption from state property tax of Indian trust lands. Response was not favorable to his opinion in the western states, and so he was forced to write yet another opinion two weeks later, wherein he again emphasized the same points.[44]

Returning Indian war veterans who had not known — or perhaps even cared — to vote before the war now found themselves barred from registering to vote on the basis of old beliefs. They began to pressure the Bureau of Indian Affairs to help them secure the vote in Arizona and New Mexico, two of the last states to bar Indians. In 1947 three Indian veterans were refused the right to register by a New Mexico judge, and they demanded that the bureau assist them in an appeal. At almost the same time a Mohave Apache veteran in Arizona was denied the right to register, and he also appealed for assistance. The National Congress of American Indians and the Bureau of Indian Affairs gathered a legal team that featured the famous Felix Cohen, and the cases went forward, the Indians eventually winning both of them in 1948.

In *Harrison v. Laveen*[45] Judge Levi Udall wrote that there was no evidence in the proceedings of the Arizona Constitutional Convention that the phrase "persons under guardianship" was intended to include Indians. In *Trujillo v. Garley*[46] Federal Judge Orie L. Phillips remarked: "We all know that these New Mexico Indians have responded to the needs of the country in time of war. Why should they be deprived of their rights to vote now because they are favored by the federal government in exempting their lands from taxation?"[47] It was a question that should have been asked decades before considering the participation of Indians in the First World War. But the timing was auspicious; no one wanted to deny voting rights to people who had served their country so recently.

Today Indians, Aleuts, and Eskimos can vote in local, state, and federal elections on the same basis as other citizens. But the old argument that Indians are not taxed is frequently raised by reactionary opponents who insist that the phrase intends a disqualification of Indian voters. Infrequently the accusation that Indians are persons legally incompetent, based on the trust doctrine for Indian lands, is also raised — again uselessly.

The Sixteenth Amendment

This amendment is the soul of simplicity: "The congress shall have power to lay and collect taxes on incomes, from whatever source derived, without apportionment among the several States, and without regard to any census or enumeration." In the popular mind the phrase "Indians not taxed" in the Fourteenth Amendment and Article 1 of the Constitution exempts American Indians from paying any form of taxes, at least without their consent or by their placing themselves voluntarily within a state or federal jurisdiction where they can be taxed. But the phrase "Indians not taxed" in fact describes the status of individual Indians within a tribal context; it does not admit of a special exemption from taxes.[48]

The exact status of Indian tribes with respect to the Internal Revenue Service code is not always clear in the sense that it seems to have evolved as part of federal policy with no clear linkages to past treaties, acts of Congress, or determinations of the status of an Indian tribe.[49] Generally Indian tribes are not taxable entities under the IRS code because they do not come within the definition of an "individual" as trusts, corporations, estates, and partnerships do. More specifically, the political status of the Indian tribe places it within the category of a government, and the IRS code does not apply to other units of government. This kind of status, however, should be related back to the aspect of sovereignty, which the United States assumed over Indian tribes in its first encounters with them.

Under the doctrine of discovery, and even under John Marshall's description of the status of Indian tribes as domestic dependent nations, the relationship of the United States with Indian tribes was a protectorate arrangement whereby the United States regulated all foreign affairs and established the rules and regulations for its citizens in their intercourse with the tribes, but it did not move further toward taking control of the political attributes of the tribe. Therefore it is doubtful that the United States ever exerted the kind of sovereignty that would have given it taxing power over Indian tribes and their income. In *McCulloch v. Maryland*[50] John Marshall not only identified the taxing power as an attribute of sovereignty but said that the power to tax involves the power to destroy. If Indian tribes, therefore, are under the protection of the United States, and their rights and property must be preserved, the Sixteenth Amendment could not apply to them at all, regardless of the clear language stating that Congress may tax from all sources of income. The United States cannot destroy an Indian tribe by taxation, for to do so would violate the trust responsibility.

Taxes on individual Indians are a little more confusing. For most sources of income that involve wages and interest, Indian individuals, since they became American citizens, are classified with all other Americans.[51] With respect to the income derived from their trust lands, however, the language of the General Allotment Act has provided a convenient peg upon which to hang a tax exemption. In section 5 of that act,[52] Congress defined a period of trust for allotments and directed that "at the expiration of said period the United States will convey the same by patent to said Indian, or his heirs as aforesaid, in fee, discharged of said trust and free of all charge or encumbrance whatsoever."[53] This provision is generally believed to exempt the land and its income from federal taxes until the Indian receives a patent in fee simple.[54] But since the allotment is a part of the tribal heritage and property, there is a good reason for Indians to argue that the Indian Citizenship Act, which exempted their rights to tribal property from the application of citizenship, is sufficient language to support a tax immunity from the IRS code. And because the period of trust on allotments has been extended indefinitely, the law is clear that income derived from trust land is not taxed.

Again with respect to the Sixteenth Amendment, the status of Indians and Indian tribes intervenes in the application of the amendment. But, as is the case with other constitutional phrases and amendments, the exclusion of Indians is not a deliberate policy decision stemming from a knowledgeable statement of the Congress. Rather, Indian exclusion is primarily the product of historical acts of the federal government accumulated at a time when it was not believed that the amendments applied to Indians.

The Prohibition Amendments

The Eighteenth and Twenty-first Amendments deal with the prohibition of intoxicating liquors for beverage purposes and the repeal of this amendment after fourteen years in 1933, respectively. Few comments need to be made about the effect of these amendments on American history. Of importance, however, is the fact that these amendments had no effect on the previously established federal prohibition of the sale of liquor to American Indians. The liquor prohibition respecting Indians was an early effort by Congress to police the fur trade and regulate commerce with the Indian tribes on the frontier. Only gradually did this prohibition come to be enforced primarily against Indians.[55]

Several treaties contained provisions specifically prohibiting the sale of liquor to Indians, and of these perhaps the most important was the Treaty of 1858 with the Yankton Sioux.[56] The Yankton reservation was allotted by an agreement on December 31, 1892,[57] which was then ratified and confirmed by Congress on August 15, 1894.[58] In the allotment agreement, the tribe ceded and relinquished to the United States their unallotted lands. Article 17 of the agreement even prohibited the sale of liquor in ceded lands adjoining the reduced reservation. It stated: "No intoxicating liquors nor other intoxicants shall ever be sold or given away upon any of the lands by this agreement ceded and sold to the United States, nor upon any other lands within or comprising the reservations of the Yankton Sioux or Dakota Indians. . . ."[59] In the 1894 ratifying act, Congress spelled out the severe punishment it would impose on those violating the treaty provision: "That every person who shall sell or give away any intoxicating liquors or other intoxicants upon any of the lands by said agreement ceded . . . shall be punishable by imprisonment for not more than two years and by a fine of not more than three hundred dollars."[60]

The prohibitory provision was tested in a 1914 Supreme Court case, *Perrin v. United States*,[61] and found to be valid. In this instance it was argued that the treaty provision, in effect, controlled the acts of the state of South Dakota, which had licensing power to permit the sale of liquor on lands under its jurisdiction. The Court found the prohibition to be a material and enforceable part of the treaty, and held that Congress, under the commerce clause, had the power to prohibit liquor introduction into Indian country.

In general, during the time when the Eighteenth Amendment was in force in the United States, violation of the liquor prohibition in Indian country was seen as a violation of federal Indian law and not as a violation of the prohibitions of the amendment. So even in a subject area in which there was uniform enforcement of the law, Indian legislation and treaties were regarded as the primary source of authority and the Constitution as a secondary source, its amendment not being regarded as having superseded existing federal Indian law. This circumstance, considering that the federal Indian liquor prohibition law arose from the treaty-making and commerce powers, would seem to argue that the treaty-making power and treaties made under this power are superior to subsequent constitutional amendments even when those amendments touch on a common subject.

Kennedy, et al. v. United States,[62] decided by the Supreme Court in 1924, is on point. In this case A. P. and John Kennedy were indicted and convicted of having whiskey in their possession in Osage County, Oklahoma, which was considered Indian country, a violation of the Act of July 23, 1892, and its amendments.[63] That act made the possession of intoxicating liquor in Indian country where liquor introduction was prohibited by "treaty or Federal statute" a criminal offense. The question before the Court was whether the Act of 1892 had been repealed, superseded, or modified by the enactment of the National Prohibition Act,[64] which had been passed to enforce the Eighteenth Amendment. After describing the purpose behind the implementation of the Indian liquor laws as well as the Eighteenth Amendment and its enforcement legislation, Justice Pierce Butler stated for a unanimous Court that "the offense charged against plaintiffs in error is not the same as any defined in the National Prohibition Act. Those portions of the Acts of 1892, 1897 and 1918, passed *for the protection of the Indian Country* . . . do not conflict with the National Prohibition Act. Both may stand" [emphasis added].[65]

More often, however, the violation of the liquor statute was a result of local politics — bootleggers bringing liquor into the reservation and being protected by local law enforcement officers. There was quite a hesitancy to indict local citizens, and so the practice was to indict the car that brought the forbidden drink into the federal enclave. Thus scholars are amused to find a series of cases such as *United States v. One Chevrolet Coupe Automobile*[66] and *United States v. One Chevrolet Four-Door Sedan Automobile.*[67]

The Twenty-sixth Amendment

In 1971 the Twenty-sixth Amendment was ratified, lowering the voting age to eighteen years partially in response to the Vietnam war and partially in recognition that times had changed and that young people were reaching maturity at an earlier age. One question that immediately came to mind was whether the amendment was applicable to Indian tribes holding their own elections, since many of the tribes when adopting the Indian Reorganization Act had simply followed the then traditional age of twenty-one when listing the qualifications for voting.

The Department of the Interior, anxious to maintain its control over the tribes since the Poverty Programs had given Indians unexpected leverage against the BIA, immediately asked for a solicitor's opinion on whether the amendment applied to tribes. In November 1971 Michael Melich wrote an opinion to the effect that the amendment applied to all laws on the basis that it was self-executing and did not need further action by the Congress.[68] Because no one wished to appear out of step with changes in American society, there was no negative reaction to the opinion.

It does present some complications, however. Melich assumed that all tribal constitutions were subject to the provisions of the Indian Reorganization Act, and therefore the amendment in its self-executing function changed tribal constitutions approved under the act's provisions. What about the tribes who adopted constitutions and merely sought the Secretary of the Interior's approval but did not come under a specific federal law? More to the point, could the amendment be extended to the Six Nations, who steadfastly refused to alter their form of government?

These questions never arose and so were never answered. Since these are provisions of tribal constitutions we are examining, how would the question of the amendment's application arise today? Undoubtedly a tribal court would have to rule that the amendment could not reach into the protected self-governing provisions that originated before the establishment of the United States. Unless willingly surrendered by the Indian nation, those provisions must remain intact.

The fact is that in many tribes, people were given adult responsibilities long before they reached the age of eighteen. Thus a wholly traditional Indian government may well base its voting franchise on a young person undergoing certain ceremonies or puberty rituals and being thereafter regarded as capable of performing adult functions within the tribe, functions that would include voting in tribal elections. For the present no one seems willing to challenge the solicitor's opinion.

This chapter closely examined a number of amendments that followed the Bill of Rights by some eight or more decades. It showed beyond a reasonable doubt that the protections outlined in these amendments, with the exception of the Fifteenth, have not been applied to tribal nations and have had — even after the unilateral extension of American citizenship to Indians in 1924 — only partial application to individual Indians. This is evident in the literal language of the cases and laws analyzed and in the perpetuation of the plenary-power doctrine, which enables the federal government to act without any constitutional restraints in its exercise of political power vis-à-vis tribal nations.

CHAPTER VIII

THE STATUS OF INDIAN TRIBES

AND THE CONSTITUTION

I N *Talton v. Mayes*[1] the Supreme Court heard an appeal by a Cherokee citizen claiming rights under the Fifth Amendment seeking to overturn a murder conviction by the Cherokee Supreme Court. The question raised by the appeal concerned the origin of self-governing powers of the Cherokee Nation. After a review of the history of the Cherokee, the court declared that "as the powers of local self-government enjoyed by the Cherokee Nation existed prior to the Constitution, they are not operated upon by the Fifth Amendment, which, as we have said, had for its sole object to control the powers conferred by the Constitution on the National Government."[2] Again, in *Native American Church v. Navajo Tribal Council*,[3] the tenth circuit court of appeals ruled that the Navajo Tribal Council could prohibit the use of peyote on the reservation because the First Amendment limitations applied only to the federal government, and the Fourteenth Amendment extended those protections only to the states. "Indian tribes are not states," the court announced. "They have a status higher than states. They are subordinate and dependent nations possessed of all powers as such only to the extent that they have expressly been required to surrender them by the superior sovereign, the United States."[4]

In a recent case, *Native Village of Venetie v. State of Alaska*,[5] a federal district court held that:

Though limited, tribal sovereignty is by no means trivial. Denomination of territory as 'Indian Country' and of a group of Indians there as a 'tribe' confers power on the leaders of such a community, and deprives the members of the tribe of the protection of the United States Constitution. As against Congress, tribal sovereignty is but a stick in front of a tank; but to the individual Indian, and in some circumstances to outsiders, the wielder of the stick may be more powerful than any state or federal official. The Constitution of the United States restrains state and federal officials, but not tribal officials acting on behalf of a tribe in 'Indian Country.' Since Constitutional safeguards do not apply, tribal sovereignty could be used in custody proceedings to deprive children or parents of fundamental rights without notice or a hearing, to foster an established religion within Indian country, or in other surprising ways, in the absence of statutory and administrative restraints. The United States Supreme Court has repeatedly affirmed that the Constitution does not restrain the exercise of tribal sovereignty in Indian country, and Congress has repeatedly exercised its plenary power to substitute statutory and administrative restraints.[6]

Dozens of other cases produced by federal and state courts have supported the same doctrine — that the Constitution and its amendments do not apply to Indian tribes.[7] Unfortunately, the Supreme Court ruled against the tribe, further restricting the application of traditional law in the protection of Indian rights and powers.[8]

This case law, as consistent as it is, deals only with the question of whether or not the Constitution and its amendments can reach through the plethora of federal Indian law and treaties and become a viable limitation on the actions of Indian tribes. In 1968, as part of the Fair Housing Act of that year, Congress included the Indian Civil Rights Act (ICRA).[9] Title 1 of this act includes some language taken from the Bill of Rights made applicable to Indian tribal governments in their relations to tribal members as well as other persons.[10] Among the rights guaranteed under the ICRA are the rights of free speech and assembly, protection against unreasonable search and seizure, the right to a speedy trial, the right to hire a lawyer in a criminal case, protection against self-incrimination and cruel and unusual punishment, and the rights to equal protection under the laws and due process. Importantly, the act excludes some constitutional provisions: for example, indictment by a grand jury (Article 5), the establishment-of-religion clause (Article 1), and the restriction against housing troops in homes (Article 3). Several of the other constitutional provisions were expressly modified in the ICRA statute. The Sixth Amendment right to have an attorney in criminal prosecutions is made provisional contingent upon the accused's ability to hire an attorney "at his own expense." Tribes are also not required to convene juries in civil trials or in criminal cases, or to issue grand-jury indictments. Additionally, tribes may discriminate in voting based on race.

The act is deceptive in many of its provisions, and even its description in Senate debate left a good deal to be desired as far as clarity was concerned. Senator Sam Ervin of North Carolina stated that the act would "confer upon the American Indians the fundamental constitutional rights which belong by right to all Americans." [11]

The irony of this situation is apparent. The Constitution does not apply to American Indians in their tribal relations. It does not protect Indian tribes. But, through a legislative act of Congress, some constitutional provisions are made an applicable part of the relationship between an Indian tribe and its members. As long as this situation exists, confusion and injustice will continue to be visited upon Indian tribes. The superior power of Congress — basically derived from its proprietorship of the land and modified by historical actions taken under constitutional authority of the treaty-making and commerce clauses — will continue to be the primary and irresponsible factor in the field of Indian affairs.

Unlike other areas of jurisprudence, federal Indian law has little logical consistency in its substance. It is a loosely related collection of past and present acts of Congress, treaties and agreements, executive orders, administrative rulings, and judicial opinions connected only by the fact that law in some haphazard form has been applied to American Indians over the course of several centuries. Federal Indian law is not related to or consistent with international law, even though it finds its most defensible context in that setting. Nor is it related to American domestic law based on the Constitution and its amendments, as we have seen demonstrated above. Indians in their tribal relations and Indian tribes in their relation to the federal government hang suspended in a legal no-man's-land. The solution to this problem — the means to bring a sense of coherent, logical consistency and historical accuracy and precedent to this subject—would be to return tribes to their political status as it existed prior to the prohibition against treaty making in 1871.

With the expansion of social programs in the 1960s and 1970s, tribal governments became an eligible sponsoring agency for many kinds of programs. In every instance in which tribes participated in these programs, they had to negotiate the terms and conditions under which they would operate them. In a related move, Congress's enactment of the Indian Self-determination Act of 1975 [12] gave tribes a more direct role in administering social services (e.g., law-enforcement programs, housing programs, health care, and schools) by giving tribal governments the option of contracting with the federal government to administer programs previously handled by the Bureau of Indian Affairs or other agencies. By 1988 Indian self-determination had evolved, for some tribes, into an opportunity to engage in tribal self-governance compacts with the federal government, which vest a larger degree of authority in the participating tribes to manage their share of federal money. [13]

Consequently, with respect to many existing programs for which tribes are now eligible, the federal government negotiates terms and conditions with them. But in the vital areas of self-government and the protection of tribal natural resources particularly, there has been only grudging recognition of the sovereign political rights and viability of Indian tribes. Thus tribes find themselves in a condition in which they have a partial responsibility for their actions but are unable to withstand the application of arbitrary pressure by the federal government and, in a growing number of cases, state governments in the most critical areas.

Because Congress in one form or another attempts to secure Indian consent before proceeding with legislation that has an impact on tribal rights, it informally recognizes that hidden deep within the American past is the requirement that Indians give their consent before a congressional act can be considered valid with respect to them. Past congressional mistakes and the willingness of succeeding congresses to repair some of the damages wrought by their predecessors shows that Congress frequently acts in haste and without due consideration of the consequences of its actions. Yet it always tries to give the appearance that even its worst blunders and most ill-considered acts had the concurrence, support, and understanding of Indian tribes.

A major step toward renewing the process of negotiation and moderniz-
ing the treaty process was taken in 1971, when the Alaska Native Claims
Settlement Act was passed.[14] Through the Organic Act for Alaska of May 17,
1884;[15] the Act of June 6, 1900, which provided for a civil government for
Alaska;[16] Alaska's statehood;[17] and a host of other federal acts spanning
almost a century, the resolution of this problem was always postponed in
favor of resolving the immediate issue at hand. But with the discovery of
tremendous reserves of petroleum on the North Slope, the problem of
native land title became a pressing issue.

After much negotiation and with the threat of prolonged litigation loom-
ing, a definitive settlement was finally reached. The state was divided into
regional areas, and corporations were established to represent the natives
in each region. To ensure fairness, one additional corporation was authorized to represent those Alaska natives who had moved to the continental
United States under government programs and on their own initiative, and
this corporation was given equal status with the northern landowning native groups. Though the bill had many shortcomings and amendments
had to be sought to adjust the terms of the settlement to changing conditions, this method of negotiating new terms to resolve long-standing legal
disputes without extensive litigation proved popular.

Since 1971 a wide variety of legal problems have been resolved using the
settlement-act format. Thus disputes over water rights, land claims, railroad rights-of-way, restoration of federal recognition, and final settlement
of boundary have all been the subject of these kinds of negotiations. Two
primary goals emerge from such settlements: the federal government attempts to repair damages for old wrongs and a proposal for future cooperative action is established. The first goal of correcting old wrongs, found
mostly in the land-claims settlements, has been reasonably generous but
has been used primarily for Indian groups not previously related to the federal government in a formal manner. The test of this new format will be a
process whereby a tribe can petition the government to review and renew
long-standing commitments and make available programs and the authority to support continuing activities of the tribe. In this manner, the two
goals can be reconciled to demonstrate a new kind of relationship between
the federal government and Indian nations.

The Constitution does not limit Indian tribes in their relationships with
the United States. That premise has been established in both American

and international law. The only modification of the idea that might be suggested is that due to the doctrine of discovery, Indian tribes, according to the United States, may only treat with the federal government and no external sovereigns. But this consideration is not material. On the other hand, it is also well established that historically the United States was restricted to the exercise of certain powers authorized by the Constitution in its relationship with American Indian tribes. But the government usurped some tribal rights at a time when Indians could least capably defend themselves, their weakness being a direct result of the United States' extending its exercise of political powers over tribes beyond those granted it in the Constitution.

As the country nears the third millennium, it is long overdue that the federal government once again restrict itself to the exercise of the only clear traditional manner of dealing with Indian tribes — the treaty relationship. The commerce clause should be authority primarily for Congress to adjust the domestic law of the United States to conform to the obligations and responsibilities accruing to the government as a result of the treaties it makes with the Indian tribes, and the property clause should be authority primarily acknowledging the unique geopolitical nature of tribes as preexisting sovereigns who live surrounded by states and the federal government, the latter-day sovereigns.

A Postscript

Since this manuscript was written, the U.S. Supreme Court has rendered two nervously anticipated decisions that dramatically reaffirmed the specific treaty rights Indian tribes reserved to themselves in the 1800s. In *Minnesota v. Mille Lac Band of Chippewa Indians* (119 S.Ct. 1187), handed down March 24, 1999, in a 5-4 ruling the Court upheld the Chippewa's 1837 treaty right to hunt, fish, and gather on 13 million acres of lands the eight Chippewa Bands ceded to the federal government in central Minnesota.

Less than three weeks later, on April 5, in *Puget Sound Shellfish Growers v. United States* (1999 U.S. Lexis 2504), the Supreme Court rejected without comment an appeal of a lower court ruling that upheld the 1855 Stevens treaty rights of twenty-one tribes in Washington to harvest shellfish on private beaches.

These two decisions — rendered within a two-and-a-half week period and coming as they do from the conservative-dominated Rehnquist Court — add impressive support to our contention that the treaty process is viable and remains the most appropriate, most fair, and certainly the clearest manner in which to identify and demarcate the rights of tribal nations.

NOTES

Introduction

1. U.S. Constitution, Art. 1, sec. 8, cl. 3.
2. U.S. Constitution, Art. 1, sec. 2, cl. 3, and the Fourteenth Amendment, section 2.
3. See the Act of June 2, 1924, 43 Stat., 253, which mandated American citizenship for all Indians who had not yet been enfranchised by prior treaty provision or federal statute.
4. Ibid.

Chapter 1

1. See Francis G. Davenport, ed., *European Treaties Bearing on the History of the United States and its Dependencies to 1698*, Carnegie Institution of Washington Publication No. 254 (Gloucester, Mass: Peter Smith, 1967): 61–63.
2. See Lewis Hanke, "The 'Requerimiento' and Its Interpreters," *Revista de Historia de América*, vol. 1 (Instituto Panamericano de Geografia e Historia: Mexico City, 1939), pp. 25–34 for a copy of the manifesto.
3. Other commentators have thoroughly examined these issues. See, *e.g.*, Lewis Hanke, *The Spanish Struggle for Justice in the Conquest of America* (Philadelphia: University of Pennsylvania Press, 1949) and *All Mankind is One: A Study of the Disputation Between Bartolomé de Las Casas and Juan Ginés de Sepúlveda in 1550 on the Intellectual and Religious Capacity of the American Indians* (Dekalb: Northern Illinois University Press, 1974); Felix Cohen, "The Spanish Origin of Indian Rights in the Laws of the United States," *Georgia Law Review*, vol. 31, no. 1 (1942); Charles Gibson, "Spanish Indian Policies," in *History of Indian-White Relations*, vol. 4, Wilcomb E. Washburn, ed. (Washington, D.C.: Smithsonian Institution, 1988): 96–102; Robert A. Williams Jr., *The American Indian in Western Legal Thought: The*

Discourses of Conquest (New York: Oxford University Press, 1990), especially Chapter 2; and S. James Anaya, *Indigenous Peoples in International Law* (New York: Oxford University Press, 1996).

4. See, *e.g.*, Yasuhide Kawashima, *Puritan Justice and the Indian: Man's Law in Massachusetts, 1630–1763* (Middleton, Conn.: Wesleyan University Press, 1986).

5. Several commentators have discussed the trust doctrine as a legal term of art that has adversely affected the rights of tribes. See, *e.g.*, Milner Ball, "Constitution, Court, Indian Tribes," *American Bar Foundation Research Journal* vol. 1 (1987), p. 62; and Petra T. Shattuck and Jill Norgren, *Partial Justice: Federal Indian Law in a Liberal Constitutional System* (Providence, RI: Berg Publishers, 1991): 115–121. And see *Lyng v. Northwest Indian Cemetery Protective Association*, 485 U.S. 439 (1988), wherein the Supreme Court flatly stated that the trust doctrine was legally unenforceable and could not shield lands considered sacred by tribes from federal activity aimed at the construction of a road.

6. 7 Stat., 13.

7. Ibid., 15.

8. See Donald A. Grinde and Bruce Johansen, *Exemplar of Liberty: Native America and the Evolution of Democracy* (Los Angeles: American Indian Studies Center, University of California, 1991), for an account of the role American Indian tribal, political, and cultural ideas played in the genesis and shaping of American democracy.

9. See *American State Papers, Foreign Affairs*, vol. 1, pp. 278–279 for the treaty between Spain and the Creek at Pensacola on May 20–June 1, 1784 and p. 280 for a treaty with the Choctaw and Chickasaw at Natchez on May 14, 1790.

10. See Alfred B. Thomas, *Forgotten Frontiers*, (Norman: University of Oklahoma Press, 1932) pp. 329–332 for a treaty with the Comanche and Spain of February 25 and 28, 1786; and Marc Simmons, *Border Comanches (Santa Fe: Stagecoach Press, 1967)*: 21–22 for a treaty with the Comanche of October 1785.

11. See David M. Brugge and J. Lee Correll, *The Story of the Navajo Treaties*, (Window Rock, Ariz.: Navajo Historical Publications, 1971) pp. 52–53; Frank Reeve, "Navajo Foreign Affairs," Part II, *New Mexico Historical Review*, vol. 46, no. 3 (1971), p. 241; and Marian Lothrop, "The Indian Campaigns of General M. G. Vallejo," *Quarterly of the Society of California Pioneers*, vol. 9, no. 3, pp. 161–205, for examples. See Annual Report of the Commissioner of Indian Affairs, 1873, p. 169 and 1875, p. 35 for reports of Mexican treaties with the Apaches.

12. *Journals of the Continental Congress*, vol. 24, May 1783, p. 319.

13. See Charles J. Kappler, comp., *Indian Affairs: Laws and Treaties*, vol. 2 (Washington, DC: Government Printing Office, 1903): 5–18 for the texts of these treaties and note the peace provisions and boundary clarifications.

14. *Journals of the Continental Congress*, vol. 34, May 1788, pp. 124–125.

15. The transcript of the Fort Laramie negotiations shows the American representatives describing the Sioux as a "small nation" with whom they did not want to go to war.

Chapter 2

1. See Grinde and Johansen, 1991.

2. See Jose Barreiro, "Indian Roots of American Democracy," *Northeast Indian Quarterly*, vol. 4–5 (Winter–Spring, 1988–1989); and Gregory Schaaf, "From the Great Law of Peace to the Constitution of the United States: A Revision of America's Democratic Roots," *American Indian Law Review*, vol. 14 (1989), pp. 323–32.

3. *Journals of the Continental Congress*, vol. 31, 1786, pp. 656–658 has a resolution dealing with Virginia's intent to invade the Indian country. The relevant part of the resolution reads:

> *Resolved,* That the State of Virginia do abstain from committing Hostilities against, making Reprisals upon, or entering into War with all or any Tribes or Nation of Indians with which the United States are in Peace or any other; and that if any Troops have been levied or Men embodied for the purpose of committing Hostilities against, making reprisals upon or entering into War with the said Indian Nations or any other the executive of the said state of Virginia do cause the same forthwith to be disbanded.

4. *Journals of the Continental Congress*, vol. 25, Saturday, September 20, 1783, pp. 591 ff.

5. See Felix S. Cohen, *Handbook of Federal Indian Law,* (reprint Albuquerque: University of New Mexico Press, 1972): 418.

6. 1 Stat., 137.

7. *Journals of the Continental Congress*, vol. 31, Monday, August 7, 1786, pp. 588–593.

8. Contained in 1 Stat., 50, Act of August 7, 1789.

9. Ibid.

10. 1 Stat., 123.
11. James Madison, in *The Federalist Papers, No. 24,* Clinton Rossiter, ed. (New York: The New American Library, 1961): 264–265.
12. "George Mason, Patrick Henry and James Monroe, in the Ratifying Convention of Virginia, 4–12 June, 1788," in *Anti-Federalists versus Federalists, Selected Documents,* John D. Lewis, ed. (Scranton, Penn: Chandler Publishing Co., 1967): 209.
13. Alexander Hamilton, in *The Federalist Papers,* No. 24, pp. 160–161.
14. *Ibid.,* No. 25, p. 163.
15. *Ibid.,* p. 165.
16. 4 Stat., 729.

Chapter 3

1. See his most famous work, *The Spirit of the Laws,* 2 vols. New and revised edition, J. V. Prichard, ed. (Littleton, Colo.: F. B. Rothman, 1991) first published in 1734. Montesquieu is mentioned much more frequently in the writings of the Constitutional fathers than John Locke, contrary to popular notions.
2. It was not simply the idea of difficulty of transportation and communication that made a large country unwieldy but also the fact that different places called forth different responses from the inhabitants. This idea, seen at that time with the rowdiness of the Kentuckians and the abortive "state of Franklin," seemed to support Montesquieu's philosophy. But Montesquieu was also cited approvingly by the Federalists because of his development of the idea of checks and balances as a constitutional mechanism to thwart any branch of government or any power within a nation from becoming absolute by being balanced or checked by another source of power within that same nation.
3. Lewis, ed. *Anti-Federalists,* 209.
4. See Earl S. Pomeroy, *The Territories and the United States: 1861–1890* (Philadelphia: University of Pennsylvania Press, 1947).
5. See, *e.g.,* Yasuhide Kawashima, "Legal Origins of the Indian Reservation in Colonial Massachusetts," *American Journal of Legal History,* vol. 13, (1969), pp. 42–56.
6. John Jay, *The Federalist Papers,* No. 3, p. 44.
7. See congressional debate on Indian removal in the 1830s, the conflict between President Andrew Jackson and the Supreme Court during the Cherokee cases; tension over Indian fishing rights in the 1960s–1990s involving

Washington and Wisconsin, the tribes, and the federal government; and the recent controversies over Indian gaming pitting some federal officials against state legislatures and governors.

8. See, *e.g.*, Samuel H. Beer, *To Make a Nation: The Rediscovery of American Federalism* (Cambridge: Harvard University Press, 1993); Thomas R. Dye, *American Federalism: Competition Among Governments* (Lexington, Mass: Lexington Books, 1990); and Paul E. Peterson, *The Price of Federalism* (Washington, D.C. : Brookings, 1995).

9. See Jules Lobel, ed., *A Less Than Perfect Union: Alternative Perspectives on the U.S. Constitution* (New York: Monthly Review Press, 1988).

10. See, *e.g.*, *Cherokee Nation v. Georgia*, 30 U.S. (5 Pet.) 1 (1831); *United States v. Holiday*, 70 U.S. (3 Wall.) 407 (1866); *United States v. Forty-three Gallons of Whiskey*, 93 U.S. 188 (1876); *Ex parte Webb*, 225 U.S. 663 (1912); *United States v. Sandoval*, 231 U.S. 28 (1913); *Perrin v. United States*, 232 U.S. 478 (1914); *United States v. Nice*, 241 U.S. 591 (1916); *McClanahan v. Arizona State Tax Commission*, 411 U.S. 164 (1973); *Morton v. Mancari*, 417 U.S. 535 (1974); *Ramah Navajo School Board v. Bureau of Revenue of New Mexico*, 458 U.S. 832 (1982). Also see *United States v. Kagama*, 118 U.S. 375 (1886), which strangely rejected the commerce clause as a basis for congressional enactment of a system of criminal laws for Indians on reservations. However, the Court sustained the Major Crimes Act on the grounds that tribes were weak and dependent and that the United States had an obligation and the power to civilize them.

11. U.S. Government, American Indian Policy Review Commission, *Final Report*, vol. 1 (Washington, D.C.: Government Printing Office, 1977), pp. 571–612.

12. U.S. Constitution, Article 2, sec. 2, cl. 2. The clause states that the President "shall have power, by and with the advice and consent of the senate, to make treaties, provided two-thirds of the senators present concur. . . . "

13. 16 Stat., 544, 566.

14. 187 U.S. 553.

15. See, *e.g.*, *Worcester v. Georgia*, 31 U.S. (6 Pet.) 515 (1832) and *Mitchell v. United States*, 34 U.S. (9 Pet.) 711 (1835).

16. *United States v. Kagama*, 118 U.S. 375 (1886).

17. There is, of course, ample evidence showing that at various times and notwithstanding the doctrine of equitable title (also known as Indian title, aboriginal title, and use-and-occupancy title), agencies of the federal government simply chose to ignore Indian land rights and acted as if the title tribes held was wholly inferior and not deserving of federal respect. See, *e.g.*, *John-*

son v. McIntosh, 21 U.S. (8 Wheat.) 543 (1823), the Indian removal period of the 1830s and 1840s, and the traumatic half-century known crudely as the General Allotment era—1880s–1930s.

18. 187 U.S. 553. For a good analysis of this important case see Blue Clark, *Lone Wolf v. Hitchcock: Treaty Rights and Indian Law at the End of the Nineteenth Century* (Lincoln: University of Nebraska Press, 1994).

19. U.S. Annual Report of the Commissioner of Indian Affairs, 1872 (Washington, D.C.: Government Printing Office, 1872): 12.

20. 72 U.S. (5 Wall.) 737, 758 (1867).

Chapter 4

1. *Cherokee Nation v. Georgia*, 30 U.S. (5 Pet.) 1 (1831) and *Worcester v. Georgia*, 31 U.S. (6 Pet.) 515 (1832).

2. See Randall B. Ripley and Grace A. Franklin, *Congress, the Bureaucracy, and Public Policy*, third edition (Homewood, Ill.: The Dorsey Press, 1984).

3. Linda Grant DePauw, ed. *Documentary History of the First Federal Congress of the United States of America*, vol. 2, Senate Executive Journal of Related Documents (Baltimore: Johns Hopkins University Press, 1974): 24. See also the discussion of the relationship between Washington and the Senate in Francis P. Prucha's *American Indian Treaties* (Berkeley: University of California Press, 1994): 70–79.

4. Prucha, *American Indian Treaties*, 76–79.

5. 4 Stat., 411.

6. See Angie Debo, *A History of the Indians of the United States* (Norman: University of Oklahoma Press, 1970): 188 for a brief discussion of this tragic event.

7. Francis P. Prucha, *The Great Father: The United States Government and the American Indian*, vol. 1 (Lincoln: University of Nebraska Press, 1984): 501–533.

8. Herman J. Viola, *Diplomats in Buckskins: A History of Indian Delegations in Washington City* (Washington, D.C.: Smithsonian Institution, 1981).

9. Francis Leupp, *The Indian and His Problem*, (1910; reprint New York: Arno Press, 1971): 207.

10. John Collier, *From Every Zenith* (Denver: Sage Books, 1963), p. 292.

11. Executive Order 11399 "Establishing the National Council on Indian Opportunity" is printed in the *Weekly Compilation of Presidential Documents*, vol. 4 (Washington, D.C.: Government Printing Office, 1968): 448.

12. See Emma Gross, *Contemporary Federal Policy Toward American Indians*

(Westport, Conn.: Greenwood Press, 1987): 65–71 for a good discussion of Nixon's Indian policy orientation.

13. See Nicholas C. Peroff, *Menominee Drums: Tribal Termination and Restoration, 1954–1974* (Norman: University of Oklahoma Press, 1982).

14. 85 Stat. 688 (1971).

15. Dwight D. Eisenhower, *U.S. Public Papers of the Presidents of the United States*, (Washington, D.C.: Government Printing Office, 1953): 166.

16. "Remarks to American Indian and Alaskan Native Tribal Leaders," April 29, 1994, in *Weekly Compilation of Presidential Documents* (1994): 941.

17. Order of May 14, 1855, in *Indian Affairs, Kappler, comp.* See volume 1, pp. 846–47. This was the first executive-order reservation. It involved lands set aside for the Ottawa and Chippewa Indians of Michigan in Isabella and Emmet counties. And see *Executive Orders Relating to Indian Reservations from May 14, 1855 to July 1, 1902* (Washington, D.C.: Government Printing Office, 1902) for a list of Indian executive-order reservations.

18. 24 Stat., 388.

19. See Secretary of the Interior Robert McClelland's letter regarding the Ottawa and Chippewa executive-order reservation in 1855 in *Executive Orders Relating to Indian Reservations*, 45–46. It was not until the U.S. attorney general spoke in 1924 that executive-order reservations were extended a protected status comparable to treaty reservations. 34 *Opinions of the Attorney General*, 181 (1924).

20. 41 Stat. 3, 34.

21. 44 Stat. 1347.

22. Act of August 13, 1946, 60 Stat. 1049.

23. 4 Stat., 729.

24. 4 Stat., 735.

25. 9 Stat., 395.

26. 64 Stat., 967.

27. 64 Stat., 1100.

28. Act of August 8, 1946, 60 Stat. 939. See Prucha, *The Great Father*, vol. 2, p. 1037.

29. Act of June 18, 1934, 48 Stat. 984.

30. P. L. 93–628.

31. P. L. 103–413.

32. *Colliflower v. Garland*, 324 F2d. 369 (9th Cir. 1965).

33. See, *e.g.*, *Lane v. Pueblo of Santa Rosa*, 249 U.S. 110 (1919); *United States v. Creek Nation*, 295 U.S. 103 (1935); *Tooahnippah v. Hickel*, 397 U.S. 598 (1970); and *Morton v. Ruiz*, 415 U.S. 199 (1974).

34. *Santa Clara Pueblo v. Martinez*, 436 U.S. 49, 56 (1978).

35. 1 Stat., 137.
36. 4 Stat., 729.
37. Ibid.
38. Treaty with the Delawares, 7 Stat., 13.
39. Act of November 2, 1921, 42 Stat., 208.
40. See Cohen, *Handbook.* See especially section 17, "Indian Appropriation Acts: 1789 to 1939," p. 88, for a short synopsis of these important congressional measures.
41. 11 Stat., 749.
42. See Prucha, *American Indian Treaties,* 238–40.
43. 16 Stat., 544, 566.
44. 314 U.S. 339 (1941). In this case the United States, as trustee for the Hualapai Tribe of northern Arizona, sued to enjoin the railroad from interfering with the possession and occupancy by the Indians of their lands. The Court held that rights based on aboriginal Indian title are enforceable against parties even when those rights have not been recognized by treaty, congressional act, or other governmental action. Equally important, the Court held that Indian title had not been extinguished even though actions by governmental officials, including Congress, had treated the Hualapais' land as public land because extinguishment of Indian title "cannot be lightly implied" and must be specifically evinced by Congress, or there must be a "voluntary cession" on the part of the tribe.
45. 15 Stat., 17. The Senators were John B. Henderson, chairman of the Committee of Indian Affairs, along with S. F. Tappan and John B. Sanborn.
46. See, *e.g.,* 41 Stat., 738 (1920), an act that authorized the Sioux to bring a claim against the United States before the court of claims.
47. Leupp, *The Indian and His Problem,* 203.
48. The Burke Act, 24 Stat. 182, an amendment to the 1887 General Allotment Act, became law in 1906. The act, introduced by South Dakota Representative Charles Burke, was a congressional response to the Supreme Court's 1905 decision, *Matter of Heff,* which held that Indian allottees became American citizens as soon as they accepted their land allotment, not at the end of the twenty-five year trust period stated in the allotment law. The Burke Act countered the *Heff* ruling by declaring that Indian allottees remained under federal trust protection and were not enfranchised until the expiration of the twenty-five year trust period. The act, however, also gave the secretary of the interior the authority to prematurely issue fee patents to so-called competent Indian allottees when the secretary determined that they were capable of "managing their own affairs."

49. Leupp, p. 206. The situation of the Five Civilized Tribes — the Cherokee, Creek, Choctaw, Chickasaw, and Seminole — is particularly distinctive in federal Indian law annals because of their allegedly more "civilized" status in the eyes of federal administrators and because of the manner in which they were removed from their original territory in the southeast and relocated to lands in present-day Oklahoma. See Angie Debo, *And Still the Waters Run: The Betrayal of the Five Civilized Tribes* (Princeton: Princeton University Press, 1942) and Grant Foreman, *Indian Removal* (Norman: University of Oklahoma Press, 1932) for outstanding accounts of two traumatic periods in the history of these nations.

50. Leupp, p. 207.

51. Leupp, pp. 211–212.

52. 384 F. Supp. 312. Affirmed 520 F. 2d 676 (9th Cir. 1975). Certiorari denied 423 U.S. 1086 (1976).

53. See David E. Wilkins, "The 'De-Selected' Senate Committee on Indian Affairs and its Legislative Record, 1977–1992," *European Review of Native American Studies*, vol. 9, no. 1 (1995): 27–34.

54. H. R. 1977, 104th Congress, 1st session, July 1, 1995, pp. 54–55.

55. *New York Times*, March 21, 1998, p. 14.

56. Authorized under Senate Resolution 79, 70th Congress, 1st session, Act of February 1, 1928.

57. 48 Stat. 985.

58. Act of July 1, 1932, 47 Stat. 564.

59. Act of April 16, 1934, 48 Stat. 596.

60. 60 Stat. 1049.

61. Act of April 11, 1958, 82 Stat. 73. Also see, *e.g.*, U.S. Congress/Senate Hearings Before the Subcommittee on Constitutional Rights of the Committee on the Judiciary, *Constitutional Rights of the American Indian*. 87th Congress, 1st session, September 1, 1961.

62. 88 Stat., 1910.

63. U.S. Senate, *Final Report and Legislative Recommendation: A Report of the Special Committee on Investigation of the Select Committee on Indian Affairs*, Senate Report No. 101–216, 101st Congress, 1st session, 1989.

64. See *Chinese Exclusion Case*, 130 U.S. 581 (1889), *Asakura v. Seattle*, 265 U.S. 332 (1923).

65. 116 U.S. 138 (1882).

66. 118 U.S. 394 (1886).

67. See, *e.g.*, Felix S. Cohen, "Indian Rights and the Federal Courts," *Minnesota Law Review*, vol. 24, no. 2 (January 1940), pp. 145–200; Charles F. Wilkinson,

American Indians, Time, and the Law (New Haven: Yale University Press, 1987); and Julie Wrend and Clay Smith, eds., *American Indian Law Deskbook* (Niwot, Colo.: University Press of Colorado, 1993).

68. See David E. Wilkins, *American Indian Sovereignty and the U.S. Supreme Court: The Masking of Justice* (Austin: University of Texas Press, 1997).

69. 21 U.S. (8 Wheat.) 543 (1823).

70. 9 How. 356 (1850).

71. 11 U.S. (7 Cranch) 164 (1812).

72. 112 U.S. 94 (1884).

73. 187 U.S. 553 (1903).

74. 210 U.S. 50 (1908).

75. 78 (11 Wall.) 616 (1870).

76. 109 U.S. 556 (1883).

77. 118 U.S. 375 (1886).

78. 198 U.S. 371 (1905).

79. 219 U.S. 346 (1911).

80. See 28 Stat. 315, which is a ratification of the 1892 agreement with the Yankton. Article 16 reads:

> If the Government of the United States questions the ownership of the Pipestone Reservation by the Yankton tribe of Sioux Indians under the treaty of April 19, 1858, including the fee to the land, as well as the right to work the quarries, the Secretary of the Interior shall, as speedily as possible, refer the matter to the Supreme Court of the United States to be decided by that tribunal, and the United States shall furnish without cost to the Yankton Indians at least one competent attorney to represent the interests of the tribe before the court.

81. 12 Stat. 765, 767.

82. See, for example, 21 Stat. 291 (1890), "An Act to carry into effect the second and sixteenth articles of the [1867] treaty between the United States and the Great and Little Osage Indians"; 27 Stat. 394 (1892), "Joint Resolution Construing Article 4 of the [1891] Agreement with the Citizen Band of Pottawatomie Indians in Oklahoma Territory; and 48 Stat. 927 (1934), "An Act to modify the effect of certain Chippewa Indian treaties . . . . " In each of these instances, the Congress acted to clarify and/or put into effect the meaning of specific treaty or agreement provisions.

83. 397 U.S. 598 (1970).

84. 420 U.S. 194 (1975).

85. Bob Woodward and Scott Armstrong, *The Brethren*, (New York: Simon & Schuster, 1979): 57–58, 359–360.

86. See, *e.g.*, Russel L. Barsh and James Y. Henderson, "The Betrayal: *Oliphant v. Suquamish Indian Tribe* and the Hunting of the Snark," *Minnesota Law Review*, vol. 63 (1979), pp. 609–640; and Vine Deloria, Jr., "Trouble in High Places: Erosion of American Indian Rights to Religious Freedom in the United States," in *The State of Native America: Genocide, Colonization, and Resistance*, M. Annette Jaimes, ed. (Boston: South End Press, 1992): 267–290.

87. 448 U.S. 371 (1980).

88. Ibid., 435.

89. Ibid., 421–422.

90. See, *e.g.*, *Cotton Petroleum Corporation v. New Mexico*, 490 U.S. 163 (1989); *Brendale v. Confederated Tribes and Bands of the Yakima Indian Nation*, 492 U.S. 408 (1989); *County of Yakima v. Confederated Tribes and Bands of the Yakima Indian Nation*, 112 S. Ct. 683 (1992); *South Dakota v. Bourland*, 113 S. Ct. 2309 (1993); *Hagen v. Utah*, 114 S. Ct. 958 (1994); *Department of Taxation and Finance of New York v. Milhelm Attea and Brothers, Inc.*, 114 S. Ct. 2028 (1994); *Seminole Tribe of Florida v. Florida*, 134 L. Ed. 252 (1996); *Strate v. A-1 Contractors*, 117 S. Ct. 1404 (1997); *South Dakota v. Yankton Sioux Tribe*, No. 96–1581 (1998); and *Alaska v. Native Village of Venetie Tribal Council*, No. 96–1577 (1998).

91. 485 U.S. 429 (1988).

92. 494 U.S. 872 (1990).

93. 374 U.S. 398 (1963).

94. 107 Stat. 1488.

95. 117 S. Ct. 2157 (1997).

Chapter 5

1. Article 9, December 24, 1818, 8 Stat., 218.

2. See, *e.g.*, Treaty with the Choctaw Indians, Sept. 27, 1830, 7 Stat., 333.

3. September 9, 1849, 9 Stat., 974.

4. Act of February 8, 1887, 24 Stat., 388.

5. Ibid.

6. Ibid., 389–90.

7. Art. 3, 1 Stat., 50, 52.

8. Act of March 3, 1871, 16 Stat., 544, 566.

9. 30 U.S. (5 Pet.) 1 (1831).

10. Besides the treaty-ending debate, the 1885 Major Crimes Act (23 Stat., 385) also became law as a rider attached to an Indian appropriation bill.

11. U.S. *Congressional Globe*, March 1, 1871, Senate, p. 1824.

12. 15 Stat., 17.

13. *Congressional Globe*, March 1, 1871, Senate, p. 1824.

14. 72 U.S. (5 Wall.) 755 (1866).

15. Ibid., p. 755.

16. *Congressional Globe*, March 1, 1871, Senate, p. 1824.

17. Ibid.

18. Ibid., pp. 1824–1825.

19. Ibid., p. 1825.

20. Ibid., p. 1822.

21. Ibid.

22. Ibid.

23. Ibid.

24. Termination was the official policy of the federal government toward a number of Indian tribes from 1953 through the 1960s. It was most clearly enunciated through House Concurrent Resolution 108, enacted August 1, 1953 (67 Stat., B132). A "terminated" tribe had its share of federal benefits, programs, and services severed.

25. 3 Stat. 380.

26. 4 Stat. 721.

27. 5 Stat. 680.

28. Kappler, vol. 2, p. 1065; see H. R. Ex. Doc. 68, 47th Congress 2d session.

29. See Sen. Ex. Doc. 16, 50th Congress, 2d session, December 13, 1888.

30. Act of September 30, 1950, 64 Stat., 1094–95.

31. Art. 12, April 29, 1868, 15 Stat., 635.

32. Act of June 17, 1954, 68 Stat., 250–52.

33. 391 U.S. 404 (1968).

34. 67 Stat., 588.

35. 397 U.S. 619 (1970).

36. 101 S. Ct. 1245 (1981).

37. *Lone Wolf v. Hitchcock*, 187 U.S. 553 (1903).

38. Ibid., p. 564.

39. *Cherokee Nation v. Hitchcock*, 187 U.S. 294 (1902).

40. 187 U.S. 553, 568.

41. Ibid.

42. See, *e.g.*, *United States v. Lopez*, 115 S. Ct. 1624 (1995); and *Seminole Tribe of Florida v. Florida*, 116 S. Ct. 1114 (1996). In these two 5-to-4 decisions, both written by Chief Justice Rehnquist, the Court rekindled a vision of dual Federalism in which the states are considered equal sovereigns to the federal

government. With regards to Congress's power to regulate commerce, in *Lopez*, which involved the 1990 Gun-Free School Zones Act, which restricted possession of firearms in school areas, Rehnquist wrote that Congress had exceeded its authority in enacting the gun-control act because "the possession of a gun in a local school zone is in no sense an economic activity that might, through repetition elsewhere, substantially affect any sort of interstate commerce" (p. 1634). Rehnquist and the bare majority made it clear that the power to regulate firearms was a police power "of the sort retained by the States" (Ibid.).

The *Seminole* case involved a provision of the 1988 Indian Gaming Regulatory Act, but it only peripherally involved tribes per se. The provision in question authorized tribes to sue states if they failed to negotiate gaming compacts in good faith with the tribes. The Court declared, however, that states were sovereign entities and as such enjoyed immunity under the Tenth Amendment and therefore could not be sued without their explicit consent.

The fact that both cases were 5-to-4 decisions indicates that the matter of redefining Federalism is far from settled.

43. 1 Stat., 49.
44. 1 Stat., 50.
45. 1 Stat., 54.
46. See the Act of July 22, 1790, "An Act to regulate trade and intercourse with the Indian tribes" (1 Stat., 137), the first of a series of temporary measures that culminated in a permanent intercourse act on June 30, 1834, 4 Stat., 729. The first of several measures creating trading houses was established by Congress on April 18, 1796, 1 Stat., 452. The trading houses were abolished by an act of Congress on May 6, 1822, 3 Stat., 679.
47. 3 Stat., 516.
48. Ibid.
49. 60 Stat., 1049.
50. U.S. Congress, Committee on Indian Affairs, House Report No. 474, *Regulating the Indian Department*. 23d Congress, 1st session, May 20, 1834, pp. 1–2.
51. Act to Regulate Trade and Intercourse with the Indian Tribes, June 30, 1834, 4 Stat., 729; and Act to Provide for the Organization of the Department of Indian Affairs, June 30, 1834, 4 Stat., 735.
52. See, e.g., Article 6 of the Treaty with the Omahas of March 16, 1854. 10 Stat., 1043, which provides for family allotments and is repeated in a number of other treaties of that year, e.g., Treaty with the Nisqually and Puyallup, December 26, 1854, 10 Stat., 1132, Article 6.

53. See "Report to the President by the Indian Peace Commission," January 17, 1868, CIA, AR, 1868. Serial 1366, pp. 496–510.
54. 109 U.S. 556.
55. See Sidney L. Harring, *Crow Dog's Case* (New York: Cambridge University Press, 1994), which traces the manipulations of the BIA with regard to the exercise of self-government by the Indians beginning in the mid 1860s.
56. 23 Stat., 362, 385.
57. 118 U.S. 375.
58. Ibid., pp. 378–79.
59. Ibid., pp. 379–80.
60. Ibid., pp. 383–84.
61. See the case law cited in note 90 in Chapter 4.
62. See 1 Stat., 549, "An Act for an amicable settlement of limits with the state of Georgia. . . ."
63. See Jill Norgren, *The Cherokee Cases: The Confrontation of Law and Politics* (New York: McGraw-Hill, 1996): 37 for discussion of this period.
64. 21 U.S. (8 Wheat.) 543 (1823).
65. Ibid., pp. 572–73.
66. Ibid., p. 574.
67. Ibid., p. 584.
68. Ibid., pp. 591–92.
69. A better reading of this doctrine can be found in *Mitchel v. United States*, 9 Pet. 711 (1835).
70. 30 U.S. (5 Pet.) 1 (1831).
71. Ibid., pp. 1, 27.
72. Ibid., pp. 1, 17.
73. Ibid., pp. 1, 53.
74. 21 U.S. (8 Wheat.) 543 (1823).
75. 187 U.S. 553 (1903).
76. 78 U.S. (11 Wall.) 616 (1870).
77. 14 Stat., 799.
78. The key question, of course, is if or when the "trust" status of Indian lands has been terminated. See, e.g., *County of Yakima v. Yakima Indian Nation*, 112 S. Ct. 682 (1992), which held that state governments and their subdivisions, the counties, could impose an ad-valorem tax on patented reservation land owned by tribes and individual Indians. While the majority held that the Yakima lands had lost their trust status, the dissent suggested the land was still in trust. However, many state attempts to impose other types of taxes on Indians inside Indian country have been defeated. See, e.g., *Oklahoma Tax*

Commission v. Citizen Band Potawatomie Indian Tribe of Oklahoma, 498
U.S. 505 (1995), concerning cigarette taxes; *Oklahoma Tax Commission v.
Sac and Fox Nation*, 508 U.S. 114 (1993), concerning vehicle excise tax and
registration fee; and *Oklahoma Tax Commission v. Chickasaw Nation*, 115
S. Ct. 2714 (1995), concerning motor fuel tax. But see *Cotton Petroleum
Corp. v. New Mexico*, 490 U.S. 163 (1989) and *Dept. of Taxation and Finance
of New York v. Milhelm Attea & Bro's.*, 114 S. Ct. 2028 (1994), which allowed
states to impose taxes on non-Indian corporations doing business on reservation lands and taxes on Indian traders who sell tobacco and tobacco-related
products to non-Indians.

79. Roy W. Meyer, *History of the Santee Sioux* (Lincoln: University of Nebraska
Press, 1967): 127–28.
80. Act of February 22, 1889, 25 Stat., 399.
81. Act of February 22, 1889, 25 Stat., 677.
82. Act of June 16, 1906, 34 Stat., 267.
83. Act of June 20, 1910, 36 Stat., 557.
84. *West's Revised Code of Washington, Annotated: Constitution of the State of
Washington* (St. Paul, Minn.: West Publishing Co., 1988): 358–59.
85. *United States v. Winans*, 198 U.S. 371 (1905); *Winters v. United States*, 207
U.S. 564 (1908); *Dick v. United States*, 208 U.S. 340 (1908); and *Antoine v.
Washington*, 420 U.S. 197 (1975) were important decisions affirming federal supremacy over state law in Indian affairs. But see *United States v.
McBratney*, 104 U.S. 621 (1882); *Ward v. Race Horse*, 163 U.S. 504 (1896); and
most recently *Crow Tribe of Indians and Thomas Ten Bear v. Repsis*, 73 F. 3d
982 (1995), which confirmed the viability of the equal footing doctrine as a
principle sufficient to elevate states' rights over federal treaty rights.
86. Act of August 15, 1953, 67 Stat., 588.
87. Act of April 11, 1968, 82 Stat., 73, 77–81.
88. *Confederated Tribes of Siletz Indians v. U.S.*, 841 F. Supp. 1479, 1487 (D. Or.,
1994).
89. Cited in David M. O'Brien, *Constitutional Law and Politics*, 2d edition,
vol. 1 (New York: W.W. Norton, 1995): 319.
90. *Wolsey v. Chapman*, 101 U.S. 755, 769 (1879).
91. Cohen, *Handbook*, 101.
92. 110 F. 3d 688 (9th Cir., 1997).
93. Ibid., p. 698.
94. Act of February 24, 1855, 10 Stat., 612.
95. Act of March 3, 1863, 12 Stat., 765, 767.
96. Act of March 3, 1891, 26 Stat., 851.

97. See Larry C. Skogen, *Indian Depredation Claims, 1796–1820* (Norman: University of Oklahoma Press, 1996).
98. Lewis Meriam, et al., *The Problem of Indian Administration* (Baltimore: Johns Hopkins Press, 1928).
99. Act of August 8, 1946, 60 Stat., 939.
100. Act of October 8, 1976, 90 Stat., 1990.

Chapter 6

1. Act of June 2, 1924, 43 Stat. 253. Of course, prior to this act, some Indians had been naturalized as U.S. citizens via treaty provisions, specific Indian statutes, or tribal-specific legislation. The 1924 act, while declaring Indians to be citizens of the U.S., also, and importantly, provided that "the granting of such citizenship shall not in any manner impair or otherwise affect the right of any Indian to tribal or other property." In other words, Indians retained their previous rights as tribal citizens to property.
2. U.S. Congress, Senate, Hearings Before the Subcommittee on Constitutional Rights of the Committee on the Judiciary, Pursuant to S. Res. 53, pt. 1. *Constitutional Rights of the American Indian.* 87th Congress, 1st session, August 29, 30, 31, and September 1, 1961, (Washington, D.C.: Government Printing Office, 1962): p. 8.
3. Generally, the double-jeopardy clause applies only to criminal cases and actually has three distinctive constitutional protections: 1) protection against a second criminal prosecution for the same offense after acquittal; 2) protection against a subsequent prosecution for the same offense after conviction; and 3) protection against multiple punishments for the same offense.
4. See, *e.g.*, Robert F. Berkhofer, Jr., *Salvation and the Savage: An Analysis of Protestant Missions and American Indian Response, 1787–1862* (Lexington: University of Kentucky Press, 1965). An interesting bit of history in this area is Missionary Ridge, which overlooks Chattanooga, Tennessee, to the east and was the site of a great Civil War battle. It received its name from a prohibition by the Cherokees against missionaries who wished to visit their village in the bend of the river below. That ridge was as close as the missionaries were allowed to come.
5. 7 Stat., 47.
6. 7 Stat., 160.
7. 31 U.S. (6 Pet.) 515 (1832).
8. Act of April 10, 1869, 16 Stat., 40.

9. Prucha, *The Great Father*, vol. 1, pp. 517–19.

10. Ibid., p. 519.

11. Ibid., p. 523.

12. Ibid., p. 524.

13. Ibid., pp. 524–25.

14. 25 Stat., 783.

15. Ibid., p. 785.

16. 30 Stat., 62, 79.

17. 210 U.S. 50.

18. Ibid., pp. 76–77.

19. 34 Stat., 1221.

20. 152 U.S. 114 (1894).

21. Ibid., pp. 117–18.

22. Eisenhower's comments are in *U.S. Public Papers of the Presidents of the United States: Dwight D. Eisenhower* (Washington, D.C.: Government Printing Office, 1953): 166.

23. Leupp, *The Indian and His Problem*, 296.

24. See Cohen, *Handbook*, p. 175, note 347.

25. Ibid., pp. 175–76.

26. This circular is reprinted in Prucha's *The Great Father*, vol. 2, pp. 951–52.

27. Act of June 18, 1934, 48 Stat., 985.

28. For a good discussion of the peyote issue, see Omer C. Stewart, *Peyote Religion* (Norman: University of Oklahoma Press, 1987).

29. *Employment Division v. Smith*, 494 U.S. 872 (1990).

30. See Robert H. Keller and Michael F. Turek, *American Indians and National Parks* (Tucson: University of Arizona Press, 1998).

31. 92 Stat., 469.

32. U.S. Congress, Committee on Interior and Insular Affairs, *American Indian Religious Freedom*, House Report No. 95–1308, 95th Congress, 2d session, June 19, 1978, p. 1.

33. 620 F. 2d. 1159, (6th Cir. 1980), cert. den. 449 U.S. 953.

34. 638 F. 2d 172 (10th Cir. 1980), cert. den. 452 U.S. 954.

35. 541 F. Supp. 785, aff'd 706 F. 2d. 856 (8th Cir. 1983), cert. den. 104 S. Ct. 413.

36. 708 F. 2d 735 (D. C. Cir 1983), cert. den. 104 S. Ct. 37.

37. 48 F. Supp. 182 (1982), aff'd 746 F. 2d 570 (9th Cir. 1985), cert. den. 474 U.S. 820 (1985).

38. 476 U.S. 693 (1986).

39. 485 U.S. 439 (1988).

40. 858 F. 2d 404 (8th Cir., 1988).

41. 494 U.S. 872 (1990).
42. In *Bowen v. Roy* the Supreme Court denied free-exercise relief to an Abenaki Indian who wanted to prevent the government from assigning his child a social security number.
43. In *Smith*, the Supreme Court essentially jettisoned the compelling interest test and held that the only independent protection offered by the free-exercise clause was in its prohibition of laws inspired by a desire to disadvantage religion, on the grounds that such laws impose an intentional burden, not merely an incidental burden, on religious exercise.
44. *Northwest Indian Cemetery Protective Association v. Peterson*, 565 F. Supp. 586 (1983), aff'd in part and vacated in part, 795 F. 2d 688 (9th Circ. 1986). This decision was overturned by the Supreme Court in 1988 in 485 U.S. 439.
45. See Deloria, "Trouble in High Places," 267–290.
46. *Northwest Indian Cemetery Protective Association v. Peterson*, 565 F. Supp. 586 (1983). Virtually all of the ensuing facts are drawn from this district-court opinion.
47. Ibid., p. 591.
48. Ibid., p. 590.
49. *Sherbert v. Verner*, 374 U.S. 398 (1963) and *Wisconsin v. Yoder*, 406 U.S. 205 (1972), which, taken together, provide protection of religious exercise by holding that the government may burden the free exercise of religion only if it is protecting a compelling interest by the least intrusive means possible.
50. 565 F. Supp. 586, 595 (1983).
51. Ibid.
52. Ibid.
53. Ibid.
54. Ibid., p. 597.
55. Canby is no novice to Indian law questions, having published a federal Indian law legal text, *American Indian Law in a Nutshell* (St. Paul, Minn.: West Publishing, 1981) that was updated in 1998.
56. 98 Stat., 1619.
57. 764 F. 2d 581, 589 (1985).
58. *Lyng v. Northwest Indian Cemetery Protective Association*, 485 U.S. 439 (1988).
59. 374 U.S. 398 (1963).
60. Lyng, pp. 451–52.
61. Ibid., p. 453.
62. Ibid., p. 455.
63. Ibid.
64. Ibid., pp. 458–59.
65. Ibid., p. 468.

66. After their firing, Smith and Black applied for unemployment compensation. The employment division of the Department of Human Resources of the state of Oregon considered their applications in a number of administrative hearings and appeals. After the first hearing, the referee determined that the claimants' use of peyote was merely a case of "poor judgement" and that the two should not be denied benefits. This decision was appealed by their employer, a nonprofit organization, Alcohol and Drug Abuse Prevention and Treatment (ADAPT), to the Employment Appeals Board (EAB), which reversed the referee's decision and denied Smith and Black unemployment benefits. The two then appealed, in separate cases, to the Oregon Court of Appeals. In a per-curiam decision, *Smith v. Employment Division*, 709 P. 2d 246 (Or. 1985), the court reversed and remanded for reconsideration in light of the companion case, *Black v. Employment Division*, 707 P. 2d 1274 (Or. 1985), which was reversed.

Each of these decisions was appealed to the Oregon Supreme Court. Oregon's high court in *Smith v. Employment Division*, 721 P. 2d 445 (Or. 1986) affirmed as modified, and the court in *Black v. Employment Division*, 721 P. 2d 451 (Or. 1986), affirmed as modified and remanded. In these cases Oregon's highest court held that while the denial of unemployment compensation benefits to the counselors after they used peyote did not violate provisions of Oregon's constitution, the court held that it did violate the free-exercise clause of the U.S. Constitution. The court, in closing, concluded that "the ingestion of peyote is a sacrament of the Native American Church, that the claimant was a member of that church and that his religious beliefs were sincerely held" (p. 454).

The employment division then sought and secured a writ of certiorari to the U.S. Supreme Court. In that decision, *Employment Division v. Smith*, 485 U.S. 660 (1988), Justice Stevens for the majority held that the combined cases had to be remanded back to Oregon's supreme court for a "definitive ruling as to whether the religious use of peyote [was] legal in Oregon. . . ." The Oregon Supreme Court in *Smith v. Employment Division*, 763 P. 2d 146 (Or. 1988), reaffirmed its earlier rulings by holding that though the state statute against controlled substances, which includes peyote, provides no exception for sacramental use of peyote, the state could not, in keeping with the federal Constitution's First Amendment, deny unemployment compensation to the two counselors. The case was then sent back to the U.S. Supreme Court, which issued its penultimate decision in 1990.

67. 110 S. Ct. 1595 (1990).

68. 110 S. Ct. 1595 (1990).

69. 374 U.S. 398 (1963).

70. 406 U.S. 205 (1972).

71. 98 U.S. 145 (1879).

72. Frederick Mark Gedicks, "Religion," in *The Oxford Companion to the Supreme Court of the United States*, Kermit L. Hall, ed. (New York: Oxford University Press, 1992): 724.

73. 110 S. Ct. 1595, 1602–06 (1990).

74. Ibid., p. 1598.

75. Ibid., p. 1600.

76. Ibid., p. 1602.

77. See, *e.g.*, *Manybeads v. United States*, 730 F. Supp. (1989); *Attakai v. United States*, 746 F. Supp. 1395 (1990); *Havasupai Tribe v. United States*, 752 F. Supp. 1471 (1990); and *Lockhart v. Kenops*, 927 F. 2d 1028 (1991), which followed *Lyng's* reading of the Religious Freedom Resolution, which held that the act was not legally enforceable.

78. In a lobbying effort predating *Lyng* and *Smith* but that was intensified after these two rulings, tribes and their supporters formed the Indian Religious Freedom Coalition and sought an omnibus congressional law that would provide comprehensive protection of Indian religious freedom severely damaged by court cases and left largely unguarded by the 1978 AIRFA. Various bills were introduced; the broadest measure would have guaranteed protection in four general areas: use of peyote, sacred sites, Indian prisoners' rights, and religious use of eagles and other animals. This omnibus measure failed, but a separate bill that focused on peyote was eventually enacted into law on October 6, 1994. The bill legalized the use of peyote throughout the United States so long as its use is connected with the practice of NAC ceremonies (108 Stat., 3125).

    In addition, during his first term President Clinton signed executive orders specifically involving Indian religious issues. The first, which became effective on April 29, 1994, dealt with eagle feathers. This measure is intended to clarify and expedite the federal process that Indians must go through before obtaining eagle feathers from the various federal agencies that receive them. The second order, signed May 24, 1996, promotes accommodation of access to sites considered sacred by traditional Indian religious practitioners. Although all the above measures are positive steps, they do not provide the comprehensive protection required to guarantee Indian religious freedom, for they are tailored responses to specific problematic areas.

79. 96–CV–063–D (1996).

80. The issue in the *Bear Lodge* case of 1996 involved a private organization.

81. 98 U.S. 145 (1878).

82. Ibid., pp. 166–67.

83. 133 U.S. 333 (1889).

84. Ibid., p. 342.

85. See *Annual Report of the Secretary of the Interior*, House Executive Document No. 1, 48th Congress, 1st session, (Washington, D.C.: Government Printing Office, 1883), pp. x–xiii. And see *United States v. Clapox*, 35 Fed 575 (D.C. Ore. 1888) and *Tillett v. Lujan*, 931 F. 2d 636 (1991), which are the only federal cases that deal specifically with the legality of these courts. These institutions in their early years were empowered by the Indian agents to arrest and convict Indians engaged in traditional cultural or religious practices. They remained the dominant law-and-order institution on many reservations until the federal government, guided by John Collier's influence in the 1930s, replaced them with more modern tribal court systems. A handful of the original Courts of Indian Offenses, later termed CFR courts (because their guidelines are charted in the Code of Federal Regulations), remain in existence on those reservations lacking established tribal governments. They have jurisdiction over all civil suits wherein the defendant is a tribal member within their jurisdiction and over all other suits between members and non-members that are brought before the courts under the stipulation of both parties.

86. 82 Stat., 77–80.

87. 2 Stat., 6.

88. 4 Stat., 729.

89. 11 Stat., 329.

90. 48 Stat., 787.

91. Cohen, *Handbook*, 174.

92. Ibid., p. 175; citing *Connors v. United States*, 33 C. Cls. 317, 323–24 (1898).

93. Felix S. Cohen, "The Erosion of Indian Rights, 1950–1953: A Case Study in Bureaucracy," *Yale Law Journal*, vol. 62 (1952–1953), p. 356.

94. Edgar S. Cahn, ed., *Our Brother's Keeper: The Indian in White America* (New York: New Community Press, 1969): 120–21.

95. 48 Stat., 787.

96. Cohen, "Erosion of Rights," 359.

97. Ibid.

98. U.S. Senate, Hearings Before the Subcommittee on Constitutional Rights of the Committee on the Judiciary, *Constitutional Rights of the American Indian*, 89th Congress, 1st session, June 1965 (Washington, D.C.: Government Printing Office, 1965): 270.

99. Ibid.

100. 545 F. 2d. 1255, 1258 (1976).
101. 435 U.S. 313, 322 (1978).
102. Ibid., pp. 326–27.
103. 342 P. 2d. 369 (1965).
104. Ibid., pp. 373–74.
105. Ibid., pp. 378–79.
106. See, e.g., *Martinez v. Southern Ute Tribe of Southern Ute Reservation*, 249 F. 2d 915 (1957); *Barta v. Oglala Sioux Tribe of Pine Ridge Reservation*, 259 F. 2d 553 (1958); *Twin Cities Chippewa Tribal Council v. Minnesota Chippewa Tribe*, 370 F. 2d 929 (1967); and *Groundhog v. Keeler*, 442 F. 2d 674 (1971).
107. 187 U.S. 553 (1903).
108. See, e.g., *South Dakota v. Bourland*, 113 S. Ct. 2309 (1993), wherein Justice Clarence Thomas, in his first Indian law opinion, stated that although Congress had not passed an express act declaring its intent to extinguish Cheyenne River Sioux tribal jurisdictional authority as recognized in the 1868 Fort Laramie Treaty, the Court ruled that Congress had so abrogated those treaty rights through implicit language in the 1944 Flood Control Act and the 1954 Cheyenne River Sioux Act, which created the Oahe Dam and Reservoir project. But as Justice Blackmun noted in dissent, "the majority, however, points not even to a scrap of evidence that Congress actually considered the possibility that by taking the land in question it would deprive the tribe of its authority to regulate non-Indian hunting and fishing on that land" (p. 2322).
109. Act of July 10, 1952, 66 Stat., 560.
110. 401 U.S. 520.
111. 401 U.S. 527.
112. This doctrine, also described as the "implied reservation of water," was established in *Winters v. United States*, 207 U.S. 564 (1908). The basic principles of the Winters doctrine are the following: 1) Congress has the power to reserve water for federal lands, which include Indian reservations; 2) when Congress sets aside land for a specific purpose, it reserves by implication a sufficient amount of water to fulfill that purpose; 3) Indian reservations, regardless of how they are created — by congressional statute, treaty, or executive order — are established with the intention of making them habitable and productive, and whatever amount of water is necessary to fulfill these goals of habitability is thereby reserved by implication for the tribe's use and benefit; 4) congressional or presidential measures that created Indian reservations must be interpreted liberally in favor of the tribe; thus even if the treaty, statute, or executive order is silent about water rights, the tribe is still

presumed to have a right to a sufficient amount of water to satisfy the reservation's purpose for the present and future needs of the resident population. See Harold Ranquist, "The Winters Doctrine and How it Grew: Federal Reservation of Rights to the Use of Water," *Brigham Young University Law Review* (1975); and Daniel McCool, *Command of the Waters: Iron Triangles, Federal Water Development, and Indian Water* (Tucson: University of Arizona Press, 1987).

113. McCarran resolution.
114. This expression first appears in *Mitchel v. United States*, 34 U.S. (9 Pet.) 311, 345–46 (1835), wherein the court wrestled with how to define aboriginal Indian land rights.
115. Act of August 8, 1946, 60 Stat., 939.
116. See, *e.g.*, Russel L. Barsh, "Indian Land Claims Policy in the United States," *North Dakota Law Review*, vol. 58(1982), pp. 7–82; Harvey D. Rosenthal, *Their Day in Court: A History of the Indian Claims Commission* (New York: Garland Publishing, 1990).
117. 348 U.S. 272 (1955).
118. 390 F. 2d. 686 (1968).
119. Ibid., p. 691.
120. Ibid., p. 694.
121. 448 U.S. 371 (1980).
122. 23 Stat., 362, 385, 18 U.S. C. 548.
123. 27 Stat., 612, 631.
124. Ibid. This provision was also written into the U.S. Code 25 and U.S. Code 175.

Chapter 7

1. 14 Stat., 755.
2. Ibid., p. 756.
3. 14 Stat., 769.
4. 14 Stat., 785.
5. 14 Stat., 799.
6. Ibid., Article 9.
7. 31 Fed. 327 (1886).
8. Ibid., p. 329.
9. Ibid.
10. July 27, 1868, 15 Stat., 264.
11. 18 Stat., 146, 176.

12. Cohen, *Handbook*, 340.
13. Act of March 3, 1875, 18 Stat., 420, 449.
14. Annual Report of the Commissioner of Indian Affairs, 1875 (Washington, D.C.: Government Printing Office, 1875): 526.
15. U.S. Senate, Committee on the Judiciary, "The Effect of the Fourteenth Amendment on Indian Tribes," Senate Report No. 268, 41st Congress, 3d session, (Washington, D.C.: Government Printing Office, 1871).
16. Ibid., p. 11.
17. Ibid., p. 10.
18. Ibid., p. 11.
19. Ibid.
20. 16 Fed. Cas. No. 8840 (D. C. Ore. 1871).
21. Ibid., p. 166
22. 2 Fed. 58 (1880).
23. Ibid., p. 61.
24. 112 U.S. 94 (1884).
25. 25 Fed. Cas. 14891 (1879).
26. 24 Stat., 388, (1887).
27. Ibid., section 6, p. 390.
28. 43 Stat., 253.
29. Administration of the Indian Office, Bureau of Municipal Research Publication No. 65 (1915), p. 17 as quoted in Cohen, *Handbook*, 155.
30. 197 U.S. 488 (1905).
31. 241 U.S. 591 (1916).
32. Ibid., p. 598.
33. For a good introduction to Indian voting, see Vine Deloria, Jr. and Clifford M. Lytle, *American Indians, American Justice* (Austin: University of Texas Press, 1983): 222–226. See also Helen L. Peterson, "American Indian Political Participation," *Annals of the American Academy of Political and Social Science*, vol. 311 (May 1957), pp. 116–126; Leonard G. Ritt, "Some Social and Political Views of American Indians," *Ethnicity*, vol. 6, no. 1 (March 1979), pp. 45–72; Daniel McCool, "Indian Voting," in *American Indian Policy in the Twentieth Century*, Vine Deloria, Jr., ed. (Norman: University of Oklahoma Press, 1985): 105–133; Glenn A. Phelps, "Representation Without Taxation: Citizenship and Suffrage in Indian Country," *American Indian Quarterly*, vol. 9 (1985), pp. 135–148; Richard L. Engstrom and Charles J. Barrilleaux, "Native Americans and Cumulative Voting: The Sisseton-Wahpeton Sioux," *Social Science Quarterly*, vol. 72, no. 2 (June 1991), pp. 388–393; Orlan J. Svingen, "Jim Crow, Indian Style," in *The American Indian: Past and Present*, Roger L.

Nichols, ed. (New York: McGraw Hill, 1992): 268–277; and Jeff Corntassel and Richard Witmer, II, "American Indian Tribal Government Support of Office-Seekers: Findings From the 1994 Election," *Social Science Journal*, vol. 34, no. 4 (1997), pp. 511–525.

Indian gaming revenues have, of course, altered the role that some tribes play in the American political process. As tribal revenues have increased, so has their ability and willingness to participate in local, state, and federal campaigns. In part, this comes from a desire to have an active role in selecting candidates who will protect tribal rights to self-determination. And in part it is both an offensive and defensive strategy — offensive in the sense that tribes want to support political candidates who have a good track record of assisting tribes and the distinctive concerns they have, defensive in the sense that as some tribes have become economically better off, this has prompted a massive backlash among many state and federal officials who are intent on curtailing if not eliminating Indian gaming operations and weakening other tribal rights as well.

A recent conference on the Gila River Reservation in central Arizona, "Arizona Indian Voters' Convention '98," (September 18–19) focused on celebrating the fiftieth anniversary of an Arizona Supreme Court case, *Harrison v. Laveen* (1948), which affirmed the right of Indians to vote in the state. Another goal of the conference organizers, several tribes in the state, was to convince the state's Indians that unless they voted in local, state, and federal elections they stood to lose not only gaming rights but other important benefits as well.

34. 442 F. 2d 674 (1971).

35. Ibid., p. 682.

36. August 1, 1937, Memorandum for the Secretary, *Opinions of the Solicitor of the Department of the Interior Relating to Indian Affairs, 1917–1974*, vol. 1, pp. 777–781.

37. Ibid. p. 778.

38. Ibid. p. 779.

39. *Porter v. Hall*, 271 P. 411, 34 Ariz. 308 (1928).

40. See Alison Bernstein, *American Indians and World War II* (Norman: University of Oklahoma Press, 1991): 138.

41. Frederic Kirgis, "Right of Franchise — State Law", *Opinions of the Solicitor of the Department of the Interior Relating to Indian Affairs, 1917–1974*, vol. 1 (GOP: Washington, D.C., n.d.): 799–802.

42. Ibid., p. 802.

43. Nathan Margold, M–31039, *Opinions of the Solicitor of the Department of*

the *Interior Relating to Indian Affairs, 1917–1974*, vol. 1 (GPO: Washington, D.C., n.d.): 990–997.

44. See Margold, "Method of Determining 'Indians not Taxed'" M–31039, Supplemental memo, in *Opinions of the Solicitor*, 997–1000.

45. 67 Ariz. 337, 196 P2d. 456 (1948).

46. A statutory three-judge federal court, New Mexico (1948) (unreported) — cited in Bernstein, 139–140.

47. Ibid.

48. Cohen, *Handbook*, 254.

49. See M. Maureen Murphy, "Taxation Within Indian Lands: The Legal Framework," Congressional Research Service Report for Congress, 87–249A (July 1987), for a general discussion of taxation within Indian country. See also Richmond L. Clow, "Taxation and the Preservation of Tribal Political and Geographical Autonomy," *American Indian Culture and Research Journal*, vol. 15, no. 2 (1991), pp. 37–62. Notwithstanding the tax-exempt status of tribes as corporate bodies, the federal government has considered and actually introduced legislation in recent years that would directly tax tribal nations with gaming operations.

    For example, in 1994 the Clinton administration briefly considered a special tax on tribal casinos to finance welfare revisions. The administration dropped the idea in the face of concerted tribal opposition. And in 1995 a House committee approved a measure that would have imposed a 34 percent corporate income tax on Indian gaming operations (*The Kansas City Star*, October 2, 1995, p. B1). That measure was also defeated, although others in Congress are continuing a push to tax Indian gaming operations.

50. 17 U.S. (4 Wheat.) 316 (1819).

51. *Squire v. Capoeman*, 351 U.S. 1 (1956).

52. 24 Stat., 388 (1887).

53. 24 Stat., 388–89 (1887).

54. The issue of state taxes of individual Indian property has been made more problematic by two recent U.S. Supreme Court rulings: *County of Yakima v. Confederated Tribes and Bands of the Yakima Indian Nation*, 502 U.S. 251 (1992) and *Cass County v. Leech Lake Band of Chippewa Indians*, No. 97–174 (1998). *Yakima* held that a county could assess an ad-valorem tax on reservation land owned in fee by individual Indians or the tribe that had originally been made alienable when patented under the General Allotment Act. *Cass County*, following *Yakima*, held unanimously that Cass County had acted properly in levying property taxes on reservation land that had originally been made alienable by Congress and sold to non-Indians but then repurchased by the tribe.

55. See Francis P. Prucha, *American Indian Policy in the Formative Years: The Indian Trade and Intercourse Acts, 1790–1834* (Lincoln: University of Nebraska Press, 1962), especially Chapter 6, "The Crusade Against Whiskey," pp. 102–138, for a good discussion about what animated the federal government's policy toward liquor and Indians. For an excellent treatment of federal Indian liquor laws prior to 1942 see Cohen, *Handbook*, especially Chapter 17. For more recent laws, see the Cohen revision, edited by Rennard Strickland et al., (Charlottesville, Va. : Michie, Bobbs-Merrill, 1982): 305–308. And see *United States v. Mazurie*, 419 U.S. 544 (1975), which upheld Congress's authority to delegate to tribal governments the power to regulate the distribution of alcoholic beverages on Indian land.

56. 11 Stat., 743.

57. 28 Stat., 314.

58. 28 Stat., 286.

59. 28 Stat., 314.

60. 28 Stat., 319.

61. 232 U.S. 478 (1914).

62. 265 U.S. 344 (1924).

63. 27 Stat., 260; as amended by the Act of January 30, 1897, 29 Stat., 506, and the Act of May 25th, 1918, 40 Stat., 563.

64. 41 Stat., 305.

65. 265 U.S. 344, 346.

66. 58 F2d. 782 (1932).

67. 41 F2d. 782 (1930).

68. Michael Melich, "The Eighteen-Year-Old Vote Amendment of the U.S. Constitution as Applied to Tribes," M–36840, November 9, 1971, in *Opinions of the Solicitor of the Department of the Interior Relating to Indian Affairs, 1917–1974*, vol. 2 (GPO: Washington, D.C., n.d.): 2041–2043.

Chapter 8

1. 163 U.S. 376 (1896).

2. Ibid., p. 384.

3. 272 F. 2d. 131 (1959).

4. Ibid., p. 134.

5. 687 F. Supp. 1380 (D. Alaska 1988): p. 1392.

6. Ibid.

7. See, *e.g.*, *Goodell v. Jackson*, 20 John. 693 (1823); *The Kansas Indians*, 72 U.S.

(5 Wall.) 737 (1867); *McKay v. Campbell,* 16 Fed. Cas. No. 8,840 (1871); *Ex parte Reynolds,* 20 Fed. Cas. No. 11,719 (1879); *United States v. Osborn,* 2 Fed. 58 (1880), *Ex parte Crow Dog,* 109 U.S. 556 (1883), *State v. McKenney,* 18 Nev. 182 (1883); *Elk v. Wilkins,* 112 U.S. 94 (1884); *Talton v. Mayes,* 163 U.S. 376 (1896); *Patterson v. Council of Seneca Nation,* 157 N. E. 734 (1927); *Toledo v. Pueblo de Jemez,* 119 F. Supp. 429 (1954); *Native American Church v. Navajo Tribal Council,* 272 F. 2d 131 (1959); *Glover v. United States,* 219 F. Supp. 19 (1963); *Groundhog v. Keeler,* 442 F. 2d 674 (1971); *Jacobson v. Forest County Potawatomi Community,* 389 F. Supp. 994 (1974); *Janis v. Wilson,* 521 F. 2d 724 (1975); *Tom v. Sutton,* 533 F. 2d 1101 (1976); *United States v. Wheeler,* 435 U.S. 313 (1978); *Santa Clara Pueblo v. Martinez,* 436 U.S. 49 (1978); *Merrion v. Jicarilla Apache Tribe,* 109 U.S. 556 (1982); *Dubray v. Rosebud Housing Authority,* 565 F. Supp. 462 (1983); *R. J. Williams Co. v. Fort Belknap Housing Authority,* 719 F. 2d 979 (1983); and *Imperial Granite Co. v. Pala Band of Indians,* 940 F. 2d 1269 (1991).

8. *Alaska v. Native Village of Venetie Tribal Government,* No. 96–1577 (1998).

9. 82 Stat., 73, 77–81; as amended on October 27, 1986, 100 Stat., 3207.

10. For a good treatment of the Indian Civil Rights Act see Donald L. Burnett, Jr., "An Historical Analysis of the 1968 'Indian Civil Rights Act,'" *Harvard Journal of Legislation,* vol. 9 (May 1972), pp. 557–626.

11. 113 *Congressional Record,* 35472 (1967).

12. 88 Stat., 2203.

13. Congress, at the behest of tribes, enacted the Tribal Self-Governance Demonstration Project as a five-year experiment in 1988 (102 St. 2296). A limited number of tribes were entitled to receive consolidated block grants that would enable them to plan and implement programs formerly carried out by the federal government. The success of the initial tribes led Congress to make this a permanent law in 1994 (P. L. 103–413). By 1996 some 53 tribes had entered into the self-governance process.

14. 85 Stat., 688 (1971).

15. 23 Stat., 24 (1884).

16. 31 Stat., 321 (1900).

17. 72 Stat., 341 (1959).

REFERENCES

Anaya, James S. *Indigenous Peoples in International Law*. New York: Oxford University Press, 1996.

Bailyn, Bernard. *The Debate on the Constitution* 1. New York: The Library of America, 1993.

Ball, Milner. "Constitution, Court, Indian Tribes." *American Bar Foundation Research Journal* 1 (1987): 1–139.

Barreiro, Jose. "Indian Roots of American Democracy." *Northeast Indian Quarterly* 4–5 (Winter–Spring 1988–1989).

Barsh, Russel L. "Indian Land Claims Policy in the United States." *North Dakota Law Review* 58 (1982): 7–82.

Barsh, Russel and James Y. Henderson. "The Betrayal: *Oliphant v. Suquamish Indian Tribe* and the Hunting of the Snark," *Minnesota Law Review* 63 (1979): 609–640.

Berkhofer, Robert F., Jr. *Salvation and the Savage: An Analysis of Protestant Missions and American Indian Response, 1787–1862*. Lexington: University of Kentucky Press, 1965.

Bernstein, Alison, *American Indians and World War II*, Norman: University of Oklahoma Press, 1991.

Brugge, David M. and J. Lee Correll. *The Story of the Navajo Treaties*. Window Rock, Ariz.: Navajo Historical Publications, 1971.

Burnett, Donald L., Jr. "An Historical Analysis of the 1968 'Indian Civil Rights Act.'" *Harvard Journal of Legislation* 9 (May 1972): 557–626.

Burt, Larry W. *Tribalism in Crisis: Federal Indian Policy, 1953–1961*. Albuquerque: University of New Mexico Press, 1982.

Cahn, Edgar S., ed. *Our Brother's Keeper: The Indian in White America*. New York: New Community Press, 1969.

Clark, Blue. *Lone Wolf v. Hitchcock: Treaty Rights and Indian Law at the End of the Nineteenth Century*. Lincoln: University of Nebraska Press, 1994.

Clow, Richmond L. "Taxation and the Preservation of Tribal Political and Geographical Autonomy." *American Indian Culture and Research Journal* 15: 2 (1991): 37–62.

Cohen, Felix S. *Handbook of Federal Indian Law*. Reprint; Albuquerque: University of New Mexico Press, 1972.

———. "Indian Rights and the Federal Courts," *Minnesota Law Review* 24: 2 (January 1940): 145–200.

———. "The Spanish Origin of Indian Rights in the Laws of the United States." *Georgetown Law Journal* 31 (1942): 1–21.

———. "The Erosion of Indian Rights, 1950–1953: A Case Study in Bureaucracy." *Yale Law Journal* 62 (1952–1953): 348–390.

———. *Felix S. Cohen's Handbook of Federal Indian Law*. Rennard Strickland, et al., eds. Charlottesville, Va.: Michie, Bobbs-Merrill, 1982.

Corntassel, Jeff and Richard Witmer, II. "American Indian Tribal Government Support of Office-Seekers: Findings from the 1994 Election." *Social Science Journal* 34: 4 (1997): 511–525.

Davenport, Francis G., ed. *European Treaties Bearing on the History of the United States and its Dependencies to 1698*. Carnegie Institution of Washington, Publication No. 254. Gloucester, Mass.: Peter Smith, 1967.

Deloria, Vine, Jr. "Legislation and Litigation Concerning American Indians." *Annals of the American Academy of Political and Social Science* 436 (1978): 88–96.

———. "Trouble in High Places: Erosion of American Indian Rights to Religious Freedom in the United States." In M. Annette Jaimes, ed. *The State of Native America: Genocide, Colonization, and Resistance*. Boston: South End Press, 1992, pp. 267–290.

Deloria, Vine, Jr. and Clifford M. Lytle. *American Indians, American Justice*. Austin: University of Texas Press, 1983.

DePauw, Linda Grant, ed. *Documentary History of the First Federal Congress of the United States of America* 2. Baltimore: Johns Hopkins University Press, 1974.

Engstrom, Richard L. and Charles J. Barrilleaux, "Native Americans and Cumulative Voting: The Sisseton-Wahpeton Sioux," *Social Science Quarterly* 72: 2 (June 1991): 388–393.

Fixico, Donald L. *Termination and Relocation: Federal Indian Policy, 1945–1960*. Albuquerque: University of New Mexico Press, 1986.

Gedicks, Frederick Mark. "Religion." In Kermit L. Hall, ed. *The Oxford Companion to the Supreme Court of the United States*. New York: Oxford University Press, 1992, pp. 717–726.

Gibson, Charles. "Spanish Indian Policies." In Wilcomb E. Washburn, ed. *History of Indian-White Relations* 4. Washington D.C.: Smithsonian Institution, 1988, pp. 96–102.

Grinde, Donald A., and Bruce E. Johansen. *Exemplar of Liberty: Native America* and the Evolution of Democracy. Los Angeles: American Indian Studies Center, University of California, 1991.

Hanke, Lewis. "The 'Requerimiento' and its Interpreters." Revistade Historia de America 1. Mexico City: Instituto Panamericano de Geografia e Historia, 1939, pp. 25–34.

———. The Spanish Struggle for Justice in the Conquest of America. Philadelphia: University of Pennsylvania Press, 1949.

———. All Mankind is One: A Study of the Disputation Between Bartolomé de Las Casas and Juan Ginés de Sepúlveda in 1550 on the Intellectual and Religious Capacity of the American Indians. Dekalb: Northern Illinois University Press, 1974.

Kappler, Charles J., comp. Indian Affairs: Laws and Treaties. 2 vols. Washington: Government Printing Office, 1903.

Kawashima, Yasuhide. "Legal Origins of the Indian Reservation in Colonial Massachusetts." American Journal of Legal History 13 (January 1969): 42–56.

———. Puritan Justice and the Indian: White Man's Law in Massachusetts, 1630–1763. Middleton, Conn.: Wesleyan University Press, 1986.

Leupp, Francis E. The Indian and His Problem. New York: Scribners, 1910.

Lewis, John D., ed. Anti-Federalists versus Federalists, Selected Documents. Scranton, Penn.: Chandler Publishing, 1967.

Lothrop, Marian. "The Indian Campaigns of General M. G. Vallejo," Quarterly of the Society of California Pioneers 9: 3 (1932): 161–205.

McCool, Daniel. Command of the Waters: Iron Triangles, Federal Water Development, and Indian Water. Tucson: University of Arizona Press, 1994.

———. "Indian Voting." In Vine Deloria, Jr., ed. American Indian Policy in the Twentieth Century. Norman: University of Oklahoma Press, 1985, pp. 105–133.

Meriam, Lewis, et al. The Problem of Indian Administration. Institute for Government Research, Studies in Administration. Baltimore: Johns Hopkins Press, 1928.

Meyer, Roy W. History of the Santee Sioux. Lincoln: University of Nebraska Press, 1967.

Montesquieu, Charles de. The Spirit of the Laws. 2 vols., 1734. Reprint; J. V. Prichard, ed. Littleton, Colo.: F. B. Rothman, 1991.

Murphy, M. Maureen. "Taxation Within Indian Lands: The Legal Framework." Congressional Research Service Report for Congress, 87–249A (July 1987).

New York Times, March 21, 1998, p. 14.

Norgren, Jill. The Cherokee Cases: The Confrontation of Law and Politics. New York: McGraw-Hill, 1996.

Peroff, Nicholas C. Menominee Drums: Tribal Termination and Restoration, 1954–1974. Norman: University of Oklahoma Press, 1982.

Peterson, Helen L. "American Indian Political Participation." *Annals of the American Academy of Political and Social Science* 311 (May 1957): 116–126.

Phelps, Glenn A. "Representation Without Taxation: Citizenship and Suffrage in Indian Country," *American Indian Quarterly* 9 (1985): 135–148.

Pomeroy, Earl S. *The Territories and the United States: 1861–1890.* Philadelphia: University of Pennsylvania Press, 1947.

Pommersheim, Frank. *Braid of Feathers: American Indian Law and Contemporary Tribal Life.* Berkeley: University of California Press, 1995.

Prucha, Francis P. *American Indian Policy in the Formative Years: The Indian Trade and Intercourse Acts, 1790–1834.* Lincoln: University of Nebraska Press, 1962.

———. *The Great Father: The United States Government and the American Indian* 1. Lincoln: University of Nebraska Press, 1984.

———. *American Indian Treaties.* Berkeley: University of California Press, 1994.

Ranquist, Harold. "The Winters Doctrine and How it Grew: Federal Reservation of Rights to the Use of Water." *Brigham Young University Law Review* (1975): 639–724.

Richardson, J. D., ed. *Compilation of the Messages and Papers of the Presidents, 1789–1897.* 10 vols. Washington, D.C.: Government Printing Office, 1907.

Ritt, Leonard G. "Some Social and Political Views of American Indians." *Ethnicity* 6: 1 (March 1979): 45–72.

Rosenthal, Harvey D. *Their Day in Court: A History of the Indian Claims Commission.* New York: Garland Publishing, 1990.

Rossiter, Clinton, ed. *The Federalist Papers.* New York: New American Library, 1961.

Schaaf, Gregory. "From the Great Law of Peace to the Constitution of the United States: A Revision of America's Democratic Roots." *American Indian Law Review* 14 (1989): 323–32.

Shattuck, Petra T., and Jill Norgren. *Partial Justice: Federal Indian Law in a Liberal Constitutional System.* Providence, R.I.: Berg Publishing, 1991.

Simmons, Marc. *Border Comanches: Seven Spanish Documents, 1785–1819.* Santa Fe, N.M.: Stagecoach Press, 1967.

Skogen, Larry C. *Indian Depredation Claims, 1796–1820.* Norman: University of Oklahoma Press, 1996.

Sorkin, Alan L. *American Indians and Federal Aid.* Washington. D.C.: Brookings Institution, 1971.

Stewart, Omer C. *Peyote Religion.* Norman: University of Oklahoma Press, 1987.

Svingen, Orlan J. "Jim Crow, Indian Style." In Roger L. Nichols, *The American Indian Past and Present.* New York: McGraw Hill, 1992, pp. 268–277.

Thomas, Alfred B. *Forgotten Founders.* Norman: University of Oklahoma Press, 1932.

U.S. Attorney's General Opinions, 1924.

U.S. Congress. House. Committee on Indian Affairs. *Report on Regulating the Indian Department*. House Report 474, 23d Congress, 1st session (1834).

——. House. Committee on Interior and Insular Affairs. *American Indian Religious Freedom*. House Report 95–1308, 95th Congress, 2d session (1978).

U.S. Congress. Senate. *The Effect of the Fourteenth Amendment on Indian Tribes*. Senate Report 268, 41st Congress, 3d session (1868).

U.S. Congress. Senate. Committee on Indian Affairs. *Survey of Conditions of the Indians in the United States. Hearings before a Subcommittee of the Committee on Indian Affairs*. 71st Congress, 3d session (1929–1927).

——. Senate. Committee on the Judiciary. *Hearings before the Subcommittee on Constitutional Rights of the Committee on the Judiciary. Constitutional Rights of the American Indian*. 87th Congress, 1st session (1962).

——. Senate. Committee on the Judiciary. *Hearings before the Subcommittee on Constitutional Rights of the Committee on the Judiciary. Constitutional Rights of the American Indian*. 89th Congress, 1st session (1965).

——. Senate. Select Committee on Indian Affairs. *Final Report of the Special Committee on Investigations of the Select Committee on Indian Affairs*. Senate Report 101–216, 101st Congress, 1st session (1989).

U.S. Congress. Special Report. *American Indian Policy Review Commission: Final Report*. Washington: Government Printing Office (1977).

U.S. *Congressional Globe*. 1871.

U.S. *Congressional Record*. 1967.

U.S. Department of the Interior. *Commissioner of Indian Affairs: Annual Reports* for the years 1872, 1883, 1891.

U.S. Department of the Interior. *Opinions of the Solicitor of the Department of the Interior Relating to Indian Affairs, 1917–1974*. Washington, D.C.: Government Printing Office, n.d.

U.S. *Executive Orders Relating to Indian Reservations from May 14, 1855 to July 1, 1902*. Washington, D.C.: Government Printing Office, 1902.

U.S. *Journals of the Continental Congress, 1774–1789*. 34 vols. Washington, D.C.: 1904–1937.

U.S. *Public Papers of the Presidents of the United States: Dwight D. Eisenhower*. Washington, D.C.: Government Printing Office, 1953.

Viola, Herman J. *Diplomats in Buckskins: A History of Indian Delegations in Washington City*. Washington, D.C.: Smithsonian Institution, 1981.

Weekly Compilation of Presidential Documents. Washington, D.C.: Government Printing Office, 1994.

West's Revised Code of Washington Annotated: Constitution of the State of Washington. St. Paul, Minn.: West Publishing, 1988.

Wilkins, David E. "The 'De-Selected' Senate Committee on Indian Affairs and its Legislative Record, 1977–1992," *European Review of Native American Studies* 9: 1 (1995): 27–34.

———. *American Indian Sovereignty and the U.S. Supreme Court: The Masking of Justice.* Austin: University of Texas Press, 1997.

Williams, Robert A., Jr. *The American Indian in Western Legal Thought: The Discourses of Conquest.* New York: Oxford University Press, 1990.

Wrend, Julie and Clay Smith, eds. *American Indian Law Deskbook.* Niwot: University Press of Colorado, 1993.

Woodward, Bob and Scott Armstrong. *The Brethren.* New York: Simon and Schuster, 1979.

INDEX OF CASES

INDEX

Devil's Tower (Wyoming), 120
Dickinson, President, 10
disclaimer clause, 91
discovery, doctrine of, 4, 5, 79, 80, 82–
    83, 89, 133, 151, 159, 161
Domenici, Senator Pete, 49
double jeopardy, 126–129, 178 n. 3
Downes, William, 120
Due Process clause, 129–132
Dull Knife, Chief, 124

Eighteenth Amendment, 96
Eisenhower, Dwight, 37, 104
elimination of executive order powers,
    38
Elk, John, 145
Eminent Domain, 133
England, 4, 5, 6, 10, 11, 13, 14, 19, 22, 23,
    26, 34, 60, 72, 81, 84, 100, 123, 130,
    133
Episcopal church, 102, 103
equitable title, doctrine of, 167 n. 17
Ervin, Senator Sam, 50, 158
executive-order reservations, 38–39,
    169 nn. 17, 19

Fair Housing Act (1968), 157
Fathers of the American Revolution,
    6, 7
"federal Indian law," 33, 158
Federalist No. 42, 18
Federalist Papers, viii, 21, 27, 51
"federalists," 18
Federally Impacted Area Act (1950), 40
Fifteenth Amendment, 96, 139, 148–
    149
Fifth Amendment, 99, 126, 129, 130,
    156
First Amendment, 99, 103, 105, 109,
    113, 115, 117, 120–121, 122, 125, 156,
    157

Five Civilized Tribes, 45, 54, 73, 76,
    140
Flathead, 102
Florida, 5, 36
Fort Berthold, 102
Fort Duquesne, 13
Fort Hall, 102
Fort Laramie treaty (1851), 44
Fort Laramie treaty (1868), 68
Fort Pitt treaty (1775), 8
Fort Stanwix treaty (1784), 10, 23
Fourteenth Amendment, 25, 51, 96,
    139, 141–148, 151, 156
Fourth Amendment, 99, 125
France, 4, 5, 6, 8, 13, 26, 34, 84, 100
Franklin, Benjamin, 13
"freedom of speech," 123
Friends (Hicksite), 102
Friends (Orthodox), 102

General Allotment Act (1887), 38, 60–
    61, 66–67, 146, 152
Georgia, 5, 15, 16, 18, 19, 20, 81, 101
Ghost Dance, 107
Gorton, Slade, 48, 49–50
government-to-government, 38
Grande River, 102
Grande Ronde, 102
Grant, U. S., 35, 37, 101
"Great Father," 34
Great Lakes, 6, 9
Great Nemaha, 102
Green Bay, 102
guardianship, 147, 149

Hamilton, Alexander, 19, 81
Hampton Institute, 125, 149
Handbook of Federal Indian Law, 92,
    123
Harlan, Justice, 54, 145
Hayden, Carl, 109

Printed and bound by CPI Group (UK) Ltd, Croydon, CR0 4YY

09/06/2025

14685839-0001